George McKendree Steele

Outlines of Bible Study

A Four-Years Course for Schools and Colleges

George McKendree Steele

Outlines of Bible Study
A Four-Years Course for Schools and Colleges

ISBN/EAN: 9783337171520

Printed in Europe, USA, Canada, Australia, Japan

Cover: Foto ©Lupo / pixelio.de

More available books at **www.hansebooks.com**

OUTLINES

OF

BIBLE STUDY.

A FOUR-YEARS COURSE

FOR

SCHOOLS AND COLLEGES.

BY

G. M. STEELE, D.D
Principal of Wesleyan Academy, Wilbraham, Mass.

LEACH, SHEWELL, & SANBORN,
Boston and New York.

C. J. PETERS & SON,
TYPOGRAPHERS AND ELECTROTYPERS,
145 HIGH STREET, BOSTON.

PREFACE.

THESE "Outlines" are designed for the use of those who desire to take a systematic course of study of the English Bible. It is intended especially for students in academies, preparatory schools, and colleges, but it will also be found useful to adult Bible-classes, and as a guide to any persons who are privately associating for the purpose of methodical study of the Holy Scriptures. The purpose contemplated is to give a good general knowledge of the character and contents of the Scriptures, using only the Bible as a text-book. The "Outlines" are not given as lessons to be learned, but as guides and suggestions of method. The plan chiefly adopted is that of analysis and syllabus, with suggestive questions.

In pursuing the studies of the several series, much is, of course, left to the discretion of the teacher. It will be found that, in cases of not greatly advanced and not largely disciplined minds, some of the lessons will be too long. In such cases, judicious selections can be made.

The work is divided into four series or courses, covering the study of four years. The first year's course embraces the Patriarchal and Hebrew history, from the creation to the end of the reign of Solomon; the second course completes the Hebrew history. There are also added outlines of the poetic and prophetic books. The third course comprises the Life of Christ as contained in the four Gospels; the fourth course embraces the history of the Propagation of the Gospel as narrated in the Acts of the Apostles and illustrated in the Epistles and the Book of Revelation.

In the Hebrew history, the Bible narratives are followed somewhat minutely, with the exception of that part of the Pentateuch containing the ceremonial law, which is only slightly treated. The poetic and prophetic books are gone over much more cursorily, and the study is more nearly analogous to the study of authors in courses in literature in our schools. It is only intended to give a good knowledge of the general character, purpose, style, and religious teachings of these books. The introductions here are much more full, both containing information not readily accessible to the ordinary student, and grouping in convenient forms some of the matter contained in the books themselves.

In the Life of Christ, it has been the design to present the events in their chronological order, and also to harmonize the different narratives. Dr. Strong's "Harmony of the Gospels" has been followed for the most part.

The treatment of the Propagation of the Gospel is similar to that of the Life of Christ — that is, it is treated chronologically, the History and the Epistles being taken together in the order of time. This gives added interest to both, as well as a pleasing variety by the change from one to the other. The introductions both here and in the Life of Christ are more full than in the Hebrew history, but they are designed to be suggestive and stimulating, not substitutive, in relation to the sacred text. The plan throughout is to keep simply to the study of the Word itself, and it is believed that there is not a question or an item anywhere in the series that contains a denominational implication, or indicates a preference for any theological party among those who regard the Scriptures as a Divine Revelation.

It will be found in practice better sometimes to vary the order of study in the "Outlines" to a certain extent. Thus in the second year's course it may be found more profitable with a certain class of students to take up the Life of Christ immediately after the conclusion of the Hebrew history, and upon its completion return to the poetic and prophetic books, as the latter demand more disciplined minds in order to a full understanding of them.

The lists of reference books given in connection with the several courses is not intended so much for the students as for teachers.

PREFACE.

To many of the former they would not be accessible, nor would they be competent to use them to advantage. With them the main purpose should be to get a correct idea of the Bible history and the Bible teachings. It is obvious that, to secure this desirable result, and to save time and work for the teacher, each member of the class should be provided with a copy of the "Outlines."

The study of the divine Word pursued in this way has been found exceedingly interesting and profitable, and has attracted much attention from those who have been cognizant of it. That the students of our American schools should become at least as well acquainted with the sources of our religion as they are required to do with those of ancient heathen nations would seem to be self-evident, even if our religion were as mythical as much of those is acknowledged to be. How much more, not only when a large majority of our citizens recognize it to be the true and only religion, but when it is made the basis of our civilization, and is implied and involved in our whole national life! Yet the ignorance of large proportions of even educated and fairly intelligent people among us, of the Bible, is painfully obvious. That some method should be devised that would make the study of these sacred writings as attractive as that of any other literature, is very desirable. That this humble attempt in this direction, if not a great success, may not prove a failure, is the hope of the compiler of these "Outlines."

The thanks of the Author and Publishers are due to the Rev. FRANCIS N. PELOUBET, D. D., for valuable suggestions in the preparation of the list of Reference Books.

WESLEYAN ACADEMY, WILBRAHAM, MASS., JUNE, 1889.

FIRST YEAR'S COURSE.

PATRIARCHAL AND HEBREW HISTORY. — FROM THE CREATION TO THE DEATH OF SOLOMON.

BOOKS OF REFERENCE. — FIRST YEAR.

GENERAL. — Smith's OLD TESTAMENT HISTORY.
  Geikie's HOURS WITH THE BIBLE.
  Milman's HISTORY OF THE JEWS.
  Stanley's HISTORY OF THE JEWISH CHURCH, 1st and 2d Series.
  Josephus' JEWISH ANTIQUITIES.
  Thompson's THE LAND AND THE BOOK. New ed., 3 vols.
  Stanley's SINAI AND PALESTINE.
  Krummacher's DAVID KING OF ISRAEL.
  Walker's PHILOSOPHY OF THE PLAN OF SALVATION.
  Professor Blakie's MANUAL OF BIBLE HISTORY.
  Sime's KINGDOM OF ALL ISRAEL.
  Cowle's PENTATEUCH.
  Cowle's HEBREW HISTORY.
  Rand, McNally & Co.'s MANUAL OF BIBLICAL HISTORY AND GEOGRAPHY.

SCIENCE. — Professor Birch's ANCIENT HISTORY FROM THE MONUMENTS.
  Professor Sayce's FRESH LIGHT FROM THE ANCIENT MONUMENTS.
  Rawlinson's HISTORICAL ILLUSTRATIONS OF THE OLD TESTAMENT.
  Bishop Walsh's ECHOES OF BIBLE HISTORY.

ON CREATION. — Professor Guyot's CREATION.
  Hugh Miller's TESTIMONY OF THE ROCKS.
  Rev. Dr. Geo. B. Boardman's THE CREATIVE WEEK.
  Charles B. Warring's THE MIRACLE OF TO-DAY.
  Professor Tayler Lewis' THE SIX DAYS OF CREATION.
  R. S. Poole's THE GENESIS OF EARTH AND MAN.
  Rev. Dr. Joseph Thompson's MAN IN GENESIS AND GEOLOGY.
  Dr. J. M. Gibson's AGES BEFORE MOSES.
  Principal Dawson's NATURE AND THE BIBLE.
  Dr. E. Burgess' ANTIQUITY AND UNITY OF THE HUMAN RACE.
  THE ORDER OF CREATION. (Discussion by Gladstone, Huxley *et al.*)
  President W. F. Warren's PARADISE FOUND.

ON THE DELUGE. — Hugh Miller's TESTIMONY OF THE ROCKS.
  Geo. Smith's CHALDEAN ACCOUNT OF GENESIS.
  Tayler Lewis in Lange's COMMENTARY ON GENESIS.
  Lenormant's ANCIENT HISTORY OF THE EAST.

ON ABRAHAM TO MOSES. — Ebers' UARDA, and THE SISTERS.
  Tompkin's STUDIES IN THE LIFE OF ABRAHAM.
  J. Oswald Dykes' ABRAHAM THE FRIEND OF GOD.
  Thornley Smith's JOSEPH AND HIS TIMES.
  Taylor's JOSEPH THE PRIME MINISTER.
  Taylor's MOSES THE LAWGIVER.
  Hamilton's MOSES THE MAN OF GOD.

THE EXODUS. — Trumbull's KADESH-BARNEA.
  Edersheim's EXODUS AND THE WANDERINGS.
  Brugsch's EGYPT UNDER THE PHARAOHS.
  PUBLICATIONS OF THE EGYPTIAN EXPLORATION FUND.
  Dawson's EGYPT AND SYRIA.
  Wardlaw on MIRACLES.
  Trumbull's THE BLOOD COVENANT.

JOSHUA TO SOLOMON. — Thornley Smith's JOSHUA AND HIS TIMES.
  Principal Douglas' THE GOSPEL IN THE BOOK OF JOSHUA.
  Miss Smiley's FULNESS OF BLESSING.
  Edersheim's SAMUEL AND SAUL.
  Taylor's DAVID KING OF ISRAEL.
  Blakie's DAVID KING OF ISRAEL.
  McLaren's LIFE OF DAVID AS REFLECTED IN THE PSALMS.
  Tuck's THE FIRST THREE KINGS OF ISRAEL.
  Maurice's PROPHETS AND KINGS.

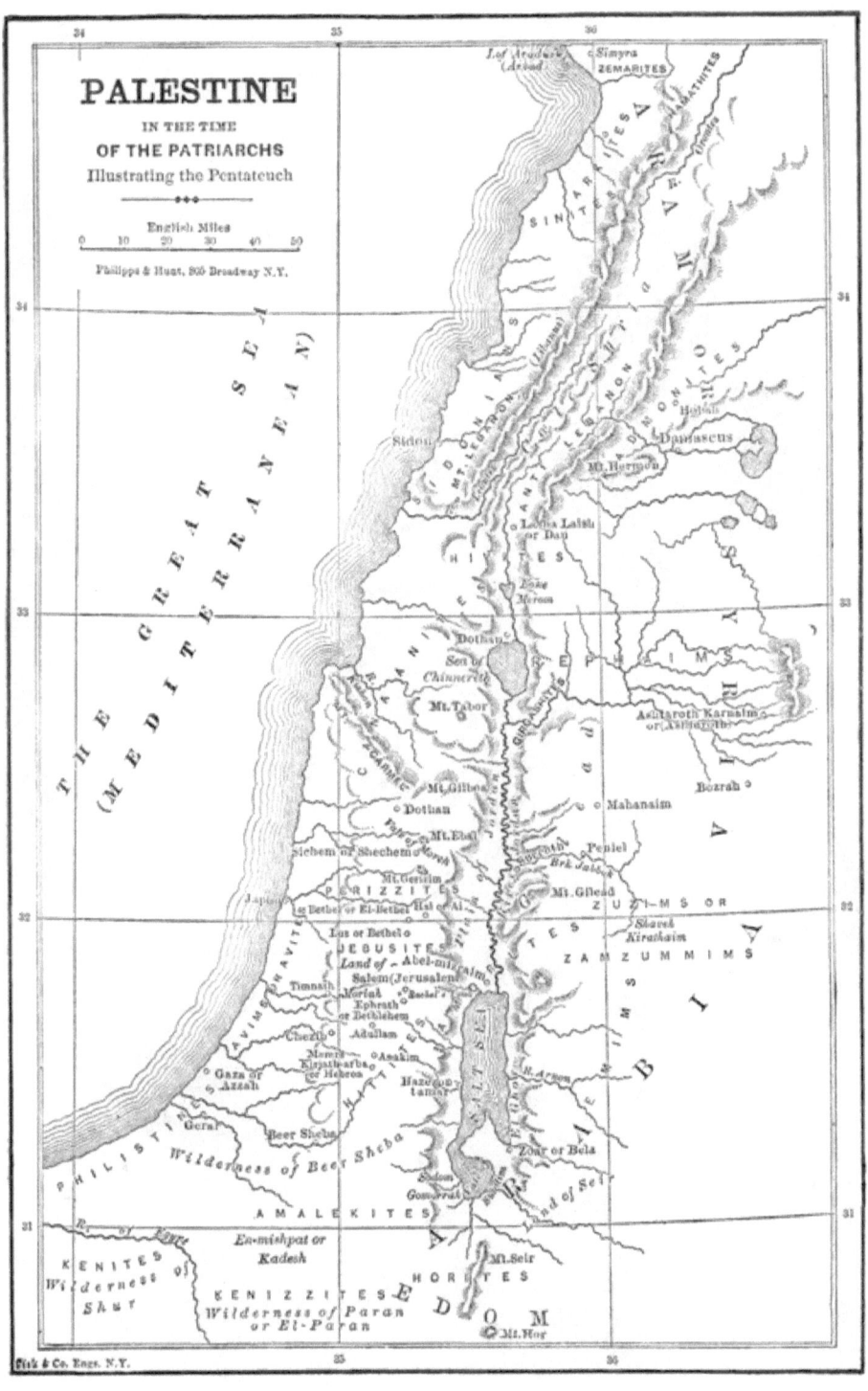

Patriarchal and Hebrew History.

I.
General Character of the Bible.

1. *Not one treatise, but several.*
There are, in all, about sixty-six different books: thirty-nine in the Old Testament, and twenty-seven in the New.

2. *A great variety in the character of the writers.*
   (a) There were about thirty of them in the Old Testament; and probably nine in the New.
   (b) Some of them lived in palaces, and some in prisons. Some were princes; some were philosophers and scholars; and others were shepherds, fishermen, or mechanics.

3. *The time covered.*
   (a) They extend over fifteen hundred or sixteen hundred years.
   (b) The earliest were probably written about 1500 B. C.; the latest about 96 A. D.

4. *Division of the books.*
   (a) Historical. (b) Poetical. (c) Prophetic. (d) Biographical. (e) Epistolary.

Some of these embrace more than one of these characteristics. Let the student, as far as possible, classify the books according to the above differences.

5. *The great characteristic object of the whole collection:* a revelation of Religious Truth from God to man.

II.
From the Creation to the Close of the Flood.

Gen. i.—viii. A. M. 1—1656. B. C. 4004—2348.

1. The opening statement of the Sacred History. Gen. i. 1.
2. Give in order the six formative periods, and what was done in each. Chap. i

3. The creation of man, the place assigned him, and the injunction laid upon him. ii.

4. The Fall of Man and the consequence. iii.

5. What promise here pointing to the Messiah? 15.

6. Story of Cain and Abel. iv.

7. Genealogy of the descendants of Adam and Seth. Names and ages of the six who lived the longest. Relation of Methuselah to Noah. Was he contemporary with Adam, and how long before the Flood did he die? v.

8. The character of men as they multiplied, and the consequence. vi. 1—7.

9. God's command to Noah. The dimensions of the Ark, in English measure. vi. 13—22.

10. The story of the Flood. vii.

11. The subsiding of the waters. The place where the Ark rested. The going forth from the Ark. God's promise. viii.

III.

From the Flood to the Call of Abraham.

Gen. ix.—xii.   A. M. 1656—2083.   B. C. 2348—1921.

1. The Divine Blessing, the Divine Injunction, and the Divine Covenant. Gen. ix.

2. The sons of Noah. How many sons had each? x.

3. Through which of the three sons came the Messiah? and through which of his sons? x., xi.

4. Give an account of the confusion of tongues. xi. 1—9.

5. Who was Abraham, and what was his character? Who were some of his ancestors? His birthplace? What important personages among his descendants? Give the account of his call, his journeyings, and the kind of life he led. xi., xii.

IV.

From the Call of Abraham to the Birth of Isaac.

Gen. xiii.—xix.   A. M. 2083—2107.   B. C. 1921—1897.

1. Separation of Abraham and Lot. Renewal of the Divine promise. xiii.

2. War of the confederates, and Abraham's rescue of Lot. xiv.

3. God's promise to Abraham concerning his posterity. Remarkable character of this promise. xv.

4. Destruction of the cities of the plain. Abraham's plea for Sodom. Lot's deliverance. Give the story. xviii., xix.

5. What do you think of the character of Lot?

V.

From the Birth of Isaac to Jacob's Journey to Padan-aram.

Gen. xxi.—xxviii. A. M. 2107—2244. B. C. 1897—1760.

Abraham's character is one of the most interesting in the Old Testament history, or indeed in any history. He is among the few great men of all time. There is a majesty and dignity about him that is seldom equaled. It is all the more remarkable, from the fact that his situation is not such as to call into exercise the great energies of a great mind. The chief traits about him are his moral courage, his extraordinary faith, his profound religious convictions, all of which are evinced in his separation from his people, and beginning a wandering life among strangers; his generosity and magnanimity, as evinced in his conduct towards Lot and on other occasions; and his dignity of demeanor, and power to command respect, which we see in his intercourse with all the princes and great men with whom he came into communication. They instinctively honored him. He appears also to have been a man of large intelligence and extraordinary wisdom. That he was not free from moral infirmities is evident; and the scriptural account sets them plainly before us, as the Bible is wont to do.

1. Age of Abraham at the birth of Isaac? xxi. 5. What great feast is mentioned, and what happened at the time? xxi. 8—21. The subsequent history of Ishmael and his race. xxv. 12.

2. The offering up of Isaac. xxii. 2—14. What virtue did Abraham manifest here in a remarkable manner? Renewal of the Divine covenant. xxii. 15—19. How many times is this covenant repeated in the history?

3. Death and burial of Sarah. xxiii. First record in history of the use of money. 8—16.

4. Selection of a wife for Isaac. xxiv. Reasons for seeking one at such a distance. xxiv. 3. The account of the journey of Abraham's servant, and what occurred at the end of it. xxiv. 10—35. Departure of Rebecca, and the meeting with Isaac. xxiv. 58—67.

5. Birth of Esau and Jacob. Difference in their character and style of life. xxv. 27.

6. How Jacob, who was the younger, came to have the pre-eminence which belonged to Esau. xxv. 29—34.

7. Isaac's sojourn in Gerar, and his false statement about his wife. His prosperity, and his trouble with his neighbors. xxvi.

8. Esau's marriage, and its effect on his parents. Why was this? xxvi. 34, 35.

9. Jacob's fraud upon his father and against his brother; his mother's influence. xxvii. 1—24. He is constituted the head of the family, and receives the paternal and prophetic blessing. xxvii. 26—29. Esau's discovery of the fraud. xxvii. 30—36. Had Esau, who had bartered away his right, any real occasion to complain? Was Jacob's deception and general conduct, therefore, justifiable?

10. The purpose to send Jacob to his mother's relatives. xxvii. 42—46. Twofold reason for this. xxviii. 1—9.

VI.

From Jacob's Journey to Padan-aram to the Selling of Joseph by his Brothers

Gen. xxviii.—xxxvii. A. M. 2244—2275. B. C. 1760—1729.

1. Jacob's journey and vision at Bethel. xxviii. 10—17. The effect of this vision on Jacob. The beginning of his religious life.

2. His arrival at Padan-aram, and what befell him there. xxix. 1—12. His sojourn with his uncle, Laban, the wages he was to have, and the fraud practiced on him. xxix. 15—26.

3. The change of Jacob's wages and his prosperity by reason of it. xxx. 27—43.

4. Jacob's departure from Padan-aram. Laban's pursuit of him, and the result. xxxi.

5. Continuation of the journey. News of the approach of Esau, and its effect upon Jacob. His prayer and precaution against hostilities. The wrestling with the mysterious stranger, and the Divine blessing. The change of name and its signification. xxxii.

6. The meeting with Esau, and its amicable result. xxxiii. 1—16. Jacob's further journey, and temporary settlement. 17—20.

7. Jacob at Bethel, and the religious reformation of his household. xxxv. 1—7. The renewal of the Divine covenant. 9—15. Birth of Benjamin, and death of Rachel. 16—20. Names of Jacob's sons. 23—26. Through which of these did Christ come?

8. Return of Jacob to his father. Death and burial of Isaac. xxxv. 27—29.

9. Esau's descendants, and their formation into a nation. xxxvi.

10. Jacob's partiality to Joseph, and its effect on his other sons. Joseph's dreams, and what they indicated. xxxvii. 3—11.

11. The plot of Joseph's brothers, and their final disposal of him. 18—28. The report made to Jacob, and his great grief. 31—35. Joseph in Egypt. 36.

12. How old was Joseph at this time?

VII.

From Joseph's Arrival in Egypt to his Death.

Gen. xxxix.—l. A. M. 2275—2368. B. C. 1729—1636.

1. Joseph becomes the slave of Potiphar, the Egyptian officer. Finds favor in his sight, and is promoted to be steward of his house. xxxix. 1—6.
2. Through the wickedness of Potiphar's wife, he is cast into prison. xxxix. 7—23. His experience there, and the remarkable incident which befell him. xl. 1—23.
3. Pharaoh's dreams, and failure of his wise men to interpret them. xli. 1—8. Joseph sent for. His interpretation, consequent exaltation, and the success that came to him. 9—44. His marriage, and the birth of his children. 45—52.
4. The famine. It extends to Canaan, and affects Jacob's family. xlii. 1, 2. The sons of Jacob going down to Egypt for corn, and their meeting with Joseph. His conduct towards them, and their return. 3—38.
5. Their second journey to Egypt, and reception by Joseph. His device to try them, and their consequent distress. xliii., xliv. His final revelation of himself, and his sending for his father's family. xlv.
6. Jacob's journey to Egypt, and his meeting with Joseph. xlvi. 1—29. The settlement of the family in Goshen. 30—34. Introduction of Joseph's father and brothers to Pharaoh. xlvii. 1—10.
7. Continuance and effect of the famine. xlvii. 13—26. Jacob's old age, and charge to Joseph. 28—31.
8. His final conversation with Joseph, and his blessing of Joseph's children. xlviii.
9. Jacob's prophetic benediction upon his sons, and his death. xlix. 1—33.
10. The burial of Jacob in the land of Canaan. l. 1—13. The apprehensions of Joseph's brothers lest he should avenge himself on them for their former ill-treatment of him. His magnanimous conduct towards them. l. 15—21.
11. Joseph's last days and death. l. 22—26.

VIII.

From the Death of Joseph to the Institution of the Passover.

A. M. 2471—2513. B. C. 1533—1491.

This period embraces nearly two-thirds of the life of Moses, one of the half-dozen most remarkable men that have ever lived. He was born of a Hebrew family while his people were slaves, and under an edict of the Egyptian king, which required every male child of his people to be put to death. By a device of his mother, he was set afloat on the river in a little chest. Being discovered by the daughter of the king, he was adopted as her son, brought up as a royal prince, and instructed in all the learning of those times. His education, combined with extraordinary natural capabilities, made him a person of great power, skill, and executive ability. How he used these in the emancipation of his people, and their organization into a nation with a system of religion which has endured unto this day, and which would have been marvelous had it been only human, is shown in the sacred narrative. But more than this is given, evincing the revelation of God to this, his chosen servant. It is from this time that we begin to get some scattered glimpses of ancient history. It was about this age that Athens is supposed to have been founded, and Troy built; also Corinth, and perhaps Thebes in Bœotia.

Exodus i.—x.

1. Original number of Jacob's family in Egypt. Their rapid increase, and the apprehensions of the Egyptians. Exod. i. 1—10.

2. The enslavement of the Israelites. Attempt of the Egyptians to prevent their increase, by slaying the male children. 11—22.

3. Birth of Moses. His mother's device to prevent his being slain. His adoption by Pharaoh's daughter, and his education as a prince of Egypt. ii. 1—10.

4. He becomes acquainted with his people, sympathizes with them, and takes their part. 11—14.

5. His flight to Midian, and residence there. 15—22.

6. Miracle of the burning bush, and God's revelation to Moses. Moses' call to be the deliverer of his people. iii. 1—22.

7. Moses' hesitancy, and God's encouragement of him. Aaron, his brother, appointed to help him. iv. 1—17.

8. Moses' departure from Midian. His meeting with Aaron, and their announcement to the Israelites. 18—31.

9. Message to Pharaoh and his defiant tone. v. 2—4. The consequent persecution of the people, and the increase of their burdens. Their discontent. 5—23.

10. God confirms his promise of deliverance, and sends Moses again to Pharaoh. vi.

11. Moses and Aaron before Pharaoh, and their miracle in his presence. vii. 1—14. *The first plague:* the water turned to blood. 15—28.

12. *Second plague.* Its effect upon Pharaoh. Its removal, and the hardening of his heart. viii 1—15.

13. *Third and fourth plagues.* Pharaoh's promise to let them go, and the violation of it. 16—32.

14. *Fifth plague.* ix. 1—7. *Sixth plague.* 8—12.

15. Solemn warning to Pharaoh. *Seventh plague.* Pharaoh's alarm. His promise, and its violation. 13—35.

16. *Eighth plague.* Its effect upon the king. x. 1—20.

17. *Ninth plague.* The wrath of Pharaoh. 21—29.

IX.

From the Institution of the Passover to the Giving of the Law.

Exod. xi.–xix. A. M. 2513. B. C. 1491.

1. The Lord's direction to Moses concerning the coming of the great and final plague. xi. 1—10.
2. Institution of the Passover. Meaning of the word, and its memorial character. A type of what? Description of the manner of its celebration. xii. 1—20. Moses' direction to the people. 21—27.
3. Destruction of the first-born in Egypt, and the consequent distress and terror of the inhabitants. Hurried departure of the Israelites, and their spoiling of their oppressors. 28—36.
4. Their first journey. The number of the people, the manner of their going out, and the importance of the event. 37—51.
5. Further instruction concerning the celebration of the event in the future. Continuation of the journey, and how they were guided. xiii.
6. Pharaoh recovers from his fright, and attempts to recapture the Israelites. xiv. 1—10. The alarm of the latter, and their reassurance by Moses. 11—14.
7. The miraculous passage through the Red Sea. The destruction of Pharaoh and his army, and deliverance of the people. 15—31.
8. The song of victory. xv.
9. Continued journeys of the liberated Israelites. Their apprehension of famine, and their murmurings. The miraculous supply of quails and manna. Directions concerning the gathering of the manna. Disobedience and its consequences. xvi. 1—36.
10. Lack of water, and its miraculous supply. xvii. 1—7.
11. First battle with a hostile nation. 8—16.
12. Visit of Moses' father-in-law, and his counsel as to the method of governing the people. xviii.
13. Moses on Mt. Sinai, and God's charge to him and the people. The awe inspired by the demonstrations about the mountain, and the evidence of the Divine Presence. xix.

X.

From the Giving of the Law to the Worship of the Golden Calf.

Exod. xx.–xxxii. A. M. 2513. B. C. 1491.

PART FIRST.

1. The Ten Commandments. xx. 2—17. (To be committed verbatim.)
2. The two divisions of the decalogue. (*a*) The first table containing duties growing out of our relations to God: *four* commandments. 2—11.

(*b*) The second, containing laws growing out of our relations to our fellow-men: *six* commandments. 12—17.

3. How are these all summed up in the New Testament? Matt. xxii. 37—39.

4. Effect upon the people of these utterances of the voice of God. xx. 18—21.

5. Sundry civil and moral ordinances given to Moses for the Government of the Israelites. xxi.—xxiii. (*a*) What four offenses are mentioned, of which the punishment was death? xxi. 12—15. (*b*) What penalty for destroying an eye, a tooth, etc.? 24, 25. (*c*) What restitution for stealing an ox or a sheep? xxii. 1. (*d*) What for other trespass or destruction of property? 5—9. (*e*) What three great annual feasts were the Israelites commanded to keep? xxiii. 14—17.

PART SECOND.

1. Account of Moses going up into the mount to meet God? xxxiv.
2. Offerings for the tabernacle and sanctuary. xxv. 3—7.
3. What three principal articles of furniture for the tabernacle are described in chapter xxv? 10, 23, and 31.
4. The tabernacle and its enclosure. (*a*) The dimensions (English measure) of the enclosure or "court of the tabernacle." xxvii. 9—18. (*b*) Dimensions of the tabernacle. xxvi. 15—22. (*c*) How was the tabernacle divided? xxvi. 33. (*d*) What was in each of the divisions? xxvi. 33—35.
5. Whence, probably, came all the rich materials for the building and decorating of the tabernacle, and for its furniture? xii. 35, 36.
6. The great apostasy. (*a*) The worship of the golden calf. xxxii. 1—6. (*b*) Anger of the Lord. 7—10. (*c*) Moses' prayer. (*d*) Moses' discovery of the idol, and its effect on him. 15—24. (*e*) The consequence to the people. 25—35.

XI.

From the Setting Up of the Tabernacle to the Appointment of Men to go and Explore the Promised Land.

Exod. xl.; Num. i.—xii. A. M. 2514. B. C. 1490.

1. The setting up of the tabernacle. Describe the divisions and the contents. Exod. xl.

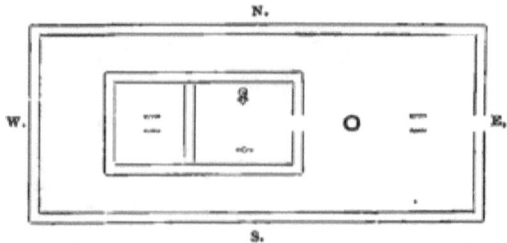

2. The numbering of the tribes. Num. i. 19—46. Were all the tribes numbered, and why? Num. i. 47—50 and iii. 11—13. Did the numbers given embrace *all* the people of the other tribes? i. 45.

3. How nearly did the numbers of the first-born males of all the tribes correspond with the number of the tribe of Levi? iii. 39 and 43.

4. Arrangement of the host into camps, and the location of the general camps in relation to the tabernacle. ii. 1—31. Where did the Levites take position? iii. 23, 29, 35, 38.

5. The offense of Nadab and Abihu. Probable cause of their sacrilegious conduct. Lev. x. 8—11.

6. The offerings of the princes of the tribes for the service of the tabernacle. What were the offerings of each? Num. vii.

7. How long after leaving Egypt before the Israelites left the vicinity of Mount Sinai? Num. x. 11. What was the occasion of their long delay, and what had occupied the time? (Last part of Book of Exodus, Leviticus, and the first part of Numbers.)

8. What was the signal for the departure of the children of Israel from any locality, and what the signal of their encamping? ix. 17. When was their signal of departure given in the wilderness of Sinai? x. 11. How long was their journey at this time? x. 33. Moses' invocation at setting out, and the halting. x. 35, 36.

9. Whither did they take their journey? Deut. i. 6, 7. What was the general direction? The character of the country? Deut. i. 19.

10. A spirit of mutiny among the people, and the cause of it. Num. xi. 4—6. How was the complaint met? 31, 32. Punishment of the people. 33. Allusion to this in Ps. lxxviii. 27—31.

11. What new feature in the government of the people was introduced? 16, 17 and 25.

12. Jealousy of Miriam and Aaron against Moses. The cause of it, and God's vindication of his servant. xii. The great characteristic of Moses. xii. 3.

XII.

From the Sending of the Spies to Explore the Land to the Invasion of Moab.

Num. xiii.—xxi.   A. M. 2514—2552.   B. C. 1490—1452.

1. Appointment of men to explore the country. Num. xiii. 1—20. Their journey. 21—25. Their report. 26—33.

2. The effect of this report upon the people. xiv. 1—4. Remonstrance of Moses and Aaron, Joshua and Caleb. 5—9. The Lord's indignation and judgment against the people, and especially against those who brought back the evil report. 11—38.

3. The too late repentance and rash undertaking. 39—45. Beginning of the forty years' wandering in the wilderness.

4. Three incidents of history during this period. (*a*) Punishment of a man for violating the Sabbath. xv. 32—36. (*b*) Mutiny of Korah, Dathan and Abiram, and their summary punishment, with the further fatal consequences. xvi. 1—35 and 41—50. (*c*) The miracle of the rods. xvii.

5. Death of Miriam. xx. 1. Who was she, and what have we previously heard about her?

6. Complaint of the people of lack of water. The miracle of the fountain in the rock. The fault of Moses and his condemnation. 2—13.

7. Close of the forty years' wandering, and the preparation for the invasion of Canaan. King of Edom refuses permission to march by the direct route through his territory. 14—21.

8. Death of Aaron, and the mourning for him. 23—29.

9. The Israelites' journey around the land of Edom. xxi. 4. Murmurings of the people, and their destruction by serpents. The Brazen Serpent. 5—9.

10 Continued journeyings toward the east of the Jordan. 10—20. First great battle, and beginnings of conquest and occupation. 21—25. Second great success, and acquisition of territory. 33—35.

XIII.

From the Conquest of Heshbon and Bashan to the Death of Moses.

Num. xxii.—Deut. xxxiv. A. M. 2552—2553. B. C. 1452—1451.

1. Alarm of Balak, king of Moab, and his device to thwart the Israelites. Num. xxii. 2—6.

2. Character of Balaam. A worshiper of the true God—a prophet—but corrupt and mercenary.

3. The negotiations with Balaam. 7—21. How are we to reconcile God's permission to Balaam to go with the messengers, and his subsequent rebuke and condemnation.

4. Account of Balaam's journey. 22—41. Balaam's prophetic utterances and the Divine overruling of his speech, and Balak's disappointment. xxiii., xxiv.

5. The Israelites lured into idolatry by their intercourse with the Moabites. xxv. 2, 3. The judgment of the Lord against them. 5—9.

6. New census of the tribes. Compare this numbering with the one at the beginning of the forty years. i. 46 and xxvi. 51. Compare also the numbering of the Levites at the different times. iii. 39 and xxvi. 62. What prediction was here fulfilled? xiv. 28—30, xxvi. 64, 65.

7. Overthrow of the Midianites, and the capture of their land and their wealth. xxxi.

8. Request of the two and a half tribes to receive the portion of their inheritance in the recently conquered territory. xxxii. 1—5. Objections of Moses. 6—15. The pledge and contract and final consent. 16—42.

9. Directions concerning the previous occupiers of the Promised Land. xxxiii. 51—56. Appointment of a commission for the distribution of the land. xxxiv. 16—29.

10. Appointment of cities of refuge, and conditions which made them available. xxxv.

11. Farewell discourses of Moses. (*a*) Recapitulation of their experience in the wilderness, and exhortation to obedience. Deut. i —iv. (*b*) Rehearsal of the Law, and injunction to keep it in spirit and in truth. v.—xxvi. (*c*) Sanctions of the Law; prophetic blessings and cursings. xxvi.—xxx.

12. Writing of the Law and the sacred memorial song, and directions as to future use of them. xxxi., xxxii.

13. Farewell blessing to the several tribes. xxxiii.

14. The vision and death of Moses. xxxiv.

15. Give an estimate of his character. (See introduction to No. VI.)

XIV.

From the Death of Moses to the General Conquest.

Josh. i.—xii. A. M. 2553—2554. B. C. 1451—1450.

1. God's charge to Joshua. i. 1—9. The note of preparation. 10, 11. The tribes which have already received their inheritance on the east of the Jordan, renew their contract to render military aid in the subjugation of Canaan. 12—18.

2. Expedition of the spies, and the aid afforded by Rahab. ii.

3. Directions for the forward movement, and the miraculous passage of the Jordan. iii. The commemorative monument. iv. 1—8, 9, 20—24. What time in the year was this passage? 18. Effect of the approach of the Israelites on the people of the land. ii. 24, and v. 1.

4. What great national rite was here renewed, and what feast was celebrated? v. 2—9 and 10.

5. What miracle ceased? 12. Confirmation of the Divine promise to Joshua. 13—15.

6. What is the meaning of the word Joshua, and of what other great name was it a type and synonym?

7. The taking of Jericho. The supernatural element in it. vi. 1—20. Rescue of Rahab. 22, 23 and 25. The predicted curse on the rebuilders of the city. 26. Was this prediction ever fulfilled? 1 Kings xvi. 34. Distance of Jericho from the Jordan? From Jerusalem?

8. The repulse at Ai. vii. 2—5. Its effect on Joshua, and the answer of the Lord. 6—15. The sin of Achan. vii. 1 and 16—23. The punishment. 24—26.

9. Conquest of Ai. viii. 1—29.

10. What injunction of Moses was here observed? Deut. xxvii. 2, 3, 8, and Joshua viii. 30, 35.

11. The confederation of the Canaanitish kings against Israel. ix. 1, 2. The device of the Gibeonites to prevent their own destruction. 3—17. What did the princes of Israel do when they found out the deception? 18—27.

12. Discomfiture of the confederate kings. Extraordinary miracle connected with the great battle. x. 1—14. Execution of the kings. 16—27. Subjugation of Southern Palestine. 28—43.

13. The northern confederation. xi. 1—9. Completion of the conquest. 10—23. How many kings did Joshua conquer on the west of Jordan? xii. 7—24.

XV.

From the General Conquest to the Death of Joshua..

Josh. xiii.—xxiv. A. M. 2554—2577. B. C. 1450—1427.

1. Was the conquest described in the previous study a complete one? Josh. xiii. 1. What parts yet remained unsubdued? 2—6.

2. What tribes had already received their apportionment and where? 8—12 and 15—32.

3. The claim of Caleb, and the grant which satisfied it. xiv. 6—15. What gave him prominence at this time?

4. Draw an outline map, and mark the prominent historical localities. xv., xvi., and xviii.

5. How many and what tribes had not yet received their allotment? xviii. 2. What censure did Joshua utter against the people, and what was the effect? 3—9.

6. What tribe after this first received its assignment, and where was it located? xviii. 11. What important cities were included in this portion? 21—28.

7. Give the remaining allotments, and point them out on the map. xix.

8. The cities of refuge, their number, location, and the design of them. xx.

9. Inheritance of the Levites; why omitted among the others, and how the omission was compensated. How many cities were assigned them? xxi. 1—42.

10. The Reubenites, Gadites, and Manassites, who had been doing military duty, released from further service and permitted to return to their places on the east of the Jordan. xxii. 1—9. What event came near causing a rupture of the nation, and civil war? 10—20.

11. Joshua's old age and final charge to the people. Exhortation to religious fidelity, and his prophetic warning. xxiii. Rehearsal of the Provi-

dential history of the nation. xxiv. 1—12. His solemn charge, his own choice, and his expressed fear for their constancy. 13—28.

12. Death of Joshua and Eleazar, and their burial. Conduct of the people at that time. 29—33.

XVI.

From the Death of Joshua to the Birth of Samuel.

Judges I.—Ruth iv. A. M. 2577–2831. B. C. 1425—1171.

During this period, we have, in the line of contemporary secular history, the institution of the Olympic and Isthmian games in Greece, the Argonautic expedition, the government of Ægeus and Theseus in Athens, the elopement of Helen, the Trojan war, the voyage of Æneas and his settlement in Italy, and the foundation of Tyre.

PART FIRST.

1. Character of the Book of Judges. (*a*) Fragmentary. (*b*) Unchronological. (*c*) To a large extent the events are local and tribal rather than national. (*d*) Still presenting a view of the character and condition of the people which is historically important.

2. State of the nation. (*a*) Somewhat unorganized and unsettled. (*b*) Destitute of any strong central administration of government. (*c*) Lacking the moral energy and religious spirit, and obedience to the Divine direction necessary to the overcoming of the heathen nations in their midst. (*d*) Therefore frequently falling into their idolatrous customs, and becoming politically subject to them.

3. Outline of the conduct and history of the people during this period. Judg. ii. 10—23.

4. The *First Apostasy* and consequent servitude. iii. 7, 8. Who was raised up to be their deliverer and ruler, and how long did he govern? 9—11.

5. The *Second Apostasy* and servitude. 12—14. The new leader and deliverer. His exploits and the victory of the people and the long peace. 15—30.

6. The *Third Apostasy*. The subjugation by the heathen nation. Character and resources of their oppressor. iv. 1—3. Peculiar character of the new leader. Means of regaining independence. Give the substance of the narrative. 4—24.

7. Song of victory. Give two or three of the notable passages. v. 4, 5, 20, 23.

8. *Fourth Apostasy*. What nation now became the instrument of punishment, and what was the condition of the people? vi. 1—6. The Divine warning. 7—10.

9. The call of Gideon. 11—26. Result of this call and its further confirmation. 27—40.

10. Account of Gideon's revolt and its success. vii. Singular test in the organization of his forces. vii. 2—8. Foreshadowing of victory. 9—14. The assault and its success. 19—25.

11. Civil dissensions and punishment of refractory cities. viii. 1—9 and 13—17. Discomfiture of the Midianite people and princes. 10—12 and 18—21.

PART SECOND.

1. The career of Abimelech. (*a*) Murder of his brothers and usurpation of the local government. ix. 1—6. (*b*) Jotham's parable and prophecy. 7—20. (*c*) Dissension and disorder and civil war. 21—49. (*d*) Death of Abimelech. 50—57.

2. Further relapses of the Israelites and the evil consequences. x.

3. Story of Jephthah and the revolt against the oppression of the Ammonites. (*a*) His early history and character. xi. 1—3. (*b*) Appeal of the people to him when in trouble, and his first answer. 4—10. (*c*) His demand of the Ammonites, and their reply and Jephthah's answer. (*d*) Jephthah's rash vow, the great victory, and the dreadful consequence of his vow.

4. The Ephraimites again make trouble, and are punished for their folly. xii. 1—6. Other judges after Jephthah. 8—15.

5. Samson's career. (*a*) His birth and consecration by his parents. xiii. (*b*) His marriage and the beginning of his exploits. xiv. (*c*) Give the chief incidents of his subsequent life and his death. xv. and xvi.

6. Micah, the graven image, and the Levite acting as priest. xvii. Expedition of the Danites, and their treatment of Micah. xviii.

7. After the infamous conduct of certain Benjaminites related in chapter xix., what did the other tribes do? xx. 1—26. The contest and its results. 30—48. The subsequent sympathy for Benjamin, and the means of restoring the tribe. xxi.

8. Give the outlines of the history of Ruth. Ruth i.—iv. Into what important relationship does this Moabite woman come to some of the chief personages of the Jewish race? iv 18—22. What other woman, a foreigner, is also supposed to have been a connecting link in the lineage of Christ? Matt. i. 5.

XVII.

From the Birth of Samuel to the Demand for a King.

I. Sam. i.—viii.   A. M. 2863—2909.   B. C. 1141—1095.

1. Chronology of this period. (*a*) Probably embraced within the forty years mentioned, Judg. xiii. 1. (*b*) Samson's life probably partly contemporaneous with that of Samuel.

2. Continued domination of the Philistines. Their geographical position, and the part of the nation exposed to them. (See map.)

3. Meaning of the name Samuel. (Asked of God.) I. Sam. i. 20. Why was this name given?

4. What vow did Samuel's mother make concerning him, and how did she fulfill it? i. 11 and 27, 28.

5. Who was Eli, and what two offices did he hold? ii. 11 and iv. 18.

6. Who assisted Eli in the discharge of his offices in his old age? Their character? ii. 12 and 17.

7. Samuel's position in the house of Eli, and his character as a child. ii. 11 and 26.

8. God's revelation to Samuel concerning Eli. iii. 1—14. The communication to Eli. 16—18. Samuel's reputation among the people? 20. Geographical signification of "from Dan to Beer-sheba?"

9. Continuation of the Philistine war. Defeat of the Israelites. The ark of the covenant brought to the camp. Disastrous result. iv. 1—11. The calamity reported to Eli, and the consequence. 12—18.

10. Effect of the presence of the ark among the Philistines. v.

11. Return of the ark; incidents connected therewith. vi.

12. Religious revival and reformation under Samuel's administration. vii. 1—6. Continued war, and defeat of the Philistines. 7—14. The government of Samuel. 15—17.

13. The people's demand for a king, and Samuel's remonstrance. The Lord's direction to grant their request. viii.

XVIII.

From the Anointing of Saul to the Call of David.

I. Sam. ix.—xvi. A. M. 2900—2941. B. C. 1005—1063.

The beginning of this period marks a radical change in the civil constitution of the Israelitish nation. The broken and partially disorganized condition of the tribes, the want of civil discipline among them and the frequent religious apostasies indicated the want of a strong central government. A monarchy would have been unnecessary for them, if they had been disposed to live together in obedience to the Divine law, under the direction of such religious teachers and judges as the Lord from time to time appointed. But, as it was evident that they would not do this, it was obviously better for them to be under a monarchy, than to go on drifting towards anarchy as they had begun to do.

1. Who was Saul, and what kind of a man was he? ix. 1, 2. Give an account of his adventures just before his call to the kingdom. 3—14. The meeting with Samuel and their communication. 15—25.

2. The anointing. ix. 26—x. 1. Samuel's predictions to Saul of the experience of a day as the signs of a Divine appointment, and the fulfillment of them. 2—16. The public designation of Saul as king. 17—27.

3. Saul's first exploit as leader of the people. xi. 1—11. His magnanimity. 12, 13. Renewal of the kingdom. 14, 15.

4. Samuel's rehearsal of history, his surrender of authority, and counsel concerning their future conduct. xii. What remarkable phenomenon in response to his words? Its effect on the people. 10—19.

5. Continuation of the troubles with the Philistines. xiii. 1—8. Saul's first transgression, and the predicted penalty. 9—14. Scarcity of weapons of war among the Israelites, and the inroads of their enemies. 17—23.

6. Daring adventure of Jonathan, and its marvelous success. xiv. 1—16. Further effects of this assault. 17—23.

7. Saul's injunction and imprecation. Jonathan's unconscious transgression. 24—30. The great victory. The faintness of the people and consequent conduct, and Saul's reproof of them. 31—34.

8. Evidence of the Divine displeasure, and the investigation. 36—44. Why Jonathan was not slain. 45.

9. Saul's success and prosperity. 47—52.

10. The doom of Amalek, and the war against that nation. xv. 1—8. Saul's second transgression. Samuel's rebuke, and Saul's defense. 9—21. The condemnation and repentance. 22—31.

11. The Lord's direction to Samuel concerning the call of David to be the future king. xvi. 1—3. The feast in Bethlehem and the quest of Samuel for David, and the anointing. 4—13.

12. Saul's trouble, and the remedy recommended. 14—16. David sent for. His musical skill, and its effect on Saul. 17—23.

XIX.

From the Anointing of David to the Death of Saul.

I. Sam. xvii.—xxxi. A. M. 2941—2948. B. C. 1063—1056.

PART FIRST.

1. Mention some of David's immediate ancestors. Ruth iv. 17—22. To what tribe did he belong? Who were some of the greatest of his descendants?

2. The Philistine war. Gathering of the armies. I. Sam. xvii. 1—3. The giant champion's defiance. 4—11. Give his height in English measure; also the weight of his coat of mail and his spear's head.

3. What was David's occupation? Give the account of his visit to the army, and what occurred on his arrival. 17—30.

4. Effect of the situation on David. His presentation to Saul, and his utterances in the king's presence. 31—37.

5. Describe the going forth of David to meet Goliath, the combat and the conquest. 31—51. Subsequent events. 51—58.

6. Beginning of the remarkable friendship of David and Jonathan. xviii. 1—4. David's situation in the service of the king. His popularity, and Saul's jealousy. The attempt to slay him 5—12.

7. His appointment to dangerous positions, under promise of being the king's son-in-law. Treachery, and further promise on condition of slaying one hundred Philistines. What did Saul hope from this arrangement? How many Philistines did David slay? 13—30.

8. The king still more openly seeks the life of David. Jonathan's good offices in his behalf. xix. 1—7.

9. David's continued success, and Saul's increasing jealousy. Attempt to slay David, and Michal's device. Finds shelter with Samuel. Saul's sending for him and finally going himself, and the result. 8—24.

10. David still a fugitive. Interview with Jonathan, and plan of the latter to secure and furnish information concerning Saul's disposition and purpose. Covenant between the friends. xx. 1—23. Carrying out of the plan, and the result. 24—42.

11. David's flight, and the affair with Abimelech the priest. xxi. 1—9. Goes to the camp of the enemy. His behavior there. 10—15.

PART SECOND.

1. Various persons resort to David, whom he forms into a company of which he becomes the chief. His disposal of his parents, and departure to a new locality. xxii. 1—5.

2. Saul's trouble about David, and appeal to his friends. 6—8. Doeg the Edomite gives information. Saul's cruel vindictiveness in the punishment of Abimelech and his friends. 9—19. Abiathar escapes and takes refuge with David. 20—23.

3. David's exploit at Keilah. xxiii. 1—6. Saul's continued persecution. 7—15. Jonathan's interview with David, and his great magnanimity. 16—18.

4. David's betrayal by the Ziphites, his escape from Saul, and summons of the latter to repel an invasion. 19—29.

5. Saul's pursuit of David with an army. Opportunity of David to avenge himself. His generous self-restraint. His revelation of himself and his disposition to Saul. xxiv. 1—15. Saul's humiliation and confession. Recognition of David's future kingship, and the covenant made. 16—22.

6. Death of Samuel, and the affair with Nabal. xxv. 1—12. David's angry purpose, and the mediation of Nabal's wife. 13—35. Death of Nabal, and the sequel. 36—42.

7. Saul again pursues David, and again is at David's mercy. David's magnanimity and religious scruples. xxvi. 1—25.

8. Goes again to the Philistines. His conduct and his fortunes among them. xxvii. 1—7. Marauding excursions. 8—12.

9. The Philistine war renewed. xxviii. 1—4. Folly and wickedness of Saul, and his condemnation. 5—25.

10. David and the Philistines. Suspicions of the latter. xxix. 1—5. Dismissed by the king. 6—11.

11. The city of David's residence destroyed, and his family and friends captured. His distress, and what he did. The pursuit, adventures on the way, and success of the expedition. xxx. 1—20.

12. Dispute concerning division of the spoil. The decision, and establishment of a permanent rule. 21—25.

13. Last great battle of Saul. His discomfiture and death, and death of his sons. xxxi. 1—7. Triumph of the Philistines. Loyal conduct of the men of Jabesh-Gilead. 8—13.

XX.

From the Death of Saul to the Complete Establishment of David's Authority over the Whole Kingdom.

II. Sam. i.—vii. and I. Chron. xi—xvii.   A. M. 2948—2964.   B. C. 1056—1040.

The character of David is one of the most remarkable, even among the eminent men of the Bible. It was complex, and, in some respects, contradictory. In the previous lessons, we have had an account of his youth and of his early manhood. During these years, he evinced great native abilities, as well as a simple faith and a profound religious purpose. These qualities were greatly developed by the extraordinary experiences through which he passed in these early years. As we find him in the following lessons, he has several marked characteristics. He has, first, military genius of a high order. Out of a partially subdued and demoralized people, he organized forces which, under his general direction, not only made the nation independent, but brought most of the neighboring tribes under wholesome fear, if not into subjugation. In the second place, he had great administrative abilities,— a genius for government. This, with his military ability, rendered him perhaps the most powerful ruler of his age, and extended his empire far beyond the previous boundaries of the nation, and made other considerable nations tributary. Thirdly, he was a man of remarkable intellectual and poetic power. His writings are among the choice treasures of Hebrew literature, and, even aside from their religious value, belong to the small class of writings destined to be valued in all ages. Fourthly, he was a man of not only lofty religious sentiments, but of profound and earnest piety. Fifthly, he was a man, nevertheless, of mighty passions and impulses, which, notwithstanding the restraints of his religion, now and then broke through their limits and carried him into grievous sins and acts fraught with peril to himself and his people. His remorse and contrition over these are indicated, both in the narrative and in some of his Psalms.

---

1. David hears the report of the battle in which Saul and his sons were slain. Punishment of the man who assisted in Saul's death. II. Sam. i. 1—16.

2. The lament for Saul and Jonathan. David's remarkable dirge. 17—27.

3. The men of Judah anoint David as king, at Hebron. His message to the men of Jabesh-Gilead. ii. 1—7.

4. Dissent of the other tribes, and appointment of Ishbosheth as king. Beginning of civil war. 8—17. Defeat and flight of the latter's army under Abner, and pursuit by Joab and Asahel. The latter slain. 18—23. End of the pursuit. 24—32.

5. Continuation of the war, and David's success. David's family. iii. 1—5. Quarrel of Ishbosheth with Abner, and desertion of the latter, who negotiates with David to bring in the dissenting tribes. 6—12.

6. Conditions of the league. 13—16. Progress of the negotiations. Abner's reception by David, and his departure to effect the conciliation of his party. 17—21.

7. Indignation of Joab at the situation. Abner pursued, brought back, and treacherously slain. David's grief and imprecation on Joab. 22—39.

8. Murder of Ishbosheth. His slayers, thinking to be rewarded, are, by David's order, put to death. iv. 1—12. The kingdom united under David. v. 1—5. Conquest of Jerusalem completed, and it is made the capital of the kingdom. 6—9; I. Chron. xi. 1—8. David's mighty men, and some of their exploits. I. Chron. xi. 9—47; II. Sam. xxiii. 8—39.

9. David's prosperity. Invasion by the Philistines, and their repulse. II. Sam. v. 10—25.

10. Removal of the ark. vi. 1—5. Disaster and admonition. 6—9. The ark with Obed-Edom, and the blessing to him. 10, 11. Its second removal, and arrival in Jerusalem. The joyful celebration. 12—19; I. Chron. xvi. 1—3. Appointments for religious service. 37—43.

11. What Psalms are likely to have been composed for this occasion? cxxxii., lxviii., xxiv. What passages in these obviously refer to this time? Give the grand refrain of the last. 7—8. With what Psalm does the song in I. Chron. xvi. in part coincide?

12. The king's purpose to build a temple unto the Lord. II. Sam. vii. 1—3; I. Chron. xvii. 1—3. David forbidden to build; the privilege to be granted to his son. 4—17. What explicit reason is elsewhere given for this prohibition? I. Kings v. 3; I. Chron. xxviii. 3. David's response and thanksgiving. II. Sam. viii. 18—29.

13. Final subjugation of the Philistines, and conquest of the neighboring nations. David's brilliant success in war. vii. 1—15. Chief officers of his government. 16—18.

XXI.

From David's Complete Establishment to the Close of Absalom's Revolt.

II. Sam. ix.—xviii.   A. M. 2964—2982.   B. C. 1040—1022.

1. David remembers his covenant with Jonathan, and shows kindness to the son of his friend. II. Sam. ix.

2. A kindly embassy to the king of Ammon is received with suspicion, and sent back with personal insult. x. 1—4. David's indignation, and the terrible punishment visited upon the Ammonites and their allies. 5—19.

3. David falls into flagrant sin, and attempts to conceal it by another, if possible, greater. The murder of Urijah. xi.

4. The prophet Nathan's parable, and the Divine rebuke and terrible judgment. xii. 1—14. Death of David's child, and the conduct of the king. 15—23.

5. Birth of Solomon. Conquest of Rabbah-Ammon. 24—31.

6. Amnon, David's oldest son, guilty of a great crime. The anger of the king, the revenge of Absalom, and his exile. xiii. 20—39.

7. Joab's stratagem to bring about the return of Absalom, and its success. xiv. 1—24. Absalom's personal appearance. His family. His restoration to the king's favor. 25—33.

8. He plots against the government, and cultivates the arts of popularity. Rebellion and insurrection. xv. 1—13. Flight of David with his family and his body-guard. 14—23.

9. The king sends back the ark, which had been taken along in the flight. He also sends his friend Hushai to Absalom, to act secretly in the king's interest, and to counteract other counsellors. 24—37.

10. Device of Ziba, who traduces Mephibosheth and obtains a reward. xvi. 1—4. Continued flight. Indignity offered to the king by one of the family of Saul. David's forbearance. 5—13.

11. Absalom enters Jerusalem. Takes counsel of Ahithophel and Hushai. 15—23, and xvii. 1—13. Shrewd and successful device of the latter. Word sent to David concerning Absalom's plans. 14—21. The two armies. Supplies for the king's troops. 24—29.

12. The battle. David's tenderness for Absalom. Defeat of the insurgents. xviii. 1—8. Absalom's death and burial. 9—19.

13. The news carried to David. 20—32. His intense sorrow and pathetic utterances concerning his son. 33.

XXII.

From the Overthrow of Absalom to the Death of David.

II. Sam. xix.—I. Kings. ii., and I. Chron. xxi.—xxix.
A. M. 2982—2989.   B. C. 1022—1015.

1. David's continued grief, and Joab's reproof. xix. 1—8. The return to Jerusalem. Incidents of Shimei, of Mephibosheth, and of Barzillai. 9—40. Jealousies and dissensions among the people. 41—43.

2. Revolt of a party under Sheba the son of Bichri. Amasa, who had been Absalom's chief captain, is commissioned to organize the troops, but is delayed. Abishai and Joab ordered to pursue the insurgents. Joab slays Amasa. xx. 1—12.

3. The rebellion crushed, and its leader slain. 13—22. Chief officers of the king. 23—26.

4. A famine and its cause. The satisfaction demanded by the Gibeonites for the cruelty of Saul toward them. xxi. 1—6. The barbarous offering to meet their demand. The touching devotion of the mother of a part of the victims. 7—11. Burial of the dead bodies with the bones of Saul and Jonathan, by David. 12—14. Exploits of David's mighty men. 15—22.

5. David's song of deliverance. xxii. With what Psalm does this substantially correspond? Mention any passages in it which strike you as remarkable.

6. David, through vanity and ambition, tempted to make a census of the military forces of his realm. Joab's remonstrance, and the king's persistence. xxiv. 1—9; I. Chron. xxi. 1—6.

7. David's repentance. The Divine message through the prophet Gad. The choice of penalties. 10—13. The king's remorse and his prayer. Directed to build an altar to the Lord. The pestilence stayed. 14—25. For what did the locality of this altar afterwards become famous?

8. Old age of David. Attempt of Adonijah to usurp the kingdom. I. Kings 1—10. Had he any natural claim to the succession? (See ii. 22, and II. Sam. iii. 4.) The matter reported to David, and his directions concerning it. 11—35.

9. Solomon anointed and acknowledged as king. The effect on Adonijah and his party. Solomon conditionally spares his brother's life. 38—53.

10. David's charge to Solomon. Gives directions concerning judgments against certain persons. ii. 1—9.

11. The particular charge concerning the temple. The preparations made, and the contributions of the people. I. Chron. xxviii., xxix. David's prayer, and grateful acknowledgment of the Divine goodness and mercy. I. Chron. xxix. 10—19. Sacrifices and rejoicings of the people, and happy inauguration of Solomon's reign. 20—25. David's death. I. Kings ii. 10; I. Chron. xxix. 28.

12. Give some of the prominent points of David's character. (See introduction to No. XX.)

XXIII.

The Reign of Solomon.

I. Kings ii.—xi., and II. Chron. i.—viii.   A. M. 2989—3029.   B. C. 1015—975.

The reign of Solomon comprises the most brilliant period of the Israelitish nation. It might be compared, in some respects, with the Augustan age of Rome, or the age of Pericles in Greece; though, in several particulars, it differed widely from them. It was, for the most part, a time of profound peace, not only throughout the nation itself; but the neighboring territories, which, far and near, had been made tributary under the reign of David, remained subject to Solomon till near the close of his reign. It appears to have been a time of extraordinary industrial prosperity, and, for the first time, we find the people engaging in a commerce which rapidly developed to large proportions.

Solomon, as well as his father, David, though in quite another way, must be set down as one of the marked men, not only of Hebrew history, but of all time. His intellectual endowments were extraordinary, especially for the age in which he lived, and the versatility of his genius was very great. While he had no opportunity to evince or cultivate, and probably did not possess the military talent of his father, his administrative ability in civil affairs appears to have been superior even to his. A man of great intuitive power, of remarkable insight into character, of comprehensive judgment and a very wide range of intelligence, he must hold his place in history among the great rulers of men. He appears to have been a man of reflective and studious habits, and, amid the overwhelming cares of his government and the multitudinous projects of improvement both in his private and in public affairs, he found time for extended literary culture and composition. The early part of his life was characterized by a marked and humble piety and communion with God. His own extraordinary prosperity, his foreign alliances, and especially his falling into that pernicious Eastern usage, which had been begun by his father, of maintaining an extensive harem and marrying many wives, at last utterly corrupted him, and led him into deplorable religious apostasy which brought disaster to his house.

His reign was about three hundred and fifty years before the building of Rome, when Minos reigned in Crete, and Athens was governed by Archons.

---

1. The party of Adonijah cause suspicions of conspiracy. The prominent men in it are put to death, or otherwise punished. I. Kings ii. 12—34. What predictions were fulfilled in the degredation of Abiathar and the punishment of Joab? I. Sam. ii. 31—36; II. Sam. iii. 39 and 27, 28.

2. Restrictions of Shimei. The violation of them, and his punishment. I. Kings ii. 36—46.

3. Solomon's piety. His public and solemn recognition of God. His prayer for wisdom, and God's answer. I. Kings iii. 3—15; II. Chron. i. 1—12.

4. Remarkable instance of his practical sagacity soon after this. I. Kings iii. 16—28.

5. Mention some of the chief officers of Solomon's government; his prime minister, iv. 5; head of religious affairs, 2; chief of the war department, 4; secretary of the treasury, 6.

6. Describe the commissary department of the government, 7—19. Evidences of prosperity, both personally and politically. Mention some of Solomon's resources, 20—28; II. Chron. i. 14—17; and ix. 13—28.

7. His intellectual endowments. I. Kings iv. 29—34.

8. Account of the preparation for building the Temple. Treaty and amicable arrangements with the King of Tyre. I. Kings v. 1—12. The number of men employed in securing the materials, and the plan of labor. 8—18. II. Chron. ii.

9. The time of laying the foundation of the Temple. I. Kings vi. 1. How long before the building of Rome? About what period of Egyptian history? Of Grecian history?

10. Dimensions of the Temple proper? vi. 2, 3, 17; II. Chron. iii. 3, 4. What were the more costly materials, and what the previous preparations? I. Kings vi. 7, 9, 15, 21, 31, 34; II. Chron. iii. 4—9.

11. Mention some of the more prominent appointments of the Temple. I. Kings vi. 19, 20; vii. 15—21, 23—26; II. Chron. iv. 1. Give the dimensions and capacity of the "brazen sea" or laver. I. Kings vii. 23—26. (A "bath" is equal to 8 gallons, 5¼ pints.)

12. How long was the Temple in building? vi. 37, 38.

13. Give some account of the dedication of the Temple. I. Kings viii.; II. Chron. v.—vii.

14. Evidences of public prosperity. I. Kings iv. 17—28; II. Chron. viii. 1—8.

15. Visit of the Queen of Sheba; her surprise and admiration of Solomon's greatness and wisdom. I. Kings x. 1—10. Commercial prosperity. 11—29.

16. The fall of Solomon, and the sad close of his reign. I. Kings xi.

17. What writings, supposed to be his, are contained in the sacred canon? What is the mournful refrain of the Book of Ecclesiastes, and how does it correspond with Solomon's career?

SECOND YEAR'S COURSE.

HEBREW HISTORY, FROM THE REVOLT OF THE
TEN TRIBES TO THE RETURN FROM THE
BABYLONIAN CAPTIVITY, TOGETHER
WITH THE POETIC AND
PROPHETIC BOOKS.

BOOKS OF REFERENCE.
SECOND YEAR.

Smith's OLD TESTAMENT HISTORY.
Geikie's HOURS WITH THE BIBLE.
Milman's JEWISH HISTORY.
Stanley's HISTORY OF THE JEWISH CHURCH, 2d and 3d Series.
Josephus' JEWISH ANTIQUITIES.
Thompson's THE LAND AND THE BOOK.
Stanley's SINAI AND PALESTINE.
Hutchinson's MUSIC OF THE BIBLE.
Sime's KINGDOM OF ALL ISRAEL.
Perowne's ON THE PSALMS.
Blakie's MANUAL OF BIBLE HISTORY.
Green's KINGDOMS OF ISRAEL AND JUDAH.
Rawlinson's HERODOTUS and EGYPT AND BABYLON.
Palmer's HISTORY OF THE JEWISH NATION.
Birch's ANCIENT HISTORY FROM THE MONUMENTS.
Rawlinson's HISTORICAL ILLUSTRATIONS OF THE OLD TESTAMENT.
Sayce's FRESH LIGHT FROM THE ANCIENT MONUMENTS.
LIFE OF ELIJAH : G. Taylor, Lowrie, Krummacher, Edersheim. Macduff.
Maurice's PROPHETS AND KINGS.
Phelps' STUDIES IN THE OLD TESTAMENT.
Taylor's DANIEL THE BELOVED.
BY-PATHS OF BIBLE KNOWLEDGE.
Rand, McNally & Co.'s MANUAL OF BIBLICAL HISTORY AND GEOGRAPHY.

HEBREW HISTORY.

I.

FROM THE REVOLT OF THE TEN TRIBES TO THE ACCESSION OF AHAB.

A.M. 3029-3071. 975-909 B.C.

A CHANGE from the power, prosperity, and glory of the kingdom under David and Solomon, becomes suddenly manifest after the close of the reign of the latter. The new king, Rehoboam, attempting to keep up the magnificent state of his father, and to make the corresponding exactions, while being incalculably inferior to him in all those qualities which command respect, and so far forth enforce obedience, soon found a large part of his kingdom in insurrection and open revolt. The secession of the Ten Tribes under Jeroboam, and the erection of a new kingdom, left the royal family with only the powerful tribe of Judah, and the small tribe of Benjamin, — a small fragment of the great empire of David and Solomon. This civil dissension gave occasion to the previously subdued nations to abjure their allegiance, and still more reduced the power of the divided nation. From this time the decadence of the people was for many years constant and rapid, and they never again regained their previous prosperity. The part that went with Jeroboam fell into idolatry and religious apostasy, and so provoked the anger of God that their condition early became very miserable. The kingdom of Judah was more faithful to their religion, though there was also great wickedness among the people.

The contemporary history of this period is mostly fabulous, and the data are very scanty. It is probable that Homer was born some time during these years, though the proof of this is by no means positive.

KINGS OF JUDAH.	B.C.	KINGS OF ISRAEL.	B.C.
Rehoboam . . .	975-958	Jeroboam	975-953
Abijam	958-955	Nadab	953-951
Asa	955-914	Baasha	951-927
		Elah	927-925
		Zimri	
		Omri	925-913

1. Give the names of the kings of Judah during the period covered by this lesson. Of Israel. What changes took place in the line of the latter?

2. Who was the successor of Solomon? What occurred at the beginning of his reign? Do you think Rehoboam acted the part of a prudent and sensible ruler? What was the result? 1 Kings xii. 1-16.

3. How many tribes seceded, and how many remained loyal? What course did Rehoboam pursue, and with what consequence? 18-24.

4. Who was made king over the seceding tribes? Give some account of his previous history. 1 Kings xi. 26, 28-33, 40.

5. What was Jeroboam's character, and what religious changes did he make? xii. 26-33. What warning did he get from the prophet of the Lord, and how did he receive it? What judgment followed? xiii. 1-6.

6. Give an account of what befell this prophet immediately after this. 11-32.

7. What was the subsequent conduct of Jeroboam? 33-44. What affliction befell him? What did he do? What answer did the prophet make? xiv. 1-16.

8. The moral and religious condition of Judah under Rehoboam? 21-24. What calamity came upon the nation? 25-28.

9. Who was Rehoboam's successor? His character? xv. 1-8. Give an account of the war between Judah and Israel. 2 Chron. xiii.

10. Who was the next king of Judah? What was his general character? Give some of the incidents of his reign. What were some of his faults? 1 Kings xv. 9-24. 2 Chron. xiv-xvi.

11. Who was Asa's successor? His character, and the character of his reign? 2 Chron. xvii. 1 Kings xxii. 41-50.

12. Who succeeded Jeroboam in the kingdom of Israel? How long did he reign? How did his reign terminate? What prophecy was fulfilled? 1 Kings xv. 25-30.

13. Who now usurped the throne? His character? What prophetic message was sent him? xv. 33; xvi. 7. Who followed Baasha, and how was the foregoing prophecy fulfilled? 8-14.

14. Who succeeded Elah? How long did Zimri occupy the throne? What events followed? The character of Omri, and the character of his reign? 15-28.

II.

JUDAH AND ISRAEL UNDER JEHOSHAPHAT AND AHAB.

A.M. 3071-3107.   909-873 B.C.

Under the reign of these two kings, both sections of the divided nation experienced a quarter of a century of peace with each, and, for the most part, of protection against the invasion of hostile neighbors. The two kings were remarkable men in their way. Jehoshaphat appears to have been a prince of decided ability, both in civil and military affairs. Under him, Judah prospered more than at any previous time after the death of Solomon. Ahab was also a man of no small power, and in many respects an efficient ruler. But he was morally weak, and was disastrously influenced by his wife Jezebel, a heathen princess, a woman evidently of great resources, but audacious and unscrupulous in wickedness. The consequence was, that the king sanctioned and encouraged the most unrighteous public conduct, and was himself led into acts of gross immorality. It is true he was not destitute of occasional compunctions of conscience. There are indications of convictions which, however, seem not to have been cherished. The nation sank into the most degrading idolatry and most abhorrent vices. The people suffered the judgments of God, but they never recovered their religious character.

KING OF JUDAH.	B.C.	KING OF ISRAEL.	B.C.
Jehoshaphat	914–889	Ahab	913–891

1. How long did Ahab reign, and over which division of the nation? His character? What source of powerful evil influence affected him?

2. What remarkable prophet suddenly appears during this reign? What judgment does he predict against Ahab and his people? 1 Kings xvii. 1. Give some account of Elijah's experience during the drought. Fed by ravens. The widow of Zarephath. What miracle did he work? 2-24.

3. After this, what was Elijah told to do? Whom did he meet? Character of this man? Give an account of his interview with the king. Describe the meeting with the priests of Baal, and the results. xviii. 1-40.

4. Elijah on Carmel. The little cloud, the great rain. 41-46.

5. Elijah's action reported to Jezebel, and its effect upon her? What was the effect upon Elijah? What followed? xix. 1-14. On what important errand was he now sent? Incidents connected with this mission. Whom did Elijah call to be his associate prophet? 15-21.

6. Give an account of the action of Ben-hadad, and the war that followed. xx. 1-21. Subsequent engagements and successes. 22-30. How did Ahab treat the conquered Ben-hadad? Was this a wise leniency? What rebuke did he receive? 31-43.

7. Give the story of Ahab's crime against Naboth. Who inspired this wickedness? What terrible judgment was uttered against both? xxi. 1-24. What description is given of Ahab? 25, 26. What was the effect of the prophet's denunciation? 26-29.

8. What was the name of the king of Judah at this time? How long did he reign? xxii. 42. His character, and the character of his reign? 2 Chron. xvii.

9. Give an account of his alliance with Ahab. What was the object,

and how was it encouraged? What contrary prediction was uttered? How did Ahab treat the utterer of this? What was the result? 1 Kings xxii. 1-37. 2 Chron. xviii. What prediction was fulfilled in the incident mentioned in 1 Kings xxii. 38? (See xxi. 19.)

10. What message came to Jehoshaphat on his return from this war? 2 Chron. xix. 1-3. What points of excellence in his administration are mentioned? 4-11.

11. What combination was made against Jehoshaphat? 2 Chron. xx. 1, 2. What measures does he adopt? The result? How was the victory brought about? The return to Jerusalem? 3-29.

12. What rebuke did he receive, and for what? 35-37.

III.

FROM THE DEATH OF AHAB AND JEHOSHAPHAT TO THE EXTINCTION OF THE HOUSE OF AHAB.

A.M. 3107-3120.   873-884 B.C.

After the death of Ahab and Jehoshaphat, both the kingdom of Judah and the kingdom of Israel entered upon a period of gradual, but more marked and rapid, decadence. This was more obvious in the case of the latter than in that of the former. The house of Ahab, by the increasing wickedness of his descendants, not only provoked the anger of the Lord against the family till the predicted curse was fulfilled in the extinction of that dynasty, but the nation had become demoralized beyond recovery. The kings of Judah, too, from this time, more frequently lapsed into idolatry, and thus brought mischief on the nation. Still the bad kings were less numerous than in Israel, and the evil consequences to the people were not as great.

In the early part of this period, Homer flourished in Greece, and Lycurgus governed at Sparta. Later, Carthage was founded by Dido.

KINGS OF JUDAH.	B.C.	KINGS OF ISRAEL.	B.C.
Jehoram	889-881	Ahaziah	891-889
Ahaziah	881-880	Jehoram	889-877
Interregnum	880-874		

1. Give an account of the reign and character of Ahaziah, son of Ahab. His accident, inquiry of a false god, meeting of the messengers with Elijah. The rebuke and prediction. The parties sent to bring Elijah, and the fatality attending them. The prophet's visit, and the death of the king. 2 Kings i. 1-18.

2. Give the story of Elijah's translation. The journey. Elisha's re-

quest. The taking away. Elisha's return and the search for Elijah. ii. 1-18.

3. Give the story of the bad water and the remedy. Of the wicked children and their punishment. 19-25.

4. Who was the successor of Ahaziah? His character? What serious event occurred near the beginning of his reign? What measures did Jehoram take to remedy the evil? iii. 1-7. What peril befell the allies? Upon whom did they call for counsel? How did he meet them, and what did he advise? What was the result? 8-27.

5. Four incidents in the prophet's life. (a) The widow in distress relieved. iv. 1-7. (b) The hospitality of the Shunamite woman, her reward, and the miraculous restoration of the dead son. 8-37. (c) The poisoned pottage. 38-41. (d) The great multitude fed with small supplies. 42-44.

6. Give the story of Naaman. v. 1-14. What reward did he offer, and how was the offer received? Of what bad conduct was Elisha's servant guilty? What was the consequence? 15-27.

7. Miracle of the axe. vi. 1-7. The Syrian war, and the miraculous aid to the Israelites through Elisha. 8-10. Attempt of the Syrian king to capture Elisha. The host smitten with blindness, led to Samaria, and delivered to the king. The latter not permitted to destroy them. 11-23.

8. Siege of Samaria, and the great distress. 24-30. Elisha threatened by the king. The messenger baffled. 31-33.

9. Elisha's remarkable prediction. The doubting officer. vii. 1, 2. Fulfilment of predictions, and the great deliverance. 3-20.

10. Further incidents relating to the Shunamite woman. viii. 1-6. Elisha goes to Damascus. Sickness of the king, and inquiry by Hazael of the prophet. The answer and startling disclosure. 7-13. Hazael's murder of the king, and usurpation of the throne. 14, 15.

11. Jehoram, king of Judah. How did he begin his reign? Whom did he marry, and what was the consequence? 2 Chron. xxi. 1-6.

12. Revolt of Edom, which had before been tributary to Judah. War and conquest by Judah, but the Edomites not wholly subdued. Continued wickedness of Jehoram. Solemn warning from the prophet. Beset with evils. Personal affliction and death. 7-20. Ahaziah's wicked reign. xxii. 1-9.

13. Jehu anointed to be king over Israel. Rejection of Ahab's house. 2 Kings ix. 1-12. Revolution in the kingdom. Jehu destroys the whole house of Ahab as predicted Jehoram cast into the field of Naboth. Ahaziah, king of Judah, being also of the family and sympathizing with them, is slain. 13-28.

14. The end of Jezebel, and the fulfilment of the curse predicted. 30-37.

IV.

FROM THE OVERTHROW OF THE HOUSE OF AHAB TO THE CAPTIVITY OF THE TEN TRIBES.

A.M. 3120–3283.   884–721 B.C.

The civil disorders became, from this time, more frequent in the kingdom of Israel. There were great wickedness and demoralization. Conspiracies, assassinations, and usurpations characterized a great part of this period. Yet there were also some symptoms of religious reformation. The prophet Hosea arose about this time, and preached powerfully and with some effect against the idolatry and general sinfulness of the nation. The style and character of his preaching are fully seen in the book of his prophecy, which should be read in connection with the historical narrative. Towards the close of the period, there was a manifest improvement in the morals of the nation, and in the character of the government. Probably the last of the kings was, in his general character, the best. But the corruption had become too great, and the health and strength of the nation had become exhausted. In the Assyrian invasion, the nation is subdued, and the people carried captive. The Jewish kingdom is involved in these calamities, but to a less extent.

During this period is the epoch of the Greek Olympiads. Rome, also, was founded by Romulus.

KINGS OF JUDAH.	B.C.	KINGS OF ISRAEL.	B.C.
Joash	873–833	Jehu	877–849
Amaziah	833–804	Jehoahaz	849–832
Azariah or Uzziah	804–752	Jehoash	832–816
Jotham	752–736	Jeroboam II.	816–775
Ahaz	736–720	Zachariah	775
		Shallum	775
		Menahem	775–765
		Pekahiah	765–763
		Pekah	763–743
		Hoshea	743–734

---

1. What was the principal condition of the treaty which Jehu made with the adherents of Ahab's family? 2 Kings x. 1–7. Give an account of what he did to the worshippers of Baal. 18–28.

2. Did Jehu maintain his character as a worshipper of the true God? What was the consequence? What disaster befell the kingdom? 29–36.

3. What disorderly proceedings took place in the kingdom of Judah about this time? xi. 1–3. How was the royal line saved from extinction?

4. Give an account of the counter-revolution. 4-21. 2 Chron. xxiii.

5. How old was the new king? How were the offices of the kingdom administered with so young a ruler? What reforms were instituted, and what improvements made under the regency of Jehoiada? 2 Kings xii. 1-16.

6. What change took place in the conduct of the king after the death of Jehoiada? What flagrant exhibition of ingratitude did he display? 2 Chron. xxiv. 15-22. What disasters followed? 23-27. 2 Kings xii. 17-21.

7. Who succeeded Jehu? His character, and the consequences to the kingdom? 2 Kings xiii. 1-9. Give some account of the reign of Joash. The interview between him and the sick prophet. Death of the latter, and the miracle at his grave. 14-21.

8. Who succeeded Joash in Judah? His character, his military success, and his relations with Israel? xiv. 1-7. 2 Chron. xxv. 1-12.

9. Give some account of the remainder of Amaziah's reign. What disasters overtook him? 2 Chron. xxv. 14-28. 2 Kings xiv. 8-20. Give an account of the reign of Jeroboam II. 23-29.

10. Who now reigned in Judah? His character in the early part of his reign? What disastrous change, and the consequences? 2 Chron. xxvi. Who was his successor? Character and exploits of his reign? xxvii. 2 Kings xv. 32-38.

11. Give the main events in the kingdom of Israel from this time to the overthrow of the nation. How many revolutions and usurpations took place? 2 Kings 8-31; xvii. 1-23. With whom was the land re-peopled, and what the effect? 24-31.

12. Who was king in Judah at this time? His character, and the character of his administration? How did he compare religiously with his predecessors? What invasion and war took place, and what was the result? 2 Kings xvi. 1-9. 2 Chron. xxviii. 6-16. How did this reign terminate? 2 Kings xvi. 10-20.

V.

THE REIGN OF HEZEKIAH OVER JUDAH.

A.M. 3283-3312. 750-721 B.C..

After the destruction of the kingdom of Israel, there were indications for a time of returning prosperity, moral as well as political, in the kingdom of Judah. Hezekiah's reign, which began six years before the event referred to, was characterized by integrity and uprightness on the part of both the king and his court, and many reforms were introduced or attempted. Still, the growing power of the Assyrian empire was pushing its encroachments, and pressing severely upon the nation, and, at one time, seemed about to destroy Judah as it had Israel. It would have done so but for the Divine interposition. As it was, the power of Judah was greatly diminished. Near the close of this reign, Babylon, for the first time, comes into noticeable relations to the Jews, by an embassy from that now rapidly developing power. To this embassy, Hezekiah, flattered by the attentions shown him, exhibited the resources of his kingdom, and the still remarkable treasures of the Temple; for which indiscretion he was rebuked by the prophet.

During this reign flourished the prophet Isaiah, a man of extraordinary intellectual and spiritual power, and perhaps the most eloquent of the Old-Testament prophets. In these days, also, Hosea, Nahum, and Micah preached and prophesied against the prevailing evils.

At this time Numa Pompilius was king of Rome; Babylon, just coming into historical note, was a viceroyalty of the Assyria of which Nineveh was the capital; Media had revolted from Assyria, and become independent; and Athens was under the rule of the Archons.

---

1. Accession of Hezekiah, and his character. 2 Chron. xxix. 1, 2. Reforms introduced. Repairs of the Temple. The Levites exhorted. Purification of neglected rooms, courts, and implements. Renewal of religious service, and appointment of proper officers, ministers, and musicians for this purpose. 3-36.

2. Great preparation for renewed observance of the Passover. Invitations sent throughout the territory of their brethren of the kingdom of Israel. How the invitation was treated by some, and heard by others. xxx. 1-12. The memorable feast. Revival influence resulting in destruction of idolatrous altars, and in the hearty devotion of the people. 13-27

3. Further combined efforts to banish idolatry. Regulation of the religious service, and its thorough re-establishment. Hezekiah's devotion and energy. xxxi. 1-21.

4. What relic of former times and temptation to idolatry was destroyed early in this reign? 2 Kings xviii. 4. Give some account of this object. Num. xxi. 5-9.

5. New enterprise infused among the people. Prosperity and victory over some of their enemies. 2 Kings xviii. 7, 8.

6. Invasion by the Assyrians. Hezekiah submits to their exactions, and pays large tribute, using the silver and gold, both of the treasury of the Temple and of its ornaments, to meet the demand. 13-16.

7. Second invasion by the Assyrians. Hezekiah's preparations for defence, both within and without the city. He also re-organizes his military forces. 2 Chron. xxxii. 1-8.

8. Siege of Jerusalem. Insulting demand of the officers constituting the Assyrian embassy, and their boastful threats. 2 Kings xviii. 17-37. 2 Chron. xxxii. 9-19.

9. Distress of Hezekiah. Message to Isaiah. The encouraging and assuring answer. 2 Kings xix. 1-7. Departure of the Assyrians for a

season, with threats of future vengeance. They return, and renew the siege. Isaiah's prophecy against them. 8-34. 2 Chron. xxxii Their miraculous defeat and utter overthrow. 2 Kings xix. 35.

10. Hezekiah's apparently fatal sickness. He is greatly afflicted, and prays earnestly. The answer through the prophet. The sign of the shadow on the dial. 2 Kings xx. 1-11. Isa. xxxviii. 1-8. Hezekiah's song of thanksgiving. 9-20.

11. His subsequent prosperity and temporary worldliness. His penitence and piety. 2 Chron. xxxii. 25-29.

12. Embassy from the king of Babylon with presents. Hezekiah's exhibition of his treasures. Isaiah's rebuke. 2 Kings xx. 12-18. Isa. xxxix. Hezekiah's death. 2 Kings xx. 21.

13. Name the prophets of this reign. Contemporary history. (See Introduction to lesson.)

VI.

FROM THE DEATH OF HEZEKIAH TO THE DEATH OF JOSIAH.

A.M. 3312-3410. 721-623 B.C.

The reign of Hezekiah was succeeded by a calamitous reaction in the condition of the nation. The reign of Manasseh, though longer than that of any other Jewish king, was, during a considerable part of it at least, the most wicked. There seems to have been no known abomination practised by any heathen nation, which, under his influence, was not imitated, if not excelled. As a consequence, the most terrible civil disasters ensued. The land was invaded, Jerusalem probably taken, and the king himself carried in captivity to Babylon. To all appearances, the end of Judah had come, as that of Israel had come thirty-five years before. But the timely and apparently genuine penitence of Manasseh, and the peaceable character of the Babylonian monarch, caused a restoration and continuance of the national life, though in a tributary relation to the conquering nation. Manasseh, after his return, undid much of the wickedness which he had committed, and introduced genuine reforms, though there was still a great lack of spiritual loyalty among the people. The reign of Amon was short and wicked. The advent of the child-king, Josiah, was signalized by a religious revival of the most marked character; and this reign appears to have been, more than any other since David's time, characterized by the deep piety of the king, and a spirit of sweeping reform among the people. The consternation caused by the discovery of the Book of the Law, — probably the Pentateuch, — which had been neglected, and perhaps lost for centuries, with its plain statements of what was required of the people, and the terrible penalties of disobedience, appears to have had a wholesome effect. But the nation had too far gone in moral decay to be more than temporarily reprieved by this reformation. The prophets Isaiah and Nahum continue till about the beginning of this period; and Joel, Jeremiah, Zephaniah, and Habakkuk begin their ministry near the end of it. The northern Assyrian kingdom becomes subordinate to the southern, of which Babylon is the capital. It was the time of the Messenian war in Greece, of Pisistratus at Athens, and subsequently of the ascendency of Sparta. In Rome, Tullus Hostilius and Ancus Martius reigned, according to the not very certain tradition; and it is also supposed to have been the period of the Horatii and Curiatii.

---

1. Who succeeded Hezekiah? What can you say of his character? 2 Kings xxi. 1, 2. How do the length and character of his reign compare with those of his predecessors? What were some of the abominable things done by him? 3-9. 2 Chron. xxxiii. 1-9.

2. What warnings and what threatenings were uttered? 2 Kings xxi. 10-15. What was the effect? 2 Chron xxxiii. 10.

3. What calamity befell the nation and the king? 11.

4. What was the effect on Manasseh? The further consequence? 12, 13.

5. What did the king do after his restoration? 14-17.

6. His death and burial. 20. What reason can you suggest why the account of this long and eventful reign is so brief and fragmentary, when there appear to have been very full details in the contemporary writings? Also, why, possibly, he was not buried with his royal ancestors?

7. The short, wicked, and uneventful reign of Amon, and his tragical death. 21-24.

8. Who was the successor of Amon? What was there remarkable about the beginning of his reign? General character of his reign. 2 Kings xxii. 1, 2. 2 Chron. xxxiv. 1, 2. Sets in operation a thorough and sweeping religious reformation. 3-7.

9. Renovation of the temple, and restoration of parts fallen into decay. 2 Kings xxii. 3-7. What important discovery was made, and what was done with it? 8-10. What was the effect of the reading of this document? 11-13. Of whom was inquiry made, and what information was given? Effect on the king and his officers? What promise was made? 11-20.

10. What public meeting took place, and what was done? xxiii. 1-3. What followed? How far did this reformation extend? What prophecy was fulfilled? 4-20. (See, also, 1 Kings xii. 32, 33, and xiii. 1-32.)

11. The great Passover celebration. 21-24. What high commendation is given Josiah? 25. Regulation of the Temple worship and service. 2 Chron. xxxv. 1-19. Did these acts of repentance and reformation save the nation, and why? 2 Kings xxiii. 26, 27.

12. What invasion took place, and what calamity followed? 2 Kings xxiii. 29, 30. 2 Chron. xxxv. 20-24. The greatness of the mourning. 25, and Zech. xii. 11.

13. The prophets of this period? Contemporary history? (See Introduction.)

VII.

FROM THE DEATH OF JOSIAH TO THE DESTRUCTION OF JERUSALEM UNDER NEBUCHADNEZZAR.

A.M. 3410–3445.   623–588 B.C.

The death of Josiah marks the virtual conclusion of the independence of the Jewish kingdom. His successors were both weak and wicked. Under them, the nation became subject first to the king of Egypt, who captured Jerusalem and deposed the king; and afterwards to the king of Babylon, from whose authority their abortive efforts to revolt brought upon them retribution, their final destruction and captivity. The records of these times are somewhat fragmentary and confused. But, besides what we find in the historical books, there are intimations and accounts of particular events in the prophets. The most noted of these was Jeremiah. He was a man of great probity, great faithfulness, and great power. In his preaching, he warned and rebuked the people for their sins so uncompromisingly that he offended the leaders, and was subject to cruel persecutions, though he compelled the respect of the less abandoned. During this period or near it, also, prophesied Habakkuk, Zephaniah, Ezekiel, and Obadiah. About this time Nineveh, the northern Assyrian capital, was overthrown, as predicted by Nahum the prophet. The Persian and Median monarchies begin to become conspicuous, and are soon after united. Draco, and afterward Solon, flourished in Athens. It was the time of the seven wise men of Greece, and of Tarquin the Elder and Servius Tullus in Rome.

---

1. Who was Josiah's successor, and what was his character? 2 Kings xxiii. 31, 32.

2. What national disaster occurred? What change in the government, and under what condition? 33–35. Compute the amount of the tribute. 33.

3. The reign and character of Jehoiakim. 36, 37. What celebrated prophet appears about this time? His description of these last two kings, and especially of the public regard in which the latter would be held. Jer. xxii. 11–17, and 18, 19.

4. His predictions of the Divine judgments. Jer. xix. 3, 4, 7–9, 15. How was he treated? xx. 1, 2. His reply to his persecutors. 3–6. The solemn warning of the prophet in the temple-court to the princes and priests. They threaten him with death, but he resolutely persists. His death sought by the king, but better counsels prevail. Jer. xxvi.

5. What further prophecy does he utter? xxvii. What remarkable prediction does he make about this time? Jer. xxv., especially vs. 11 and 12. See also xxix. 1–10. Dan. ix. 1, 2. 2 Chron. xxxvi. 21.

6. What great invasion takes place, and what results? 2 Kings xxiv. 1. 2 Chron. xxxvi. 6, 7. Dan. i. 1-6.

7. Subsequent conduct of Jehoiakim, and condition of the nation. 2 Kings xxiv. 1-4. A great fast proclaimed about this time. Baruch reads, in the hearing of the people, the prophecies of Jeremiah written in a book. The princes hear of it, and ask for the reading to them. Report being made to the king, he hears it read, but destroys it. Sequences. Jer. xxxvi.

8. Give some account of the reign of Jehoiachin (or Coniah). What calamity befalls the nation? 2 Kings xxiv. 10-16.

9. Who succeeds Jehoiachin, and what was the character of his reign? 17-19. Jer. xxi. His rebellion, and Jeremiah's counsel. 2 Kings xxiv. 20. Jer. xxix. 1-14.

10. Give an account of the final catastrophe, and the condition in which the land was left. xxv. 1-21.

VIII.

INCIDENTS DURING THE CAPTIVITY.

A.M. 3445-3497. 588-536 B.C.

There is no consecutive history of the nation during this period. Still, from the fragmentary accounts, and the allusions in the prophets, we get a tolerably correct notion of what transpired. It appears that nearly all the chief men of the nation, all the skilled artisans, and the more desirable individuals in all classes, together with the flower of the military forces, were removed from the country. The cities were depopulated, and the larger ones destroyed. The captives were placed in different localities, — a large proportion of them in Babylon and its vicinity, but many also in the distant provinces. The poorer and less influential of the people were permitted to remain in the land, and provision was made for their protection and government. But there appear to have been dissensions among them from the beginning, and mutinous quarrels were attended with assassinations. There had been for some time an Egyptian party; and this party after a time prevailed, and, against the warning and remonstrances of the prophet Jeremiah, they emigrated with a large proportion of the remnant of the people to Egypt, leaving the land more desolate and abandoned than had been intended.

The people who went into captivity under Nebuchadnezzar appear to have been, for the most part, in comfortable conditions, though some of them were subject to hardships and serious persecutions. But the fact that they were captives, and that their land was desolate because of their disobedience and rebellion, wrought in them a desire to return, and made them penitent and contrite.

The great prophets of this period were Ezekiel and Daniel. The extraordinary visions of the former, and his exhortations and predictions, had a powerful influence in preparing the nation for its restoration. The narratives of Daniel form the minor historical incidents of the period, while his prophecies have a world-wide and far-reaching significance.

The union of the Persian and the Median kingdoms, forming the great Medo-Persian monarchy, is the great contemporary event. This issued in the defeat of Crœsus, king of Lydia, and the end of his kingdom; also in the overthrow of the Babylonian empire, and its absorption by the Medo-Persian. It was the age of Pisistratus in Athens, and of Servius Hostilius in Rome. Thales, Anaximander, and Æsop flourished in these days.

---

1. What arrangement did Nebuchadnezzar make for the government of the remnant left in Judah? 2 Kings xxv. 22-24.

2. How was this appointment apparently received by the chief men who were left in Judah? Jer. xl. 7, 8. What counsel did Gedaliah give them? 9, 10. What other parties gathered to him? 10-12.

3. What suspicions were excited concerning some of these men, and how did Gedaliah regard the matter? 13-16.

4. How did this alliance eventuate? xli. 1-3. What further outrages were committed by the insurgents? 4-10.

5. What counter-revolution took place? 11-15. Where did the recovered remnant settle, and for what reason? 16-18.

6. To whom did the leaders go for advice, and what did they promise? xlii. 1-6. What counsel and warning did he give them? 7-18. What did he say about their insincerity, and the punishment of it? 19-22.

7. How did they receive this message, and what did they do? xliii. 1-7. What did Jeremiah predict? 8-13.

8. Can you mention any other events which belong to this period? (See Daniel, Esther, etc.)

IX.

FROM THE DECREE OF CYRUS, PERMITTING THE RETURN FROM THE CAPTIVITY, TO THE CLOSE OF EZRA'S OFFICIAL MISSION.

A.M. 3468-3547. 536-457 B.C.

The prophet Jeremiah had predicted, about the beginning of the reign of Jehoiakim, 610 B.C., that the people of Judah should be carried captive to Babylon, and that their captivity should last seventy years. Though the destruction of Jerusalem did not occur till some twenty years after this, yet the fact, that, in the three or four years from the utterance of this prediction, Nebuchadnezzar conquered the Jews, and began to send many of the people to Babylon, makes it evident that the period is to be reckoned from this point, or about 606 B.C. We have, in this lesson, the notice of the completion of the seventy years; the proclamation of the Persian king, now sovereign of Babylon and all its dependencies; and the account of the return of the first instalment of the children of the captivity, comprising about fifty thousand persons. We have the history of the restoration of their worship, and the building of the temple, with the opposition and malicious interruptions to which they were subject. The record is broken, and not continuous. After the completion of the temple, there is an interval of nearly sixty years, of which we have no information. Then there is an account of Ezra's journey with two thousand men, and the regulations and reformation introduced by him as governor or viceroy of the king of Persia. It is evident that there was no intention of restoring the independence of the nation. It was, and for many years continued to be, a province of the Persian empire. The history closes abruptly, and is not resumed again till many years afterward in the Book of Nehemiah.

To this period unquestionably belong the incidents recorded in the Book of Esther. (See No. XI.) It seems to be given to exhibit and illustrate the fact, that, while a small proportion only of the Jews returned to Palestine, there were multitudes scattered abroad throughout the countries of the Gentiles, and in various provinces of the Persian empire, preserving their distinct nationality, and keeping up their religious observances. We get from this a pretty fair idea of the relation of the Jews to the other nations, and learn from it that, though in exile, they usually enjoyed a good degree of freedom.

It is believed by a large number of the best authorities, that the King Ahasuerus, who is so conspicuous in this narrative, was the Xerxes whose invasion of Greece resulted so disastrously. It was in this invasion that occurred the battle of Thermopylæ, and that of Salamis, and the defeat of the Persians at Platæa and Mycale. The scriptural narrative has reference to a time subsequent to the return of Xerxes.

Within this period, embracing nearly a century, lived many noted historical characters, — Confucius, Zoroaster, Pythagoras, Sophocles, Miltiades, and Cimon, and, later, Pericles. Great events, too, took place, — the overthrow of Tarquin the Proud in Rome, and the establishment of the Roman republic, and the battle of Marathon. Among the Jews, Zechariah and Haggai were the prophets.

---

1. What important event took place soon after the conquest of Babylon by the Medes and Persians, which greatly effected the fortunes of the Jewish people? Ezra i. 1. Who issued the proclamation, and what was its purport? i. 1-4. Its effect? 5, 6. Did the king do any thing else to further this object? 7-11.

2. What does the catalogue of names in Ezra ii. represent? How many were there in all? 64-67. (See Introduction.) What further aid was furnished towards the enterprise? 68, 69.

3. What took place a few months after the return? iii. 1-7. What in the second year? 8-11. How were some of the people affected? 12, 13.

4. What trouble arose, and from what source? What followed on this account? What was the effect on the Persian government, and on the plans of the Jews? How long was the work delayed? iv. 1-24.

5. What prophets exercised their office in these times? v. 1. What influence did they exert? Zech. i. 1-6; iv. 1-10, etc. Hag. i. 1-11; ii. 1-9. The effect? Ezra v. 2.

6. Conduct of the enemies? 3-6. What did they do further? 6, 7. Purport of the letter? 8-17.

7. Action of the Persian government? What was the result? vi. 1-6. Commandment of the king to the intermeddlers? 7-12.

8. What was the consequence? Give some account of the festivities at the completion of the temple. 13-22.

9. How long a period elapses here without any record? (Introduction.) Give an account of appointment of Ezra, and commission given him by the king. vii. 1-20. What further orders were given by the king? 21-26.

10. What was the number of men? (Introduction.) Where did they gather, and what was done there? viii. 15-23. Mention some of the treasures collected. 24-27. What was done on the arrival at Jerusalem? 31-36.

11. What condition of affairs did Ezra find at Jerusalem? ix. 1, 2. How did it affect him? 3-11. What did he do? 12, 13.

12. Effect upon the people? x. 1-4. What was done? 5-19.

X.

THE STORY OF ESTHER.

A.M. 3468-3547.   536-457 B.C.

1. In the Book of Esther, what remarkable story is told of the Persian king and his queen? Esth. i. With what king in profane history is Ahasuerus supposed to be identical? (See Introduction to No. IX.)

2. Who was Esther, and what wonderful experience came to her? ii. 1-20. Who was her guardian and counsellor in this matter?

3. What animosity was felt by the king's prime minister against Mordecai? The cause of it? What plan of revenge was devised by Haman? iii. Effect on Mordecai and the Jews? iv. 1-3.

4. Give an account of Mordecai's communication with Esther on this subject. What difficulties were in the way of Esther's influence? How did the struggle in her mind result? Give the account of her meeting with the king, and what followed. 4-17. Effect on Haman, and the advice of his wife? v.

5. Give an account of the reward of Mordecai for the service previously rendered the king. The advice of Haman, and his terrible humiliation. vi.

6. What was the final outcome of all this? vii.–x.

XI.

THE ADMINISTRATION OF NEHEMIAH.

A.M. 3545-3547. 446-434 B.C.

Between the period embraced in the last lesson and the beginning of the present, there is an interim of about ten or twelve years. The main topic of the treatise of Nehemiah is the rebuilding of the walls of Jerusalem. Connected with this, is an account of the bitter opposition of the Samaritans and the neighboring tribes, and of the moral disorders prevailing among the Jews. The Babylonian captivity appears to have entirely cured the nation of its idolatrous proclivities. The evil tendency now was to amalgamate with the tribes surrounding them, and thus by intermarriage to obliterate the distinct and peculiar Jewish nationality. The chosen people would have thus been reduced to the conditions of the mongrel tribes now inhabiting the old Israelitish territory at the north of them, and the idea of a theocratic government would have been done away. It appears to have been the Divine intention not so much now to restore the political independence of the Jews, as to preserve the pure national stock with their religious economy intact as a continuance of that preparation for the coming of the Messiah which had been going on from the beginning.

It was with this motive that both Ezra and Nehemiah exerted themselves so strenuously against the admission of aliens, and the intermarriage with Gentiles. To this end, it was necessary to make Jerusalem the religious capital of the race, and to both rebuild the temple, and fortify the city with walls.

The period of the present lesson covers only about twelve years, and concludes the sacred annals of the Jewish people. After this time, as we learn from secular history, the Jews were still subject to the Persian empire until the conquest of Alexander about a century later, when they came under his dominion. After the breaking up of his empire, it fell by turns under the sway of the Seleucian kings of Syria and the Egyptian Ptolemies. There were various revolts, and attempts at independence. In one of these, the Jews were conquered by Antiochus the Great, and subsequently by Antiochus Epiphanes, who committed various acts of abominable cruelty. After this came an heroic period, in which the Maccabæan or Asmonæan family flourished, and performed extraordinary exploits, achieving for a brief period actual independence, and some national prosperity. About 63 B.C., Judæa became a Roman province. Twenty years later Herod was made king, though his kingdom was tributary to the Romans. It was under this king that the advent of our Saviour took place.

Nehemiah's mission to Jerusalem, and administration of the government there, was under the reign of the Persian King Artaxerxes Longimanus. It was about the time of Cincinnatus and the Decemviri in Rome. It was the time of the acme of Grecian civilization, when Pericles yet ruled at Athens; the time of Socrates, the greatest of philosophers; of Euripides and Aristophanes, great dramatists; of Phidias, the noted painter; and Thucydides, the historian. It was also the period of the Peloponnesian war.

---

1. What important personage now appears in the Jewish history? Where was he, and in what situation? Neh. i. 1-11; ii. 1. How long was this after the events of the last lesson? (Introduction.)

2. What report came to Nehemiah concerning matters in Judæa? Neh. i. 1-3. What was the effect upon him? What did he do? 4-11.

3. Nehemiah's communication with the king, and its result? ii. 1-8. What occurred on the journey? 9-11.

4. What survey did he make, and what did he ascertain? 12-16. What did he counsel the people to do? How did the enterprise affect their hostile neighbors? 17-20.

5. What impression does the account of the workers and the division of labor give you of the general interest in the cause? iii.

6. What hostilities and opposition were incurred? Give an account of the measures resorted to by enemies, and the precautions taken. iv. 1-23.

7. Of what moral improprieties were many among the higher classes accused? v. 1-5. How did Nehemiah treat the case? Reformation of these abuses. 6-19.

8. What was done by the hostile Gentile chiefs to hinder the work? vi. 1-10. What treachery manifested itself? Did this permanently prevent the carrying out of the enterprise? 12-19.

9. Give an account of the re-organization of the government. vii. 1-5. What follows? 6-73. What was the number?

10. What public meeting took place, and for what purpose? Who was the reader and expounder? viii. 1-8. How was the occasion celebrated? 9-12. What new festival was established? 13-18.

11. What took place still later in the same month? ix. 1-3. Give some account of the exercises. What were some of the topics of the prayer offered? What covenant was made? 4-38.

12. What were some of the provisions of the covenant? x. 29-39.

13. What arrangements were made for re-peopling Jerusalem? Assignment of work? xi. and xii.

14. What abuses and disorders were subsequently developed? xiii. 1-5. Where was Nehemiah at this time? 6. What did he do on his return? 7-9. What other sins did he rebuke? 10-32.

15. Give a brief account of the subsequent history of the Jews to the time of Christ. Contemporary events. (Introduction.)

THE POETIC AND PROPHETIC BOOKS.

THE POETIC AND PROPHETIC BOOKS.

I.

THE BOOK OF JOB.

This has been supposed to be one of the most ancient of all existing writings in any language. It is thought by many to be prior even to a portion of the Pentateuch. But the best recent authorities place it somewhat later. Its author is unknown. The narrative comprises only a small part of the book, and is a very simple story, though containing some remarkable incidents. Briefly, it is the history of a man of superior mental endowments, of lofty moral sentiments and godly life, who had also been greatly prospered in his temporal relations. It had been insinuated by the great adversary of human souls, that Job's piety was of a mercenary kind, prompted only by the motive that it would give him worldly advantage. It was the sneering intimation, heard sometimes even in our day, that there is no such thing as disinterested goodness, and that every man is virtuous only so far as virtue is likely to pay. To refute this low and unworthy theory, seems to have been one of the great objects of the book. Another object was to show, that, contrary to the popular notion then and sometimes since prevailing, worldly prosperity is not always in proportion to moral goodness, nor is adversity any sure indication of wickedness on the part of its victim.

It is upon this latter point that Job's three friends differ from him, and the larger part of the book is taken up with its discussion. They insist that he must have been guilty of some wickedness, or these afflictions would not have come upon him. He vindicates himself from this aspersion; and, though sorely perplexed and despondent because of God's dealings with him, asserts his integrity, and avows his faith in God to the last extremity. "Though he slay me, yet will I trust in him." Still, Job's language at various points seems to imply that he regards God as somehow dealing unjustly with him. Doubtless this is the " cry of the human," in its pain and anguish, and its necessary ignorance of the ways of God.

Of the twenty-nine chapters comprising the discussion between Job and his accusing friends, Eliphaz, who is the leading speaker on the adverse side, takes up four, Bildad three, and Zophar two. The other twenty are occupied by Job. Elihu, who appears to have been a younger man than the others, listens with respectful silence till his elders have concluded, and then speaks at length on the subject under discussion. He frankly rebukes Job for so justifying himself as to imply an impeachment of the Divine justice: and is, at the same time, indignant at the three friends that they have failed to answer him. In this discourse, more than in the utterances of the others, there are gleams of a clearer light, and tokens of a higher faith, — an actual, though vague, discernment of the disciplinary nature of temporal afflictions, and a confidence, that, in some way which could not then be understood, the Divine Wisdom would so determine things that those which now appear to be evil would result in good to the believing and obedient soul.

The four chapters which contain the utterances of the voice of God, set forth in sublime language the Divine greatness and power and wisdom and excellence, and show how little competent man is to understand God's ways, or to judge concerning his acts.

---

1. The antiquity of the book. General character of Job. The two leading objects of the book. Names of the persons represented in it, and the parts taken by them. (Introduction.)

2. The story of Job. (*a*) In what part of the world is it laid? (*b*) Job's temporal condition? (*c*) His family? (*d*) Satan's accusation, and its implied meaning? (*e*) The first affliction? Did his faith fail, or his piety diminish? What did he say in view of his losses? i. 21. (*f*) The second calamity, and how he received it? ii. 7-10.

3. For what purpose did Job's friends come to him? How long did they sit with him, and in what manner? ii. 11-13.

4. How large a part of the conversation that ensued is taken up by the three friends respectively? What cause is assigned by them for Job's afflictions? Is their theory of human sorrow a correct one? How does Job defend himself? Is he wholly correct in his view of the situation? What excuse can be made for some of his utterances? (Introduction.)

5. The reason of Elihu's long silence? xxxii. 6. What is his feeling, in view of the discussion? xxxii. 2, 3. In what respect are his views better than those of the others, and how does he differ from them? (Introduction.) What do you hold to be the true doctrine of which Elihu seems to catch some glimpses?

6. Who is the chief speaker in the last chapters of the book? The nature of the utterances, and the teachings implied? The character of the writings in these chapters?

7. What is the nature of the writing of the principal parts of the book? The character of the poetry? Let each student bring in any passages which strike him as remarkable either for their imagery or sentiment.

8. The condition of Job in his last days? Whose part in the controversy did God most condemn?

II.

THE PSALMS.

This is the largest collection of Hebrew poetry now in existence. It is also one of the most remarkable poetical collections in the world. It does not, as we are apt to judge, belong to any one period of Hebrew history; though the larger part of it may doubtless be assigned to a period about 1050 to 990 B.C. But the remainder ranges from about 1500 to 450 B.C. The popular opinion ascribes the entire authorship to David; but, though probably considerably more than half of the psalms are his, it is nearly certain that a large proportion of them were due to other authors, both before and after the time of the royal poet. One bears the name of Moses; others, of Asaph and the sons of Korah; while others still have been ascribed to Hezekiah and to his successors. The final collection and arrangement was probably made by Ezra about 450 B.C.

Formerly, there were five divisions, or books, of which the following is the plan: —

1. Psalms almost entirely of David's composition, embracing i.-xli.

2. Those apparently in the main by the sons of Korah, though several of these also were by David: xlii.-lxxii.

3. Compositions principally by Asaph: lxxiii.-lxxxix. There are reasons for believing that many of these psalms were composed about the time of Hezekiah.

4. This book comprises the remainder of those written before the Captivity: xc.-cvi.

5. The last book is made up of those songs which pertain to the Captivity and the return from it: cvii.-cl. They are mostly anonymous, and, like the fourth book, are liturgic in style.

Indications of an original and intentional division of this kind are seen in the peculiar form of doxology used at the end of the several terminal Psalms of the respective books.

The psalms may be grouped, again, according to their different objects or kinds, as follows: —

1. Hymns of praise: viii., xviii., xix., civ., cxlv., cxlvii., etc.

2. National hymns: lxxviii., cv., cvi , cxiv., etc.

3. Temple hymns, or psalms for public worship: xv., xxiv., lxxxvii., etc.

4. Hymns relating to trial and calamity: ix., xxii., lv., lvi., cix., etc.

5. Messianic psalms: ii., xvi., xl., lxxii., cx., etc.

6. Hymns of general religious character: xc., cxxxix., xci., cxxi., cxxvii.

The chief general characteristics of these writings are, —

1. Lyric poetry. 2. Devotional, — that is, adapted to religious worship

They constitute the Hymn-book of the Hebrew church. 3. The third and fourth characteristics, though not so general, are that they are *patriotic* and *prophetic*. By lyric compositions are meant such as may be set to music, and can be accompanied by an instrument.

Several of these songs have peculiar characteristics. The most remarkable of these is the cxix. (*a*) It is the longest by far of all the collection. (*b*) It is divided into sections, named after the letters of the Hebrew alphabet in order. (*c*) The several verses of each section in the original all begin with the letter designating that particular section. (*d*) The subject of the psalm is the excellence of the Divine Law; and every verse of the whole psalm, with two or three exceptions, alludes to this in some form.

Psalms cxiii.-cxviii. constituted a prominent part of the service in the Passover celebration. They comprise what was known as "The Great Hallel." It is this which is alluded to in Matt. xxvi. 30, in the account of Christ's last Passover with his disciples, where it is said, "They had sung a hymn."

The religious character of the Psalms is most marked and definite. The following are some of the more prominent religious characteristics: (*a*) The one infinite, all-wise, and omnipresent personal God is recognized. (*b*) The universality of his love and providence and goodness. (*c*) Abhorrence of all idols, and rejection of all subordinate divinities. (*d*) Prophetic glimpses of the Divine Son, and of his redeeming work in the earth. (*e*) The terrible nature of sin, the Divine hatred of it, and God's great judgments on transgressors. (*f*) The possibility of forgiveness, the Divine mercy, and the duty of repentance. (*g*) The beauty of holiness, the importance of faith, and the privilege of the soul's communion with God. (*h*) While there is a less wide range of spiritual thought and sentiment than in the New Testament, and a less clear conception of the future life, there are still such exalted views of the nature of spiritual religion and of the glory that is to be revealed as are scarcely found in any other utterances previous to the advent of Christ.

FIRST PART.

1. What is there remarkable about the general character of this book? To what period of Hebrew history does the authorship of the larger part of it belong? Extent of the range of time in which the remainder was written. By whom were most of the psalms written? The names of some of the other writers? (For information on these and many of the following topics, see Introduction.)

2. How did the Jews anciently divide this collection? Give the limits of the divisions, and their respective authors, so far as known. How does each final psalm of the first four parts end, and what may it indicate?

3. Different kinds of psalms as forming another series of groups. Give the several characteristics of these groups, and cite some of the particular

psalms in each. (Some of these may be read, and their peculiarities pointed out.)

4. On what occasions in our modern religious worship is the xc. most frequently used? What is the character of the xxiii.? Of the xcvi.? Of the cv. and the cvi.? Of the lvi.? Of the ii. and the lxxvii.?

SECOND PART.

1. What are some of the chief characteristics of these compositions? What is lyric poetry? Devotional poetry? What do we use in our modern religious service that corresponds to the Hebrew psalms?

2. State some of the peculiarities of the cxix. psalm. What is its subject, and what singularity of repetition does it have?

3. What especial and noteworthy use was accustomed to be made of Psalms cxiii.-cxviii., and what remarkable allusion in it do we find in the New Testament?

4. What are the chief religious characteristics of these writings? How do their spiritual conceptions compare with those of the New Testament?

5. On what occasions were the following psalms not improbably composed? ii. (2 Sam. xv.), xxiv. (2 Sam. vi. 12–17), lvi. (1 Sam. xxi. 10–15), lxxv. and lxxvi. (2 Kings xix. 32–37), cix. (1 Sam. xxii. 9–23), lxxiv. (2 Kings xxv. 2–18), lx. (2 Chron. xviii. 11–13).

6. What is the subject of the xxiii.? Of the lxxxiv.? Of the ciii.? Of the cxxxiii.? Of the cxxxvii.? What doctrines concerning the Divine character do you find implied in the following: viii., xix., xxxiii., xlvi., xciii., cxv., cxxxix.?

III.

THE BOOK OF PROVERBS.

Among us the general meaning of the word *Proverb* is a pithy, sententious maxim of homely wisdom, familiarly known, and apt to be often repeated. In the Hebrew and other Oriental communities, it had a somewhat wider signification. Originally its import was not unlike that of a *parable*, and the two words are sometimes used in the Bible for the same form of utterance. The primary idea is that of comparison or simile; and even when nothing of this kind is formally present, it is often implied. Thus, in the book before us, we have such expressions as "A merry heart doeth good like a medicine;" "The words of a tale-bearer are as wounds;" "A brother offended is harder to be won than a strong city." But we find also in this book other forms of the proverb, both of those in which no comparison is expressed, and of those which run into the parabolic style of extended illustration.

There is also another meaning of the term *proverb*, of frequent use in the Bible, but which hardly applies to any thing in this collection. It is that of a "by-word" or a reproachful saying, one in which the conspicuous wickedness or folly of an individual is extant as a comparison and warning.

The Book of Proverbs is popularly attributed to Solomon as its author, and there is no well-established reason for doubting that most of it is due to him. In the part admitted on all hands to have been compiled by him, it is not unlikely that some maxims extant before his time were gathered up by him and put in written form, while most of the utterances were his own.

The book is written in Hebrew verse. A considerable proportion, though not all of it, is in the form of *parallelisms*. This was the most common form of poetic expression among the Hebrews. The principle is that of a two-line stanza, containing two expressions pertaining to the same subject. Parallelisms are of three kinds: —

1. *Synonymous*, in which the same thought is presented in different words, as, —

"What is man, that thou art mindful of him?
And the son of man, that thou visitest him?" — Ps. viii. 4.

"He that loveth pleasure shall be a poor man:
He that loveth wine and oil shall not be rich." — Prov. xxi. 17.

2. *Antithetic*, where the former member is illustrated by some opposition of thought in the second, as, —

"It is an honor for a man to cease from strife:
But every fool will be meddling." — Prov. xx. 3.

"A wise son heareth his father's instruction:
But a scorner heareth not rebuke." — xiii. 1.

"A prudent man foreseeth the evil, and hideth himself:
But the simple pass on, and are punished." — xxii. 3.

3. The *antithetic* or *epithetic*, in which the second member, instead of repeating the first or giving the obverse of it, adds something to it, as, —

"He appointed the moon for seasons:
The sun knoweth his going down." — Ps. civ. 19.

There are some parts of the book which are cast in none of these forms, yet the versification is everywhere maintained.

There are four distinct divisions of the book, as follows: —

1. Chaps. i.-ix. In this the style is hortatory as of an elder to a younger person, as indicated in the repeated expression "my son." The instructions conveyed are consecutive and continued through extended passages, though the imagery is highly poetic, and the parallelisms are frequent.

2. Chaps. x.-xxii. These form the nucleus or kernel of the book, and consist apparently of utterances by a single author, who at the outset is announced to be Solomon. (x. 1.) Here almost every verse is independent.

There is no consecutive thought, and generally each verse might stand anywhere else as well as in its present connection. There is a kind of appendix to this division (xxii. 18-xxiv.), which is sometimes reckoned as a division by itself. This is again partly hortatory, and for many of the exhortations reasons are assigned.

3. Chaps. xxv.-xxix. purport to be a collection of proverbs of Solomon copied in the time of Hezekiah, from some existing writings. The probability is that these were written or collected by Solomon, but not arranged at the time of his death, in connection with the others. They are less finished in style, and there appear among them series of utterances having a more or less obvious thread of connection.

4. The last two chapters appear to be the work of later writers, of whom little is known. They comprise three parts: (*a*) The words of Agur, the style of which is distinct from all the rest of the book. (*b*) The didactic poem of or for King Lemuel, in which the poetic parallelism is maintained. (*c*) The remarkably beautiful alphabetical ode in praise of a virtuous woman. This is acrostical, each several verse beginning with a letter of the Hebrew alphabet in order, and there being the same number of verses as letters in the alphabet.

The book abounds in instructive thought. Some of the prominent topics are the praise of wisdom, which is here closely cognate with piety; of integrity, diligence, filial obedience, modesty, and justice; also reprobation of sensuality, intemperance, and indolence.

---

1. Meaning of the term *proverb*? By whom is most of this book supposed to have been written? Character and style of its composition? What is meant by parallelisms? Give examples of synonymous parallelisms other than those in the Introduction. Of antithetic parallelisms.

2. Give the general divisions of the book. How does the first division differ from the second? Mention the particular distinctions of the others.

3. What are some of the prominent topics of the book? What is meant by *wisdom* as used here? Can you show how it is closely allied to religion? Point out any passage in which the intimate relation is seen.

4. What remarkable and sustained personification do you find in viii. 12-36? Find as many passages as practicable which speak of the rewards of virtue and piety.

5. Cite some passages which show the evils of sloth or indolence. Of wine-drinking and drunkenness. Of tale-bearing. Of family contention.

6. What is said of a man who rules his own spirit, or of self-control? Of contentment? Of a good name? Of disobedience to parents? Of fitly spoken words? Of a beautiful woman who lacks discretion? Of things little, but wise?

7. What peculiarity about the last twenty-three verses of the last chapter? What is here described? Mention some of the beautiful things said.

(These exercises can be varied to any extent at the discretion of teachers.)

IV.

ECCLESIASTES AND THE SONG OF SOLOMON.

These two books have probably occasioned more trouble to biblical students than any other parts of the Bible. The interpretations which have been given of them have been widely diverse, and there has been no general agreement as to the main design of either. Still, they contain many lofty sentiments and important truths, which could not well be spared from the treasury of religious thought.

The impression given by the opening verse of the Book of Ecclesiastes, and by certain passages in it, is that it was written by Solomon. There are also several allusions to the character and condition of the person represented by the writer, which seem to corroborate this impression. But there are several indications which point to a later authorship. The style is not that of Solomon's other writings, nor one which corresponds with the age of Solomon. It seems to belong to a period of less culture and refinement.

It is not improbable that it was written about three or four centuries after the time of Solomon, by some writer who, with a legitimate and proper motive, simply personated that famous king whose name among the Jews was almost a synonyme, not only for wisdom, but for all that is great in humanity. The object also may have been to set forth the experience of this great man as illustrating the result of successful worldliness and self-gratification as contrasted with the outcome of the higher wisdom implied in a godly life.

The earlier and larger part of the book is chiefly occupied with a gloomy view of life, often of a morbid character, and sometimes bordering on the contemptuous. It is enigmatical, and abounds in riddles and paradoxes. It is also mysterious and unsatisfactory. The key-note and the dismal refrain is, "Vanity of vanities; all is vanity." But even here are occasional rifts in the cloud, broad gleams of a great reconciling truth which yet somehow is connected with a higher style and better philosophy of human life. This comes out clear and satisfactory in the closing chapters. There, it appears that man was made not for this world alone, and not for selfish achievement or gratification, but with reference to some great plans of God for him, which are to be realized by obedience and devotion to the Divine service.

This, then, is apparently the scope of the book; the utter vanity and unprofitableness of human life, in so far as it consists in the mere gathering of worldly wealth, wisdom, or power, the pursuit of earthly pleasure; this, because it brings more pain and sorrow than gratification, and involves more evil than good. Having thus dwelt at length on this experience of a mere worldly man, who, nevertheless, in this instance, rises occasionally above his worldliness, the writer sets forth a better style of life — a life of obedience to God, and trust in his overruling and directing power and wisdom; the satisfaction in the consciousness of right-doing; a feeling that out of all the apparent evil in the world will come untold good to the obedient soul. There is not the bright and vivid conception of the future life which we find in the New Testament, but there is a faith which anticipates some glory yet to be revealed.

The Song of Solomon has given rise to a still larger variety of opinions than Ecclesiastes: the divergency of views has also been larger and less reconcilable. It is called in the title the "Song of Songs," implying the superlative estimation in which it was held when it was first written. The most probable theory concerning it is, that it is an eclogue or idyll, a "Song of loves," representing, now in dialogue and now in monologue, the love of a youth and maiden. These express their mutual affection in the minute and sensuous imagery usual among the Orientals, but uncommon among modern and western nations. Many think it to have been written to celebrate the nuptials of Solomon and Pharaoh's daughter, and not a few of the allusions give force to this hypothesis.

It is supposed to have a spiritual significance, referring primarily to God in relation to his people Israel, and ultimately to Christ and his Church The latter relationship is frequently prominent in the New Testament (See Mark ix 15; John iii. 29; 2 Cor. xi. 2; Rev. xix. 7; xxi. 2, etc.) There are many passages of exquisite poetry, as well as many which are applicable to the highest and purest spiritual experience.

---

1. What peculiarities in common have these two books? What of value do they both contain?

2. What is the first impression concerning the authorship of Ecclesiastes? Mention some passages in which this is indicated. i. 1-12, 13; ii. 4-10.

3. The more recent opinion concerning its authorship, and the time in which it was written? Was there any moral impropriety in the writer's personating Solomon? What was there in Solomon's character and general reputation which would naturally suggest the use of his name in such a representation?

4. What appears to have been the general design or object of the book, and what are its moral teachings? How does the former part regard life? What view is presented in the latter part?

5. What is the great refrain of the former part? i. 2; ii. 26, etc. On what supposition concerning human life is this true? Do you think that to a merely worldly and selfish man, there is as much of good as evil in this world?

6. What is the final summing up of the whole matter? xii. 13. What references to a future judgment do you find? xi. 9, and xii. 14.

7. Give the substance of the exhortation in the first part of the last chapter. What is meant by "The keepers of the house"? "Those that

look out of the windows"? "The grinders"? "The almond tree"? To what does the whole imagery apply?

8. *The Song of Solomon.* What strong expression in the title of this book, and what does it import? Who is personated as the writer and one of the principal actors?

9. What are the general character and style of the book? To what higher purposes is it supposed to relate, and what application is made of many passages in it? Where do we find this relationship expressed in the New Testament? (See citation in Introduction.)

10. What passage is often used to figure the relation of the saved soul to Christ? ii. 3 (last clause), 4. The beauty and glory of the Church? vi. 4, 10. How is the advent of spring described? ii. 11, 12. The strength of love? viii. 7.

V.

THE PROPHET ISAIAH.

The word *prophet* is used in the Bible to indicate a variety of characteristics: 1. There is implied the popular notion of one who is able, through some supernatural ability, to discern the future, and foretell events which are to transpire subsequently. 2. It signifies a person employed in the utterance of public religious discourses, something analogous to our modern preacher; and this was in large part the office of the Old-Testament prophets. Some of them were like our modern reformers, and others were even evangelists or revivalists. 3. They also exercised the functions of scribes, and wrote the histories of their times, the annals of their nation, and the biographies of the kings and great men. A very large proportion of the books of the Old Testament were written or compiled by the prophets.

The prophetic books of the Old Testament are usually reckoned in two divisions, — the major and the minor prophets. The former embrace those under the names of Isaiah, Jeremiah, Ezekiel, and Daniel; the latter, the remainder. All these books are written largely in the poetic style.

The prophet Isaiah is, next to Moses and David, the most impressive and powerful of the Old-Testament writers. He lived at Jerusalem in the times of the kings Uzziah to Hezekiah inclusive; and it is thought by some that he continued till the time of Manasseh, by whom he was put to death by being sawn asunder. But of this there is no authentic information. For a great part of his life his relation to the government seems to have been something like that of a modern court-preacher, or chaplain to the king, although there was probably no such actual office. He was a man of powerful intellect, great integrity, and remarkable force of character. In his preaching he was earnest, brave, and unflinching. His writings are characterized by unusual strength, and, at the same time, by unusual beauty; and, though he is often profound, he is seldom obscure. The book abounds in passages of remarkable eloquence and of lofty poetry.

Of the character and contents of the book, we notice the following particulars: (*a*) Warnings and threatenings against his own people for their apostasy and wickedness. (*b*) Historical sketches of the times in which he lived. (*c*) Prophecies concerning the deliverance of the Jews from their captivity. (*d*) Messianic prophecies, or those pertaining to the coming of Christ. (*e*) Predictions of God's judgments on other nations. (*f*) Anticipations of the future glory and prosperity of the Church. (*g*) Discourses urging moral and religious reformation. (*h*) Poetic effusions of praise and thanksgiving.

There are many remarkable predictions which have already had their fulfilment — some of them not long after their utterance, and others centuries subsequently. Instances of these are the judgments of God upon individuals and nations, as in the case of the king of Israel and the Israelitish nation, vii.; the overthrow of Sennacherib, x. and xxxvii.; the disasters and desolation which should overtake Babylon, Damascus, Egypt, Moab, and Idumæa, xiii., xv., xvii., xix., and xxxiv. (see especially xiii. 19-22, and xxxiv. 10-17, for most marvellous and vivid descriptions of the final fate of Babylon and the densely populated portions of Idumæa — descriptions to the verity of which at this very day travellers testify, though at the time of their utterance they must have seemed far less likely to be true than if uttered now concerning London or New York); the overthrow of the Jewish nation, and their subsequent restoration; and the clear setting forth of the mingled grandeur and humiliation of the earthly life and character of the Messiah. It was this which had been overlooked by the Jewish rulers and learned men, which, nevertheless, the apostles used with great success to demonstrate the identity of Jesus with the promised Deliverer.

None of the Old-Testament writers are so often quoted in the New Testament as Isaiah; and there is none whose vision is so broad, or whose conceptions reach to so great a height. His views on the subjects of man's moral condition, the need of a Redeemer, the possibilities of the race, the grand consequences of redemption, and the doctrine of Divine Providence, are not much surpassed by those of even Paul himself. On the last point, he has several passages setting forth the manner in which God uses even wicked men to execute the Divine judgment, while for the wicked and selfish dispositions evinced by them in the exercise of this agency, he holds them amenable, and often punishes them for those sins. A notable illustration is the case of the Assyrian king. x. 3-19.

FIRST PART

1. Some of the significations of the word "prophet" as used in the Bible? Division of the prophetic Scriptures?

2. How does the prophet Isaiah rank among the sacred writers? Give

some account of his life, and relation to the government and the times in which he lived. Some of his chief personal and literary characteristics.

3. Character and contents of the book? Quotations from this book in the New Testament? Any remarkable predictions, and their fulfilment?

4. Isaiah's moral and religious views as compared with those of New-Testament writers? On what subjects is he especially clear and pronounced?

5. Give his remarkable statements concerning the Assyrian king, and the use which God may make of a wicked man as an agent, while at the same time he holds him responsible for his wickedness. x. 3–19. Show how these statements (6 and 12) harmonize.

6. Mention a few of the express predictions of the Messiah as fulfilled in the character of Jesus. ix. 6, 7; xi. 1–4; xliii. 1–4; liii.; lxi. 1–3; lxiii. 1–3, etc.

SECOND PART.

1. What complaints does the prophet make of the wickedness of his own people? i. 2–4; lix. 1–8, 12–15; lxv. 2–7. What particular sins are rebuked? iii. 18–23; v. 20–23; x. 1, 2; xxviii. 1, 3, and 7; lxv. 3–5. What punishments are threatened? i. 28, 30, 31; ix. 18–20; xxix. 1–6, etc.

2. Against what other nations are judgments predicted? xiii., xv., xvii., xix., xxiii., xxxiv., xlviii. What remarkably vivid description of the fate of Babylon is given? xiii. 19–22. What was the rank and character of Babylon as a city? Has the prediction in its minute details been verified? What prediction concerning some of the cities of Idumæa or Edom? The present condition of this whole region?

3. Passages predicting the restoration of the Jews from captivity. xliii. 1–7; xlix. 18–23; li. 3–5, 22, 23; lii., etc. What remarkable prediction concerning the conqueror of Babylon, and the deliverance from the captivity? xliv. 27, 28; xlv. 1, 2. How long was the time of Isaiah before that of Cyrus?

4. Mention some of the more notable passages portraying the future glory of the Church, and the spiritual prosperity of the race. xi. 6–9; xl. 1–5; liv. 11–14; lix. 19–21; lx.; lxv. 18–25.

5. Discourses on moral and religious reformation. i. 16–19; v.; xxxiii. 1–8; xlviii.; li. 17–20; lix. 1–16.

6. Poetic effusions of praise, thanksgiving, and adoration. xxv.; xxvi.; xl. 9–31. Point out in the last passage the grand descriptive statements of the power and wisdom of God. What illustration is given which, even in the light of ancient astronomy, was highly indicative of the Divine majesty and greatness, but which, in the light of modern science, inconceivably magnifies these attributes? 26. Further instances under this topic? lxiii. 7–19.

7. What glowing religious discourse do you find touching the richness, freeness, and greatness of the Divine grace and its effects? lv., lvi.

VI.

JEREMIAH AND LAMENTATIONS.

629-538 B.C.

Jeremiah, the second of the great Old-Testament prophetic writers, lived in the last part of the sixth and first part of the fifth century before Christ. The beginning of his ministry appears to have been a little before the middle of the reign of Josiah, and a short time previous to the terrible calamities which overtook the nation. His prescience of these disasters, from the first, filled his soul with painful apprehensions, and gave a mournful character to his utterances. But not only the evil which he foresaw distressed him, but also the disobedience and apostasy of the people. His moral sensitiveness was very great: he was devoutly religious, and all impiety was painful to him. He was also of a deeply sympathetic nature, and the sufferings of his people, although in consequence of their sins, filled him with sorrow. There are few instances in history of a man who so shrank from giving pain to his fellow-men, and yet who so boldly, uncompromisingly, and faithfully rebuked the people of his charge. To a man so sensitive, sympathetic, and conscientious, dwelling among a people whose corrupt practices and widespread wickedness had provoked the wrath of heaven, and to whom any faithful preaching was unpopular and repulsive, and yet who was himself called to denounce the judgments of God, and to prophesy disaster and overthrow, his position was one of threefold difficulty and trouble. Yet, with a courage seldom paralleled in the moral history of the world, he fully declared the Divine message.

Of course, so far as personal safety was concerned, this was not a dangerous office during the life of the godly Josiah. But after the death of this king, under the inglorious reigns of his sons, he was subjected to great indignities, and suffered bitter persecutions. Many times his life was threatened, both by the king and the princes, and he but narrowly escaped. But he still persisted in declaring the Divine truth concerning his people. Under Divine direction, he not only rebuked the people for their sins, and showed them the now inevitable consequences of their conduct, but he gave them instructions concerning their relations to their enemies. Assuring them that these would prevail against them, and would destroy the city and carry them captive, he urged them to submit, and accept such terms as would be offered, and thus make their subjugation as tolerable as possible, promising them that after a definite period of seventy years there would be a release, and permission to return.

The contents of the book of the prophecy may be divided as follows: 1. Discourses in rebuke of the wickedness and degeneracy of the Jews. 2. Prophecies concerning the nation. 3. Sketches of national and personal history. 4. Prophecies concerning other nations. 5. Predictions of the restoration. 6. Prophecies of the Messiah, and the future glory of the Church.

The Book of Lamentations, the authorship of which is commonly ascribed to Jeremiah, is a collection of elegies on the overthrow and desolation of Jerusalem, and the nation of which it was the capital. The larger portion of the poems are acrostic; that is, each verse begins with a letter of the Hebrew alphabet following the alphabetical order. The third chapter has the further peculiarity that each letter is three times repeated, thus giving sixty-six instead of twenty-two verses. The last chapter does not fall entirely into the acrostical form.

The calamities bewailed strictly correspond to those narrated in the preceding book, and also in the last part of the Books of Kings and Chronicles. The sentiment, though intensely and at times painfully sad, is beautiful in expression, and the book abounds in the finest imagery.

FIRST PART.

1. When did Jeremiah exercise the prophetic office? How does he rank among the prophetic writers of the Old Testament?

2. What was the condition of the Jewish nation at this time? What befell it before the close of Jeremiah's ministry?

3. Mention some of the leading traits of this prophet's character. Give some of the characteristics of his writings.

4. What were there in his constitution, and in his relation to the people, that made his office burdensome and painful?

5. How were his messages for the most part received, and how was he himself treated by those to whom he ministered? Did he on this account desist from his vocation?

6. How is the book divided as to the subjects contained in it?

7. What were some of the sins and vices of which the prophet accused his countrymen? ii. 12, 13, 27, 28; iii. 20; vi. 13, 14; xix. 4, 5; xxiii. 10. What terrible denunciation does he utter against the covetous king? xxii. 18, 19.

8. What remarkable example is given of fidelity to the precepts of a father respecting strong drink? xxxv.

SECOND PART.

1. What strong figurative expression does the prophet use to indicate the greatness of his grief at the moral condition of his people? xix. 1, 2.

2. What are some of the evils predicted against the people because of their iniquities? xix. 7-9; xxxiv. 3-5; xxi. 4-6. (Other examples may be selected at discretion.)

3. Mention some of the other nations against which the Divine judgments were predicted. xxv. 18-25, xlvi., xlvii., xlviii., xlix., l. What explicit prophecy concerning the future of the then magnificent Babylon? li. 37. Do we find any thing similar to this in any other prophet? Has the prediction been fulfilled?

4. What promises of the restoration of the Jews from their captivity? xxxii 37-44; xxxiii. 7-14; xxix. 10.

5. What predictions concerning the Messiah and the Messianic times? xxiii. 5, 6; xxxiii. 14, 15

6. What is the general character of the Book of Lamentations? What was the occasion of its composition? What peculiarity of composition is found in most of the poems? What special characteristic in the third chapter?

7. How would you characterize the general sentiment and tone of the book? Select a few of the more striking passages, and show their application to the actual facts of history. (These may be read or committed.)

VII.

EZEKIEL.

595-534 B.C.

The first part of Ezekiel's ministry was probably contemporaneous with the last of Jeremiah's. Like the latter, the former belonged to the priestly class, and was himself a priest, as well as a prophet. He appears to have been of the number of the better classes who were carried into captivity with King Jehoiachin in the first invasion by Nebuchadnezzar. A portion of these had their residence assigned them upon the river Chebar, not very far from Babylon. It was here, and not in Jerusalem, that Ezekiel exercised his entire ministry, his presence in the latter place being only in visions or by the spirit.

Ezekiel was a man of powerful but peculiar intellect. Less symmetrical and less attractive in general than Isaiah, and less uniform in the flow of his thought than Jeremiah, he is yet at times scarcely inferior to either of them. While there is not that shrinking sensitiveness which we find in Jeremiah, he has the same abhorrence of sin, and the distress occasioned by the wickedness of his people is none the less. His indignation and boldness of utterance almost surpass any of his predecessors.

Ezekiel is distinguished from the other prophets in the method by which he exercises or manifests his prophetic gift. He is rather a seer of visions than a predictor of events; yet these visions are symbolic either of future events, or of existing facts and conditions. The nature of this form of presentation renders much of the writing obscure. The character of the types, and the visions, make a part of the book similar to John's Revelation in the New Testament. He would be a rash man who would confidently undertake the complete interpretation of either. Probably the time for the full understanding of much contained in both is not yet come.

Still, only portions of the book are of this character. The prophetic addresses to the people are popular as well as powerful, while his predictions of the Divine judgments on the nations, and especially those relating to Tyre and Egypt, are of remarkable eloquence.

The contents of the book may be divided as follows (see McClintock & Strong's Cyclopædia): 1. Call to the prophetic office. i.-iii. 15. 2. Symbolic visions indicating the national catastrophe. iii. 16-vii. 3. 3. Visions representing God's rejection of the people for their apostasy and idolatry, with intimations of subsequent restoration. viii.-xi. 4. A series of discourses rebuking the sins of the people, and the errors prevalent among them. xii.-xix. 5. Another series of discourses, setting forth the guilt of the nation and their consequent condemnation, and indicating that this judgment was at hand. xx.-xxiii. 6. Discourses at the time of the final siege of Jerusalem, which he announced at the very commencement, though distant many weeks' journey, and prediction of the final result. xxiv. 7. Prediction of God's judgments against several heathen nations. xxv.-xxxii. 8. Prophetic representation of the triumph of God's kingdom in the earth. xxxiii.-xxxix. 9. Symbolic representation of Messianic times or the latter-day glory.

---

1. Who was Ezekiel? Where did he exercise his ministry? Give some of the characteristics of his writings. How did he differ from Isaiah and Jeremiah?

2. How may the contents of the book be divided?

3. The condition of the Jewish nation at this time? What was the occasion of their calamities? ii. 3-5. Do nations prosper when they persist in great wickedness?

4. What peculiar designation is given to Ezekiel? iii. 1, 4, 10; v. 1; vi. 2, etc. To whom is this expression applied in the New Testament?

5. What do you learn concerning the duties and responsibilities of a minister, under the figure of a watchman? iii. 17-21. Does this apply, to any extent, to every religious person?

6. What Hebrew proverb does the prophet cite, the sentiment of which, in certain of its applications, he repudiates? xviii. 2, etc. What is the meaning of it? In what sense is it true, and in what false?

7. What doctrine do we find concerning individual responsibility in relation to sin and repentance? xviii. 4, 20, 21-28.

8. Mention some of the Gentile nations against which Ezekiel prophesied. xxv.-xxxii.

9. What remarkable descriptions do you find concerning the wealth and luxury and beauty and commerce of Tyre? xxvii. 4-25; xxviii. 13, 14. What predictions are made? xxvi 3-21, especially 4, 5, 14; and

xxvii. 36. Where was Tyre? Of what nation was it the capital, and what was the place occupied by this people in history? Have these predictions been fulfilled?

10. What is said concerning Egypt and its punishment? xxix., xxx. Is there any thing in the modern character of Egypt which justifies some of the statements of the prophet? (See xxix. 15, and other passages.)

11. What remarkable vision of Ezekiel is frequently applied to modern religious conditions? xxxvii.

VIII.

DANIEL.

595-534 B.C.

The Book of Daniel records a number of interesting events which properly belong to the period of Hebrew history covered by the Babylonian captivity. They might have been better on some accounts considered under that head. But as some of these events have also a prophetic bearing, and as history and prophecy are somewhat closely intermingled here, it seems better, on the whole, to take the whole work together.

The prophetic parts of the book are marked by a definiteness and clearness which we scarcely find in any of the other prophets; though, even here, there are some predictions the design of which it is yet difficult to determine. This is particularly the case with those in chaps. xi. and xii. Some of these have been made the basis of curiously minute calculations relating to a great variety of historical developments. Many have thought they found in them clear intimations of events and series of events in modern history reaching into the present century, and determining the time of the final consummation previous to the second coming of Christ. But probably these prophecies had their principal fulfilment in the times and relations of the Jewish nation before the first advent, while, at the same time, containing intimations of the character and development of the Messianic kingdom.

However it may be with these passages, a very large proportion of the book contains unusually definite statements concerning events then future. The interpretation of Nebuchadnezzar's dream in chap. ii., and the vision of the four beasts in vii. and again in viii., are of this kind. These indicate the succession of four great world-empires, or widely conquering forces; viz., the Babylonian, the Medo-Persian, the Grecian, and the Syrian, the last anticipating and ultimately merging in the Roman. It was doubtless one of those double intentions of prophecy of which we find many examples. Among the marvellous instances of extraordinary power in which human wisdom and Divine inspiration mingled among the Hebrew worthies, are the interpretation of Nebuchadnezzar's second dream, where the prophet courageously indicated that monarch's sins and the fearful punishment about to overtake him; also, the interpretation of the writing on the wall, announcing to the terrified Belshazzar the instant doom of himself and his empire.

But the most interesting portion of the book, to Christian readers, is the explicit prophetic statement of the time of the coming of the Messiah. ix. 24-27. By the prophetic symbolization of days for years, and weeks for corresponding periods, we have 490 years from a designated event as the period at the end of which the Messiah should close his mission. This is found to correspond to the facts as verified in the appearance and crucifixion of Christ.

FIRST PART.

1. Who was Daniel? What should you think of his family connection and personal appearance? What distinction was shown him and his three friends in their early youth? i. 1-6. What objections were urged to the diet and training to which they were to be subjected? What was done, and the result? Dan. i. 1-20.

2. What extraordinary event occurred in which Daniel's ability was called into requisition? ii. 1-45. The consequence to Daniel and his friends? 46-49.

3. Nebuchadnezzar's golden image, and his decree concerning its worship. The refusal of Shadrach, Meshach, and Abednego, and their heroic conduct. Give the narrative. iii. 1-30.

4. The second dream of Nebuchadnezzar, and the impotence again of his magicians. iv. 1-7. Daniel's bold exhortation and rebuke to the king, and his remarkable interpretation. 8-27. Fulfilment of the vision and prediction. The king's humiliation and acknowledgment. 28-37.

5. The grand banquet of Belshazzar. Profanation of the Jewish sacred vessels. v. 1-4. Appalling apparition, and the mysterious inscription. Daniel's interpretation, and announcement of Belshazzar's doom and the overthrow of his kingdom. 5-28.

6. Babylon taken by Cyrus. End of the Assyrian empire. The Medo-Persian extended over the whole eastern world. 30, 31.

7. Give such account as you can of the walls and fortifications of Babylon. How was the city taken? Mention some of the prophecies concerning its destruction. Jer. li., especially 1-4, 7-12, 27-32, 37. Isa. xlv. 1-3, xlvi.; also xiii. 19-22.

8. Before these events, what king had reigned in Babylon besides Nebuchadnezzar and Belshazzar? and what event of Jewish interest occurred in his reign? 2 Kings xxv. 27-30.

9. Daniel's eminence under the reign of Darius. The jealousy of the princes, and the conspiracy against him. Dan. vi. 1-19. Give an account of the affair. The mortification of the king, and the deliverance of Daniel. The final outcome. 10-25.

SECOND PART.

1. What remarkable vision did Daniel have in the first year of Belshazzar? vii. 1-14. What did the four beasts symbolize according to the interpretation given to Daniel? What most remarkable character is assigned to that which is symbolized by the fourth beast? What was to overthrow and supersede all these? 15-28.

2. What remarkable vision do you find described as appearing to the prophet two years later? viii. 1-12.

3. Give some account of the prayer of Daniel near the beginning of the reign of Darius, — its objects, its character, and its spirit. ix. 4-15. For what did he specially ask? 16-19.

4. What answer was given him, and what remarkable event is predicted? 20-27. Reckoning prophetic time as a year for a day, how many years are these seventy weeks supposed to symbolize? What is the decree for the restoration of Jerusalem, here referred to? Ezra vii. 11-26. How long before Christ's birth was this? How long before the crucifixion?

5. What befell the prophet two years later? x. 1-3. What vision did he have? 4-6. What comforting words were spoken to him? 11, 12.

6. What is predicted to take place in some remote future? What great doctrine of Christianity seems to be expressed here? xii. 1-3.

7. Going back over all the prophecies and visions of Daniel, while there is much that is not easy to understand, what important outlines of history are discernible? What four great world-empires seem to be foreshadowed? (See Introduction.)

IX.

THE MINOR PROPHETS.

The books of the twelve minor prophets are not arranged in chronological order. Jonah, who lived before any of the others, is placed fifth in the list, while both Joel and Amos were probably anterior to Hosea. All these prophets exercised their office during the decadence of both divisions of the Israelitish nation, and most of them after the beginning of the great calamities which came upon the people for their sins.

HOSEA.

785-725 B.C.

This prophet lived during the most troublous times of the Israelitish monarchy. It was a time when revolutions and usurpations were the order of the day in governmental ranks, and when idolatry and fearful immorality prevailed among the people. Hosea's ministry was perhaps the longest of any on record, extending over a period of more than sixty years. With one or two exceptions, he is the only one of the prophets who devotes himself almost exclusively to the Ten Tribes, rather than to the Jewish division of the nation.

The method of instruction followed by Hosea is singular, and much care is needed in the interpretation of his writings. Some of them, if taken in a strictly literal sense, might seem to involve positive immorality on the part of the prophet. But these doubtless are largely figurative, or capable of such explanations as would exclude all inconsistency of conduct. It may be that the debased condition of the people was such that only the most bold and startling illustrations of their sinfulness could have aroused them to a sense of their situation. The prevailing type is that of a wife who has been unfaithful to her husband, and has made herself very vile. The apostasies and growing wickedness of the people, together with the abominations which had become common, are set forth with great power and vividness. With these are mingled pathetic representations of the great love of Jehovah for his disobedient children. The style is abrupt, uneven, and often inelegant, but highly poetical, and abounding in metaphors. More than any other of the prophets, Hosea resembles our modern reformers and revivalists.

---

1. Give the names of the minor prophets. In chronological order, which is first? How do some of the others rank relatively as to time?

2. During what stage of the national history did they all exercise their office?

3. In what times did Hosea live, and how long before Christ? What about the length of his ministry? To which division of the nation did he devote himself?

4. What concerning his method of instruction? What is the prevailing type by which he illustrates the sin of the people? What feeling does God express, notwithstanding their vileness? What is Hosea's style?

5. What were some of the sins denounced by the prophet, and what consequences were predicted? iv. 1-3. What cause of destruction is mentioned? 6.

6. What exhortations to penitence and reformation do you find? x. 12, 13; xiv. 1, 2, 3, 9, etc. What pathetic entreaty to the people to turn to God? xi. 8. What despairing utterance concerning the nation? iv. 17. Is it good to be let alone of God?

7. What beautiful and tender sentiments are expressed towards those who repent of their backslidings? xiv. 4-7. What affectionate desire is indicated in regard to his people? xi. 1-4.

X.

JOEL AND AMOS.

JOEL.

800 B.C.

This prophet must have lived somewhat earlier than Hosea, and probably exercised his ministry in the time of Joash, king of Israel, and Amaziah, king of Judah. The writings of this prophet are not extensive, but they are of considerable interest. The main subject of his prophecy is the terrible judgments of God which were to come upon the people for their persistent disobedience. But he predicts repentance and reformation and consequent restoration. Through all these, he seems to have grand visions of the glory of the Messianic times, and the prosperity of the people of God.

The proximate events which answered to the chief predictions, were a grievous drought, and a plague of locusts which so devastated the land that the inhabitants were in great distress. This led to repentance and reformation on the part of the people, and consequent deliverance. But, doubtless, these were meant also to symbolize on a larger scale the future of the nation, and they contained intimations of more extensive calamities which should issue in a more radical and permanent reformation. They also look forward, in a general way, to the establishment of the Christian Church and its triumph in the earth. To this refers the glowing passage in chap. iii., quoted by Peter on the day of Pentecost.

AMOS.

787 B.C.

This prophet was obviously of humble origin, having been in his youth a herdsman and a gatherer of sycamore fruit. He had not been educated in the schools of the prophets, nor received any special training for the prophetic office. His residence and probable birthplace was Tekoa, about twelve or fifteen miles south from Jerusalem. The larger part of his ministry was among his own people, in the kingdom of Judah; but he at one time visited the Israelitish dominion, and preached powerfully against the idolatry of the land, and predicted dire judgments because of it. On this account, Amaziah, the idolatrous priest of the altar at Bethel, complained of him to the king, and drove him out of the country. vii. 10-17.

The style of Amos is clear and forcible; the imagery is homely and apt, much of it drawn from rustic and agricultural usages. The following are the more obvious divisions of the book: 1. A denunciation of the sins of the neighboring nations. i. 1-ii 3. 2. Description of the moral condition of Judah and Israel. ii. 4-vi. 14. 3. A reflection upon the previous discourses, and a narration of the prophet's visit to Bethel, and declaration of the impending punishment of the wicked nation and the false priest. vii. 1–ix. 10. 4. A forward look to the time of the Messiah's kingdom, and the happiness of God's people. ix. 11–15.

---

1. The time of the prophet Joel? What can you say of his writings? What predictions have had a literal fulfilment, and of what were the predictions symbolical?

2. What is said concerning the effect of the drought, and the plague of the insects? i. 4, 12, 16, etc.

3. What description is given of the locusts and their devastations? i. 6, 7; ii. 2–10. What measures were proposed to avert the evil? i. 14; ii. 12–17. What consequences promised? 19–26.

4. What prediction of remarkable events which were to occur in later times, and which was quoted in the New Testament as being then fulfilled? ii. 28–32.

5. What was the condition in life of the prophet Amos? At what time, and where, did he live? Where did he exercise his prophetic office? The effect of his mission to the kingdom of Israel? vii. 10–17.

6. The general style of the book? The divisions of the treatise?

7. Against what nations does the prophet denounce the Divine judgments? i. and ii.

8. What illustrations of the greatness and power of God are given? iv. 13; v. 8; ix. 2, 3, 5, 6.

9. What instances of transgression and sin are cited? ii. 8; iv. 1; v. 7; vi. 4–6. What promises of peace and prosperity in the latter days are made? ix. 13–15.

XI.

OBADIAH, JONAH, MICAH, NAHUM.

OBADIAH.

585 B.C.

The prophecy of Obadiah is comprised in the shortest book in the Old Testament, consisting of a single chapter of only twenty-one verses. We have no account of the man, and can only judge concerning him by what we gather from his brief writings. He probably prophesied about 585 B.C., or some time between the destruction of Jerusalem and the overthrow of Edom. So much is evident from the fact, that while he predicts the latter, and indeed makes it the main subject of his prophecy, he alludes to the indifference, or perhaps the practical sympathy with the enemy, which was manifested by Edom in the time of Jerusalem's calamity. 11-14. For this, among the wickednesses of Edom, he declares her overthrow by the same power which had laid Judah low.

The most remarkable passage is the closing one, in which the prophet announces the future glory of Jerusalem or Mount Zion, and the great prosperity of God's people, thus doubtless figuring the spiritual triumphs of the Church of Christ.

JONAH.

862 B.C.

This prophet, though the fifth in the order of arrrangement of the minor prophets, appears to have lived and exercised his sacred office many years before any of the others. We find the first mention of his name in the time of Jeroboam II., king of Israel, where he prophesies the restoration of certain extensive territories which had been wrested from the kingdom by neighboring nations. 2 Kings xiv. 25. A few ancient writers maintained that he was the son of the widow of Zarephath who was miraculously restored by Elijah. Others have attempted to identify him with the young man of the sons of the prophets sent to anoint Jehu. But these are evidently fanciful conceits, having only the slenderest foundation of conjecture.

The book is mainly a narrative of the prophet's experience when sent on a special religious mission, and the concomitants and consequences, rather than the ordinary utterances of the prophetic mind. The extraordinary supernaturalisms embodied in the book have made it the object of infidel assault and much profane wit. But they are chiefly based on false conceptions of the facts, which, though remarkable, are in no sense contradictory or inconsistent.

The character of Jonah attracts attention by reason of such unexpected weakness in a chosen messenger of the Lord, sent on a solemn and important errand. Yet a charitable consideration of all the circumstances will lead to some mitigation of our condemnation, though not to a very high estimate of the prophet's character.

MICAH.

756-697 B.C.

Of this prophet very little is known. He appears to have been contemporary with Isaiah, Hosea, and Amos, and perhaps others of the minor prophets. It is probable that the utterances of which his book is composed were made during the latter part of the period usually assigned to him, or about 720-710 B.C. The subjects are of the same general character with most of the prophecies of this period. They contain warnings concerning the national wickedness, and threatenings of punishment, together with somewhat indefinite yet confident predictions of the Messianic times and triumphs. The prediction concerning the precise place of Christ's birth is the most important and remarkable of his utterances, and was accepted by the Jewish rabbis and doctors as conclusive. It was on the authority of this prediction that the announcement of the place was made to Herod.

The book appears to have three divisions, each marked at the beginning by the formal exhortation, " Hear ye ; " each also commencing with rebukes and threatenings, and ending with a promise.

NAHUM.

713 B.C.

Of Nahum's personal history, no more is known than of that of Micah. Probably the two prophets were contemporary, and that they exercised their office about the same time. Yet the subjects are widely different, as were doubtless the places of their birth. It is thought by the most reliable authorities that Nahum was a native of Galilee, and that, when the captivity of the Ten Tribes began, he escaped to Judæa, and was in Jerusalem at the time of the Assyrian invasion under Sennacherib. The appalling and miraculous catastrophe of that invasion, and the destruction of the army, were perhaps the occasion when the Spirit moved him to prophesy against Nineveh, the renowned and mighty capital of the Assyrian empire. This is the subject of the book, and is treated in a bold, fervid, and eloquent manner. Of the literal fulfilment of these predictions in the destruction of Nineveh about a century later, there is abundant evidence. The discoveries made during the present century by Layard and others among the ruins of the buried, and for ages forgotten, city, confirm the correctness of the prophet's vivid descriptions.

---

1. What peculiarity is there about the Book of Obadiah? At what time did he prophesy, and against what particular city?

2. Of what does he accuse the Edomites? 11-14. What vision of the future glory of Israel is set forth, and to what does it probably have reference? 17, 18, 21.

3. What is there remarkable about the time and place of Jonah in relation to the other minor prophets? What are some of the not very probable traditions concerning him? What mention of him do we find in Hebrew history?

4. Give the main facts of the narrative. What are some of the obvious elements of the prophet's character?

5. What can be said of the prophet Micah? At about what time did he prophesy, and who were his contemporaries?

6. Some of the prominent topics of the book? How are the three divisions of it marked?

7. Some of the accusations and threatenings against Israel and Judah? i. 6, 7, 9; ii. 2, 4; iii. 1-4.

8. What more prosperous conditions are predicted after these judgments? iv. 1, 2. What oft-quoted utterances are found here? 3, 4.

9. What remarkable prophecy concerning the place of the Messiah's birth? v. 2. Where, and on what occasion, is this quoted in the New Testament?

10. How much do we know of the personal history of Nahum? The probable time of his ministry?

11. The subject of his prophecy? Of what empire was Nineveh the capital? How did it rank among cities, and what was its general character?

12. What event of historic interest and importance had occurred in Nahum's time, in the relations of the Assyrians to the Jews?

13. What striking features of the Divine character are set forth at the beginning of this prophecy? i. 2, 3, 7.

14. How is Nineveh described, and what is intimated concerning the energy and enterprise of the city? iii. 1, 2.

15. To what condition was she doomed? 3, 7, 11, 12. Were these predictions fulfilled? Is any thing known of Nineveh in these latter times?

XII.

HABAKKUK, ZEPHANIAH, HAGGAI.

HABAKKUK.

626 B.C.

This prophet was doubtless a contemporary of Jeremiah, though no account of him is given, either in his own writings, or in any of the historical books. It is evident that he preached to the people some little time at least before the overthrow of the nation; since he denounces the peculiar sins of that period, and predicts the Chaldæan invasions, setting forth in vivid language the characteristics of the invaders. i. 6-9. The style is highly poetical, and the imagery very fine. The first two chapters have the form of a dialogue between the prophet and the Divine Ruler. The third chapter is a prayer, or psalm, which, for grandeur of poetic conception and sublimity of expression, is seldom equalled in the literature of any language.

ZEPHANIAH.

630 B.C.

We have the genealogy of Zephaniah and the time of his ministry clearly stated in the opening passage of his written prophecy. As he predicted the fall of Nineveh, and as that city was destroyed about the middle of the reign of Josiah, the prophecy must have been made in the earlier part of that reign. He is supposed to have been a contemporary of Habakkuk, and also of Jeremiah.

The book begins with a denunciation of terrible judgments upon the people for their idolatry pride, and wickedness. Afterward great calamities are predicted to the surrounding nations. The book closes with a call to repentance, and a promise of future restoration and peace.

HAGGAI.

520 B.C.

This prophet was of the number who returned from the captivity, under Zerubbabel, according to the decree of Cyrus. He exercised his office during the troublous times of the rebuilding of the temple, and the re-organizing of the community, While we have not any more knowledge of Haggai's personal history than of the prophets who preceded him, we have unusually explicit information concerning the time of his preaching. We are told, not only in what year he prophesied, but in what month, and on what day of the month. Three such dates are given, and all of them within the space of four months, in the second year of Darius.

After the death of Cyrus the returned Jews were hindered in their work of reconstruction by the interference of the hostile Samaritans and others, and for sixteen years almost nothing was done. On the accession of Darius Hystaspes, he renewed the decree, and gave aid to the Jews. But years of inactivity had dulled their zeal, and it required the rebukes and exhortations of the prophets to stir up their interest and enthusiasm. This furnished the chief occasion and object of Haggai's ministry. In this, too, he and his co-laborers were successful: and the grand undertaking was in a few years successfully accomplished.

---

1. What was the time of Habakkuk's ministry? What evidence have we that he preached before the overthrow of Jerusalem?

2. What can be said concerning the style and form of the writing?

3. What do we know as to the morals of the people? i. 3, 4. How are the Chaldæan invaders described? ii. 2.

4. What expression do we find here that is used to illustrate the clearness of gospel truth? ii. 2. What words are often quoted to express the essence of Protestant Christianity? 4. What rebuke is given to those who tempt others to drunkenness? 15.

5. Character of the last chapter? Give some of the more highly poetical passages. What formula of extraordinary faith do we find here? iii. 17, 18.

6. What is recorded concerning Zephaniah? In whose reign did he prophesy? What reason have we for placing his ministry in the earlier part of this reign?

7. Give the chief topics of the book. How does the prophet represent the coming judgments upon the people? i. 14, 15, etc.

8. How does he describe the future condition of Nineveh? ii. 14, 15. How does this correspond with the facts?

9. What encouraging prospect is held forth concerning the future of Jerusalem, and what does it probably signify? iii. 14-20.

10. The time of Haggai's ministry? How long a time do his published prophecies cover? The political condition of the people at this time? The occasion of Haggai's addresses and exhortations?

11. What does he urge the people to do? What reproach does he utter? i. 4, 9.

12. What was the effect of his preaching? i. 14, 15. Do we find any confirmation of this in the historical books? Ezra vi. 14, 15.

XIII.

ZECHARIAH AND MALACHI.

ZECHARIAH.

520-487 B.C.

Like Haggai, Zechariah appears to have been of the company of fifty thousand who first returned from the captivity under the leadership of Zerubbabel. He was associated with Haggai in actively encouraging the people to rebuild the temple, and in urging the religious motives thereto. (Ezra v. 1; vi. 14.) There is reason for believing that he was at this time a young man (ii. 4), and therefore that he was born during the captivity. There are also indications that, like Jeremiah and Ezekiel, he was of the order of the priests.

The first date in the book we find to be in the same year in which Haggai's prophecies were uttered. The second date is about two years later. The last part of the book is probably much later still, and has been by some authors supposed to be written by some other author or authors.

The contents of the book may be embraced in four divisions: 1. The Introduction, comprising the first six verses. 2. A series of visions, which are intended, for the most part, to encourage the people with promises of future prosperity as a consequence of reformation and obedience. These extend to the end of the sixth chapter. 3. The third division comprises chaps. vii. and viii., and discusses the question of keeping up the days of fasting and humiliation which had been observed by the Jews several times in the year during their captivity. Mingled with the discussion are many reflections of a moral and spiritual character, growing not inaptly out of the subject. 4. The last division contains denunciations against some of the contemporary nations, and promises of prosperity to God's people, with various predictions concerning Christ.

MALACHI.

397 B.C.

Of the personal history of the last of the Old-Testament prophets, nothing is known, except of the time of his ministry as indicated by his writings. This must have been about one hundred years after the time of Haggai and Zechariah. The temple is spoken of as then existing, and so must have been already rebuilt. He speaks also of "the governor" (i. 8), the same term being used as in Nehemiah and nowhere else; and it must therefore have been during the administration of that eminent ruler. This is further evident from the fact that the vices and immoralities which he rebukes are the very same that Nehemiah was striving during the latter part of his official life to abolish.

It appears, that after the secure re-establishment of the Jews in their own land, and the rebuilding of the temple, and fortification of the city, the people had grown irreligious and selfish and sensual. They had not relapsed into idolatry; but their vices were largely such as we see to-day in some professedly Christian communities, where a spirit of carnality and worldliness has come in, and where vital piety has given place to formality, carelessness, and general neglect of duty. He severely reproves the priests who dishonor God by their indifference and hypocrisy. He also rebukes the popular sins of the times. He pointedly alludes to the coming of the Messiah, and gives some of the characteristics of his coming. The prophecy and Old-Testament canon end with the prediction of the final catastrophe, and the promise, that, before that, there shall appear the forerunner to prepare the people for Christ's advent.

---

1. With whom was Zechariah associated during a part of his ministry? At what time in his life was this? Where was he probably born?

2. What dates do we have in the book itself determining the times of a portion of its contents? What differences of opinion have there been about the latter part of the book?

3. Give the general divisions of the book.

4. Give some account of the visions in the second part.

5. What inquiry was made of the prophet by some of the leaders? vii. 3. What had been their custom during the captivity? vii. 5; viii. 19. What does the prophet represent as of far greater value than outward fasting? vii. 9, 10; viii. 16, 17.

6. What pleasant picture does he make of the future prosperity of God's obedient people? viii. 4, 5.

7. Against what nations does Zechariah predict judgments? ix. 1–6.

What Messianic prediction do we find? ix. 9. Where do you find the fulfilment of this?

8. What is the tone of the prophet towards his people in chaps. x., xi., and xii.? What remarkable promises are made? xiii. 1, 2; xiv. 7-9. What expression is used to indicate the general diffusion of, and reverence for, piety in the latter days? xiv. 20.

9. How long after the time of Haggai was that of Malachi? What reasons are there for this opinion? Who was the ruler at this time? Have we any later Old-Testament scripture than this?

10. What are some of the sins denounced, and how do they compare with those described by Nehemiah? Mal. ii. 8, 11; Neh. xiii. 23-27, 29; Mal. iii. 7-9; Neh. ix. 34, 35.

11. What kind of offerings does the prophet rebuke them for bringing to the Lord? i. 8, 13. What should we *always* offer to the Lord?

12. What declaration is made concerning the universal diffusion of true religion? i. 11. What prediction of the forerunner, and of the Messiah, and what is indicated as the real character of the Messiah's mission? iii. 1-3.

13. What distinction is made between the future destinies of the wicked and of the righteous? iv. 1, 2. With what predictions does the prophecy and the Old-Testament canon close? What effect would follow the rejection of the overtures? Was this fulfilled in the case of the Jews?

THIRD YEAR'S COURSE.

THE LIFE OF CHRIST.

BOOKS OF REFERENCE.

THIRD YEAR.

Farrar's LIFE OF CHRIST: also by Abbott, Hanna, Beecher.
Robinson's HARMONY OF THE GOSPELS.
Strong's HARMONY OF THE GOSPELS.
G. W. Clark's HARMONY OF THE GOSPELS.
Smith's NEW TESTAMENT HISTORY.
Geikie's LIFE OF CHRIST: also by Hanna and Abbott.
Edersheim's LIFE AND TIMES OF THE MESSIAH.
Stalker's LIFE OF CHRIST.
Bernard's PROGRESS OF DOCTRINE.
Stowe's HISTORY OF THE BOOKS OF THE BIBLE.
Gregory's WHY FOUR GOSPELS?
Tulloch's THE SUFFERING SAVIOUR.
Thompson's LAND AND THE BOOK.
Andrew's LIFE OF CHRIST (for order of events).
Wallace's BEN HUR.
Selah Merrill's GALILEE IN THE TIME OF CHRIST.
Stapfer's PALESTINE IN THE TIME OF CHRIST.
Bruce's TRAINING OF THE TWELVE.
Eggleston's CHRIST IN LITERATURE.
Hackett's ILLUSTRATIONS OF SCRIPTURE.
Farrar's MESSAGES OF THE BOOKS.

MIRACLES OF CHRIST.—Trench ON THE MIRACLES.
  Bruce's MIRACULOUS ELEMENT IN THE GOSPELS.
  Wardlaw ON THE MIRACLES: also MacDonald, Howson.

PARABLES.—Trench ON THE PARABLES: also Arnot, Guthrie, Calderwood, Cummings.
  Bruce's PARABOLIC TEACHING.

THE LIFE OF CHRIST.

I.

Historical Antecedents.—Birth of John and of Jesus.

In the studies heretofore occupying our attention, we have had a pretty full account of the Israelitish and Jewish nations down to the fourth century before Christ. A very brief sketch during the intervening centuries, gathered from secular sources, is given in the Introduction to Number XXXII. of Hebrew History. It is important to recollect at this point that all this history is a history of the world's preparation for the coming of our Lord Jesus Christ on his mission of human redemption.

The Roman power, the fourth of the great world empires described and predicted by Daniel, (ii. and vii.,) had now reached its summit. It had extended its sway over the larger proportion of the then known world. Though its successes had wrought deep and disastrous corruptions in its great cities, this period was outwardly that of its greatest brilliancy. Wealth was abundant; arts, letters and commerce flourished as never before. The Emperor, Augustus Cæsar, was perhaps in most respects the greatest and most generous of his line. The territory under his sway was in round numbers nearly three thousand miles in length and from one to two thousand in breadth.

Judea lay at the south-western extremity of these domains. This country and its inhabitants had passed through many and extraordinary vicissitudes since the restoration from the Babylonian captivity. Till within a few years it had been under the rule, real or nominal, of the Asmonean princes, descendants and successors of the great Maccabean family, members of which had performed such heroic exploits, and had achieved and for a time maintained the independence of the nation in the second century B. C. About 63 B. C., Judea had been made tributary to the all-conquering power of Rome, and Antipater, a noble but crafty Idumean, had been by Julius Cæsar made procurator, though there was still a nominal government under one of the Asmonean house. Herod, the son of Antipater, after the death of Cæsar, by various means ingratiated himself with the authorities at Rome, and was appointed king over a territory embracing substantially the whole of Palestine. His recognition by the people was achieved only after a fierce war and much bloodshed. He was a man of powerful character, and vast energy and enterprise were displayed by him in the establishment of his government and the maintenance of his authority; but he was one of the most vindictive, cruel and violently wicked of princes. He slew his own sons out of jealousy, and put to death his beautiful, virtuous and accomplished wife Mariamne for the same cause. We see this character exemplified in his order for the slaughter of all the children in Bethlehem that he might make sure of the infant Jesus, the predicted and feared "King of the Jews."

The nation, however, was in a fairly prosperous condition. Herod had built and beautified many cities, and almost reconstructed the Temple at Jerusalem. Almost for the first time for centuries the descendants of the Twelve Tribes occupied the whole of their ancient territory under a consolidated government, and it was the fullness of time for the advent of the Messiah.

Luke i. 5—80; iii. 23—38. Matt. i. 1—23.

1. At what different points of time do the Evangelists begin their accounts of the Life of Christ? Coincidence between the beginning of the Old Testament and the beginning of John's Gospel in the New.

2. Grounds of the expectation among the Jews that a Divine Person would appear among them at some period of their history, who would be a Redeemer and Restorer. Gen. xlix. 10. Numbers xxiv. 17. Deut. xviii. 15. Isa. ix. 6 and 7; xi. 1—10. Micah v. 2. (Give also other passages of similar import.)

3. Meaning of the words *Messiah* and *Christ*.

4. Coincidence between the ending of the old Testament and the beginning of Mark's Gospel in the New. Mark i. 1—3. Malachi iii. 1; and iv. 5 and 6. Other predictions fulfilled in John the Baptist. Isa. xl. 3—5; Luke iii. 4—6.

5. Incidents connected with the birth of John the Baptist.

(a) His parentage and lineage. Character of his parents and office of his father. Luke i. 5—9.

(b) How many courses of priests were there for the temple service, and to which of these did Zacharias belong? I. Chron. xxiv. 7—18. (See v. 10 and compare with Luke i. 5.)

(c) The vision and announcement. Luke i. 11—17. The unbelief of Zacharias and the penalty incurred. 18—20.

(d) The birth and naming of the child. Cessation of Zacharias' affliction and his prophetic song. 57—79.

6. The genealogy of Jesus. Matt. i. 1—16. Luke iii. 23—38.

(a) What difference do you find in these two lists?

(b) Mention some of the more distinguished names, and give a brief account of them.

(c) Is the genealogy that of Joseph, or of Mary?

(d) What reason is there for supposing that Mary also belonged to this line? Lu. i. 27 and 32.

7. The annunciation. Lu. i. 26—38.

(a) The Angel's visit. Where was Mary's residence? Its geographical situation.

(b) The announcement, and the consequent wonder in the mind of Mary.

(c) The predicted character of the child.

8. Joseph's relation to Mary and his embarrassment. The prophecy concerning the manner of Christ's birth and its fulfillment. Isa. vii. 14. Matt. i. 22, 23.

9. The prescribed name of the child, and its meaning? Matt. i. 21. What others of the same name had appeared in previous great crises of the national history? Num. xxvii. 18—21; Haggai. i. 1, and Zech. iii. What was the difference between the salvation under the former Joshuas and that under Jesus? Matt. i. 21.

10. What other name had been applied to the future child, and its signification? Isa. vii. 14. Matt. i. 23. John i. 14.

11. The decree of the Roman government for the taxing or the census of all the subjects of the empire. Lu. ii. 1. The journey made necessary to Joseph and Mary by this decree. The length of the journey.

12. What previous allusions to Bethlehem are found in the Hebrew history? Gen. xxxv. 19; I. Sam. xvi. 1 and 4. What eminent ancestor of Jesus was born there? How far was it from Jerusalem?

13. The birth of the child. Where was he laid after his birth, and why? Lu. ii. 7.

II.

The Infancy.

The visit of the Wise Men from some region at the east of Judea, is one of the remarkable and yet most mysterious events connected with the birth of Jesus. There have been many inquiries and speculations concerning the character and the coming of these seekers after the new-born child; but all that is essential to be known is doubtless implied in the narrative. They were in some sense representatives of the gentile world bringing a welcome to the Saviour not of the Jews only, but of the whole human race. They represented more than the Roman Empire, for they evidently came from beyond its limit. The title applied to them in the original record indicates that they came from the banks of the Tigris and Euphrates, where astronomy was early cultivated, and where the prevailing heathenism had taken on the form of worship of the heavenly luminaries. There were doubtless among such worshipers some who still cherished amid the corruptions of their religion traces of the One God, the Father of Lights, and spiritual conceptions of the truths of the primal revelations.

This would seem also to be implied in the "Star" given for their guidance. This, unquestionably, was a supernatural light, attracting the attention of those whose expectation of a coming Deliverer had already been excited by other means. For we have abundant evidence from authentic secular history that a wide-spread impression, both in the Roman world and beyond its limits, affected a certain class of persons—vaguely and indefinitely, it is true, but still really,—that a remarkable personage was about to appear, born somewhere in the East, and by many, as by these Wise Men, in Judea. Whether this had come from the Jews dispersed far or near among the nations, or from the influence of the Spirit of God, operating upon the minds of the more devout among the heathen, or, as is more likely, by both these causes, the fact seems well established.

The magi, guided by the star, had come to Judea, and already had the conviction that the new-born child was a royal personage and the "king of the Jews." At Jerusalem, examination of the written prophetic revelations showed that the Messiah was to be born at Bethlehem; and thither, still guided by the celestial light, they resorted, and found the young child. The gifts they presented indicated that these foreigners were persons of very great distinction and wealth. They also imply not only homage given to a royal personage, but offerings to a Divine being which also coincides with the "worship" spoken of. "Ages before, a prophet from the same regions had predicted the Messiah by the sign of 'the star that should arise out of Jacob;' and while these sages watched the heavens with the reverence of worshipers, it pleased God to use their own ideas as the source of new light."

Luke ii. 8—38. Matt. ii. 1—18.

1. To whom outside of the family, and by whom, was the first announcement of the birth of this child? How was the announcement made? Lu. ii. 8—14. What did the shepherds do, and what did they find? 15—18.

2. The presentation in the Temple. Lu. ii. 22—24. What was the law concerning the offering on such an occasion? Lev. xii. 6 and 8. Why did the mother of Jesus bring two doves or two young pigeons, instead of a lamb?

3. Simeon's meeting with the child, and his previous revelation concerning it. Lu. ii. 25, 26. His utterance concerning the character of the child. 29—32; 34, 35.

4. The greeting of the aged prophetess Anna. 36—38. What do these prophetic declarations indicate concerning the character of the child?

5. Visit of the Wise Men. Matt. ii. 1—12.

   (a) From what region are they supposed to have come? (See Introduction.) About how far, probably, from Palestine?

   (b) Was there any expectation, outside of the Jewish race, of the advent of a mysterious royal and Divine person?

   (c) What guided them in their search?

   (d) Fulfillment of prophecy in this coming. Isa. lx. 3.

   (e) The arrival at Jerusalem and the inquiry there, the excitement of the people, and Herod's jealousy lest his authority might be disturbed.

   (f) The examination of the prophetic records by the priests and scribes, and the decision that the predicted Messiah must be born at Bethlehem.

   (g) Herod's strenuous and hypocritical charge to the magi.

6. The finding of the child by the strangers, who bestow gifts and offer worship. 9—11. What does the character of the gifts brought indicate concerning the condition of the bringers? What do their offering and their worship show? (See Introduction.)

7. The Wise Men warned, and Herod baffled. 12.

III.

Childhood and Youth.

Soon after the flight of Jesus and his parents to Egypt, the cruel and tyrannical King Herod died. The strong, compact, and, in some respects, powerful monarchy which he had created, embracing the whole of ancient Palestine, and which he had hoped to perpetuate in his own family, virtually came to an end with him. The scepter had departed from Judah, for Shiloh had come. Indeed, the reign of Herod had only been by permission of the imperial Roman government; and though there was a strong semblance of independence, yet the influence of Rome was constantly felt.

Herod, by his will, had virtually divided the kingdom among three of his sons. Though Archelaus was named as his successor, and had the central government of Judea, Idumea, and Samaria, Herod Antipas was to be made governor or tetrarch of Galilee and a portion of Peraea, while Herod Philip held the similar office of ruler of the north-eastern portion of the country beyond Jordan. Even this disposition of the government was of no avail, till it had the sanction of the Emperor Augustus. It was substantially confirmed, though Archelaus was not permitted to take the title of king, and after a few years, for his maladministration, was wholly displaced, and Judea became a Roman province, with governors or procurators appointed by the emperor. Pontius Pilate was one of those appointed about A. D. 26, and it was under his administration that the crucifixion of our Lord took place. The government of Herod Antipas, the ethnarch of Galilee, was milder and less disquieting to the parents of Jesus than that of Archelaus, and for this reason they preferred to return to their old residence in Nazareth.

Matt. ii. 13—23. Luke ii. 39—52.

1. The flight to Egypt. The parents of Jesus divinely informed concerning the purpose of the king, and directed to take the child to Egypt. 13—15. How long a journey would this probably be?

2. Herod's wrath at the defeat of his plot. His infamous decree, and its execution. 16—18.

3. The return from Egypt and settlement at Nazareth. Matt. ii. 19—23. Lu. ii. 39.

    (a) What had taken place during the absence in Egypt?

2

(b) Who was now ruler in Judea? Was his jurisdiction as extensive as that of his father had been?

(c) Why did the parents of Jesus turn aside from Judea, and go to Galilee? Who was the ruler here, and how did his government compare with that of Archelaus.

4. Character of Jesus as a child. Lu. ii. 40. What is especially noteworthy about the accounts of these early years of Christ's life? (See Introduction to No. V.)

5 The annual visit of his parents to Jerusalem. Lu. ii. 41. What feast was the occasion of this visit and what was its origin? How many public feasts were the Jews required publicly to celebrate? Ex. xxiii. 14—17. Indications of the religious character of Joseph and Mary.

6. What occurred when Jesus was twelve years old? Lu. ii. 42, 43.

(a) What was there remarkable about the situation in which his parents found him? 46, 47.

(b) The effect upon them, and his mother's mild reproach. 48.

(c) His answer and its significance. 49.

7. What is the sum of all that we know concerning the subsequent childhood and youth of Jesus? 51, 52.

8. Is there any thing extraordinary about this profound silence of all the Evangelists concerning the early years of so remarkable a person.

IV.

The Herald and Usher.

During all these years, John, the son of Zacharias, appears to have dwelt in the "desert,"—that is, the sparsely settled hill-country of Judea to the west of the Dead Sea. There were a very few cities and villages in this region, and in one of these his parents had dwelt at the time of his birth. But he evidently sought the solitudes apart from the towns, and lived an ascetic life, disciplining himself for his ministry to the people to prepare them for the coming of the Messiah. At about thirty years of age,—the age at which the priests entered upon their public work, he opened his mission in these same regions, going gradually to the north where the Jordan comes down above the Dead Sea. Here he would meet occasional companies of travelers, and to them he began to preach. The extraordinary character of his message, and his rude raiment of camel's hair cloth fastened with a leather girdle,—the traditional prophetic garb,—and his abstemious primitive diet, together with the fervor and power of his preaching, attracted attention and occasioned the resort of multitudes to see and hear him. The excitement appears to have been very great, and the conviction produced by this ministry was almost universal throughout all Judea and much of the neighboring country.

We have no detailed account of John's method, nor more than brief fragments of any of his discourses, and a summary statement of his main topics. The selfishness and wickedness of the people were denounced, and repentance and reformation were enjoined as a preparation for the coming of the Messiah, whom he announced as immediately at hand. The baptism which he administered to all who accepted his exhortations, was simply symbolic of the putting away of the defilement of sin, and the purpose of a clean life. This ministry began about six months before the public career of Jesus opened, and continued for some time, though probably not many months, after. John, who had gradually made his way up the Jordan, came at last into the jurisdiction of Herod Antipas, and, for the bold reproof which he administered to that prince for his criminal conduct, was by him thrown into prison and shortly after executed.

We shall meet frequently with the designation Pharisees and Sadducees. These were two distinct and prominent religious parties among the Jews. The Pharisees were strict formalists and legalists, though to the letter of the law they had added many traditions and fanciful casuistic interpretations. Their religion was ritual and mechanical, and utterly incompatible with the liberty and spirituality of genuine godliness. They were bigoted and exclusive to an extraordinary degree, and would not eat and drink with the masses of the people. A large proportion of them rigidly adhered to their doctrines, and carefully observed all the petty artificial rules which they had laid down for themselves. They were not socially aristocratic, but they were morally and religiously so, assuming a higher sanctity than others. Nor were they connected exclusively with the wealthier classes. These facts gave them great influence with the masses of the people.

The Sadducees disagreed in all prominent points with the Pharisees. But the great, marked characteristic of their sect, was the denial of the resurrection of the dead and of spiritual existence. This party embraced a considerable proportion of the wealthy and cultivated Jews.

There was also the sect of the Essenes, about which, however, little is said in the Evangelists. They appear to have been more devoutly and spiritually religious than either of the other parties.

Luke iii. 1—17. Matt. iii. 1—11. Mark i. 1—5. John i. 1—34; iii. 27—36.

1. What changes had taken place in the civil government of Palestine since the birth of Christ? (See Introduction to No. III.) At what time did John the Baptist begin his ministry? Lu. iii. 1.

2. The burden of his preaching. Matt. iii. 8; Mark i. 5; Lu. iii. 3. The meaning of the words *repent* and *repentance*. Was there any large occasion in the character of the people for this kind of exhortation?

3. The localities of his religious gatherings. Matt. iii. 1 and 5; Mark i. 4, 5; Lu. iii. 3 and 7. What was the nature of the country in this vicinity, and what its direction from Jerusalem? (Introduction.) Were these meetings, in any respects, like certain modern religious gatherings?

4. The attendance upon John's preaching. Matt. iii. 5; Mark i. 5. What parties are especially mentioned? Matt. iii. 7. What was the character of these respective parties? (See Introduction.)

5. The vigorous rebukes addressed especially to the members of the two chief Jewish parties. Matt. iii. 7—10; Lu. iii. 7—9. What were the people, therefore, generally admonished to do? How is genuine repentance and conversion likely to evince itself? Matt. iii. 8; Lu. iii. 8. Will a godly parentage or ancestry avail any thing necessarily towards one's justification? Matt. iii. 9, 10; Lu. iii. 8.

6. Instruction, as to practical conduct, to various classes of inquirers. Lu. iii. 10—14. Who were the publicans, and what was the cause of their unpopularity? Was their calling essentially improper?

7. Excitement of the people at the nature and powerful effect of John's ministry. Their eager and interested questionings. Lu. iii. 15; Jno. i. 19.

8. His prompt and modest denial of any claim of his own to the Messiahship. Jno. i. 20—23. His testimony concerning Christ. Matt. iii. 11; Mark i. 7; Lu. iii. 16, 17; Jno. i. 26, 27.

9. John the Baptist's introduction of Christ, and further testimony concerning his character. Jno. i. 15—18, and 29—34. Also, Jno. iii. 27—36. What extraordinary titles are here applied to Jesus? What profound significance is attributed to *the lamb*, in the Jewish ceremonial service?

10. What does John the Evangelist say of the personage concerning whom John the Baptist gives this testimony? Jno. i. 1—14. Taken in connection with the Baptist's declarations, what may be gathered from these statements concerning the previous existence, mission and Divine character of Christ?

V.

Preparation of Jesus for the Beginning of His Ministry.

In studying the Life of Christ, we need to take into careful consideration the character of the records from which we derive our information. These are comprised in four brief treatises known as "gospels," written severally by men who lived in the time of Christ, two of them by his immediate companions, and the other two by persons most intimate with his apostles. Altogether they do not occupy as much space as the one-half of an ordinary twelve-mo book, and they severally average scarcely so much as a moderate modern pamphlet.

They do not profess to be biographies or complete lives of Jesus; but are rather fragmentary and somewhat disconnected memoirs or collected reminiscences. Yet they so set forth the prominent facts and characteristics of this remarkable life, that the world has received a vivid impression of a grand, unique and perfect human person, the greatness of whose humanity can be accounted for only on the supposition that it was also Divine.

Three of these memoirs, though entirely independent of each other, appear to have been written from nearly the same point of view, and present in large measure the same facts. For this reason they are called the *synoptical* gospels. These reminiscences are, for the most part, confined to Christ's

Galilean experience. John, the fourth Evangelist, appears to have written some time after the others. His work is to a considerable extent supplementary to theirs. He gives more full information concerning Christ's ministry in Jerusalem and Judea, and dwells more upon the spiritual character and doctrines of the new dispensation.

One remarkable characteristic of these writings, is their freedom from any literary intention. The writers seem to give to the world such facts of Christ's career as will convey a clear impression of his character and his object in coming to the world. They give no connected or protracted doctrinal discussions. They are as simple and free from all preconceived theories and theological or philosophical bias as it is possible to conceive. They do not even profess to give their statements of facts in a wholly logical or chronological order; but only as the events come uppermost in their minds and press for expression, do they utter them.

Another characteristic is the silence of all these writers about many things on which multitudes of people, reasonably or unreasonably, desire information. There is not the least attempt to gratify a vulgar curiosity, or to indulge in any spirit of gossip. We have nothing at all about Christ's personal appearance, and only the most meager information about his childhood and youth. Two of the Evangelists do not allude to any event in his life till the beginning of his public career. Only one of them gives us the slightest glimpse of him during the twenty-eight or nine years between his infancy and his baptism; and that one speaks only of a single event in that long period. Yet out of these records of only a small fraction of a not very long life comes an influence affecting humanity more powerfully than all other lives together since the world began!

Matt. iii. 13—17; iv. 1—11. Mark i. 9—13. Luke iv. 1—12. John i. 37—51; ii. 1—12.

1. Jesus leaves his home in Nazareth, and resorts to the place near the Jordan where John the Baptist was holding his convocation. He presents himself as a candidate for baptism. Matt. iii. 13; Mark i. 9.

2. John's objection to performing this office for one whom he recognizes as his spiritual superior. Matt. iii. 14. Can any other reason be given why it might be deemed unnecessary for such an one as Jesus to be baptized with the baptism of *repentance?*

3. Jesus overrules the objection, on the ground of ceremonial propriety. 15.

4. The extraordinary occurrence immediately consequent on the baptism. Relate what was seen and heard. Matt. iii. 16, 17; Mark i. 10, 11; Lu. iii. 21, 22. How old was Jesus at this time? Lu. iii. 23.

5. Under the direction of the Holy Spirit coming upon him especially at his baptism, Jesus goes into the desert of Judea, far from human habitations, and exposed to wild beasts, he fasts forty days. Matt. iv. 1, 2; Mark i. 12, 13; Lu. iv. 1, 2.

6. The great conflict with Satan. Matt. iv. 2—10; Lu. iv. 2—11.

(a) Jesus, after the long fasting, tortured with hunger, is urged to exert his miraculous powers for his personal gratification. An appeal to physical appetite. The answer to this solicitation.

(b) Appeal to selfish sensationalism and the desire for human praise. How is this met?

(c) Appeal to selfish ambition,— the desire of power. His prompt rebuke of the infamous suggestion.

(d) The refusal throughout to cherish a willful and wayward spirit in preference to a patient and self-denying one.

7. Do we find other instances, in the Bible, of a forty days' religious seclusion and fasting at important epochs? Ex. xxiv. 18; xxxiv. 28; I. Ki. xix. 8.

8. The ministry of angels. Matt. iv. 11; Mark i. 13; Lu. iv. 12.

9. After his return from his great spiritual conflict, Jesus is sought by two of John the Baptist's disciples, who had heard their master's testimony concerning him. Jno. i. 37—39. Andrew finds his brother Simon, and introduces him to Jesus, who bestows upon him the new name of Peter.

10. The calling of Philip. The introduction of Nathanael, and his conversation with Jesus. 43—51. What do you infer from Nathanael's remark about Nazareth as to the reputation of that city? 46. What title does Nathanael give to Jesus, and how does Jesus designate himself? 49 and 51. Where was the probable residence of all the disciples who had now joined themselves to Jesus? 44.

11. The marriage at Cana. Jno. ii. 1—11. The distance of Cana from Nazareth? What does the attendance of Jesus upon this social festivity indicate as to his character and disposition? The exhaustion of the supply of wine, and what was done by the direction of Jesus, and the result. 3—10. What evidence is there that this was a genuine and not an apparent transformation? 10.

12. Was this transformation natural or supernatural? 11. How does a miracle or supernatural event differ from a natural event? (See Introduction to No. VI.

13. The visit to Capernaum. 12. In what direction and how far from Nazareth was this place?

VI.

Christ's First Public Appearance in Jerusalem.

A conspicuous characteristic of Christ's ministry was the miraculous power which he exercised. A miracle may be defined as an event not explicable on the basis of merely natural laws or causes, but requiring a power above nature, indicating a divine agency and certifying a divine authority in the person performing the act, and never occurring except in attestation of some religious movement. It was the firm belief among intelligent Jews that no genuine miracle could be wrought but by the power of God, and that this power was never granted except to a good man. Hence the miracles wrought by Christ appeal with demonstrative force to all candid men. Thus Nicodemus: "No man can do these miracles that thou doest, except God be with him." Prejudiced partisans and enemies of Christ endeavored to destroy the force of them by impeaching their genuineness. But their reasoning was so palpably superficial and inconsequential, that it required little effort to refute them. It was to these works as credentials of this divine authority, that Christ so frequently referred; and to the Jews, and in that age, they were so incontestable, that they could not well be rejected without guilt.

Attention is asked to some characteristics of these miracles. 1. They were never wrought for the personal gratification either of Jesus or of his friends. 2. They were never allowed to minister to mere curiosity. 3. They were never performed as mere tests of individual power, nor in response to a sensational demand. 4. They were, almost without exception, in the way of some benevolent ministration to the afflictions of men.

John ii. 13—25; iii. 1—20.

1. Jesus, according to his custom, goes to Jerusalem on the occasion of the passover next after the beginning of his ministry. Jno. ii. 13. Explain the origin and nature of this memorial, and its relation to Christianity.

2. Astonishment and grief of Jesus at the profanation of the Temple to the uses of secular commerce. He drives out the traders and speculators. The dignity and force of character in him which prevented resistance. 14—16.

3. The pious zeal manifested excites the admiration of his few friends, and the jealousy of the multitude. The latter demand of him a sign,— some evidence of his authority for this extraordinary action. 17, 18. His answer; their cavilings; the impression on his disciples. 19—22.

4. Having taught, and wrought some miracles, many were convinced of his divine character and mission; but, owing to their vague and carnal conceptions, he did not commit himself to them.

5. Visit of Nicodemus. Jno. iii. 1. Who was he, and what estimate do you form of his character?

6. His recognition of Christ's miracles and consequent divine power. 2.

7. The chief topic of Jesus' conversation with Nicodemus, and the ruler's failure to apprehend its real spiritual import. 3—8. What designation do Christians of this age give to the change here implied? By what power is it effected? 5, 6 and 8.

8. Jesus' assertion of the sacred truth of his teaching, and reference to his authority as evinced by his exercise of supernatural power; also, his sole ability to reveal these truths, and the reluctance of men to receive them. 9—13.

9. The great doctrine of Redemption by Christ as the Son of man and the Son of God. 14, 15. Greatness of the divine love. 16. Men condemned, not so much because of their natural condition or past sinfulness, as because of the rejection of the Redeemer. 17—20.

VII.

The Close of John the Baptist's Ministry.—Jesus among the Samaritans.

The Samaritans occupied the portion of Palestine between Galilee and Judea. The inhabitants of the regions both to the north and south of them were orthodox Jews, while they themselves were reckoned as aliens, or at best as unworthy of religious fellowship. They were, in reality, the descendants of the inhabitants which had been colonized in the depopulated country of the kingdom of Israel, after the conquest of that nation by Shalmaneser, king of Assyria. The former inhabitants had been carried away captive, and others from various Assyrian cities, had been sent to occupy the land. It is not unlikely that a remnant of the Israelites still remained. A mongrel race was formed, and it was thought best to conform to the religion of the land, though they still worshiped their own idols. On the return of Judah from the Babylonian captivity, the Samaritans claimed national and religious affinity with them, and asked to be allowed to participate in their religious enterprises. This was peremptorily refused, and henceforth there was an irrepressible enmity between the two sections of country and kinds of people. Gradually the idolatry of the Samaritans gave way to more exclusive monotheism, and a temple was built on Mt. Gerizim as a rival to that at Jerusalem. The people came to claim that theirs was the purer Hebrew faith. The animosity was great between the Jews and Samaritans, and even the common courtesies of life were often denied. Christ himself, though rebuking the bitterness and hatred of the two peoples, yet regarded the Samaritans as aliens, or as not comprised among the covenant people. Still they appear to have cherished similar hopes and expectations concerning the Messiah to those of the Jews.

Jno. iii. 22—36; iv. 1—44. Matt. xiv. 3—5; iv. 12—17. Mark vi. 17—20; i. 14, 15. Lu. iv. 14, 15.

1. Jesus leaves Jerusalem, and goes into the rural sections of Judea, near the Jordan, not far from the place where John the Baptist was holding his assemblies. Jno. iii. 22, 23.

2. A little spirit of rivalry and jealousy apparent among the disciples of John, when they hear of the people coming to Jesus. They appeal to their master, who readily reiterates his declaration of his own subordinate character, and the divine mission and character of Jesus. 25—36. Give some of the more striking utterances. 30, 35 and 36.

3. Herod's interest in John and his regard for him, and John's influence over him. Mark vi. 20. What changed all this? Matt. xiv. 3, 4; Mark vi. 17—19; Luke iii. 19, 20. What indication does this give of John's character as a preacher?

4. What was the result? At whose instigation? Why did not Herod put John to death? See above; also, Matt. xiv. 5. What relation was this Herod to the one who was king at the time of Christ's birth?

5. Jesus departs to go to Galilee. What two reasons are given for his leaving Judea? Jno. iv. 1, 2; Matt. iv. 12; Mark i. 14. In what condition does he return? Lu. iv. 14.

6. The halt for rest and refreshment near Sychar, in Samaria. Jno. iv. 4—6. What was there noted about this spot? What allusions to it in the Old Testament? Gen. xxxiii. 19, and xlviii. 22; Josh. xxiv. 1.

7. Who were the Samaritans, and what was their relation to the Jewish religion and to the Jews? (Introduction.)

8. Conversation with the woman at the well. Jno. iv. 7—26. Why was the woman astonished at his request? 9. To what did this request for water lead? 10—15. What proof of supernatural power did Jesus give in this conversation? 16—18. What great spiritual doctrine did he announce? 20—24. His first announcement of his Messiahship. 25, 26. Is it any way singular that it should have been made at this time and place?

9. Return and surprise of the disciples. 27. They are mystified at his refusal to eat. His reference to spiritual things in reply. 31—38.

10. The effect of his teaching on the Samaritans. 39—42.

11. Arrival in Galilee. Was Jesus likely to be more popular there than elsewhere? Jno. iv. 44. The beginning of his more special ministry. The burden of his preaching. The effect. Jno. iv. 43, 44; Mark i. 14, 15; Matt. iv. 17; Lu. iv. 14, 15.

VIII.

Jesus at Cana Again, and at Nazareth.

Galilee was the name of the northernmost of the three sections into which Palestine was divided, in the time of Christ. It had originally designated, as the name implies, a little circle or circuit round about Kedesh in the tribe of Naphtali at some distance north of the Lake of Tiberias. It embraced the twenty cities which Solomon had given to Hiram, king of Tyre, in payment for service in the building of the Temple, but which Hiram had rejected, applying to them the term "cabul," disagreeable or dirty. I. Kings ix. 11—13. The region had been largely inhabited by other than Jews; hence the term "Galilee of the Gentiles." Later, the territory so designated gradually increased in extent, till it embraced the whole Plain of Esdraelon down to a line some distance below the Sea of Tiberias. During the Babylonian captivity, it was no doubt wholly occupied by Gentiles. But, by the time of Christ, these had in great measure given place to Jewish or Israelitish families returning from the dispersion, though doubtless there were still some communities of aliens among them.

It appears that the Jewish inhabitants of this region were less cultivated than their brethren in Judea; that their dialect was ruder, and that they were affected, to some extent, with the character of their heathen neighbors, though their religious faith was uncorrupted, and the simple forms of the synagogue worship were preserved in their purity.

It was in the cities, villages and hamlets of this extensive territory that a very large proportion of Christ's ministry was exercised; and he appears to have traveled over, not only the densely populated Plain of Esdraelon and the shores of the inland sea, but sixty or seventy miles farther north to the border of Phœnicia and the neighborhood of Cæsarea-Philippi, near the foot of Mount Hermon.

John iv. 46—54. Luke iv. 16—31. Matt. iv. 14—16.

1. The second visit to Cana. Jno. iv. 46. What had taken place at a former visit?

2. Relate the remarkable event which occurred at this time. 47—52. (a) The distance of Cana from Capernaum? (b) The rank of the man who came to Jesus asking help for his child? (c) The rebuke of Jesus to the eager curiosity of the people. 48. (d) What appears to have been the state of the father's mind? (e) Did Jesus do just what the man asked him to do, or did he take some other method of meeting his want? 50. (f) Do you see in this any special relation of his action to the morbid curiosity of the multitude? (g) What time in the day did the disease abate? How long before the father's return? What does this length of time indicate on the part of the father? (h) The consequence in the relations of the family to Christ?

3. Jesus' return to the city where his home had been. Lu. iv. 16. What took place on the Sabbath? 17. What was the synagogue? Can you think of any reason why Jesus, more than any other man, should have been expected to address the people?

4. What passage did he read from the Hebrew scriptures, and where is it found? 18, 19. To whom had the Jews uniformly applied this description? To whom did Jesus apply it? 20, 21.

5. How did his actions affect the people? 22. His discernment of their expectations and desires. 23.

6. Did he meet that expectation? What did he say in reference to it? 24—27. What do these words imply? Would miracles among this people have been productive of any profitable result, and why?

7. The effect upon the people. 28, 29. What was the reputation of Nazareth? Jno. i. 46. Did their action, on this occasion, agree with their reputation?

8. The frustration of their evil purpose. 30.

9. Jesus' change of residence. Matt. iv. 13; Lu. iv. 31. What was their part of the country called? Matt. iv. 15. What prophecy was fulfilled? 14—16; Isa. ix. 1, 2.

10. Give some account of Galilee. (See Introduction to this number.)

IX.

Christ's Ministry in the Neighborhood of the Western Coast of the Galilean Lake.

There has been much discussion, especially in modern times, on the subject of *demoniacal possessions*,—of which there are many instances in the narrative of Christ's life and work. There are three leading theories. The first makes the accounts of these merely symbolical, and having no basis of fact. The possession of the devils is, according to this theory, only representative of the prevalence of evil in this world; and their casting out, the overthrow of this evil by the power of truth. But evidently this is a part of the mythical theory of the Bible held by Strauss and others, and must fall with that theory.

The second view is, that the condition of the afflicted was caused by some species of epilepsy, or some cognate disease, generally accompanied by insanity. Those that hold to this theory, of course, reject all notions of any spiritual personality controlling the "possessed," and claim that Christ and his apostles in treating these cases only adapted themselves to the notions prevailing at the time among the Jews. But certainly this was not at all in accordance with Christ's method in dealing with Jewish superstitions, traditions and errors. He was accustomed to repudiate and openly rebuke them. His method, too, of direct and personal address to these agencies, indicated that he regarded them as actual, conscious intelligences, independent of their victim. That, as such, they were regarded by him as malevolent and vicious, there is no doubt.

The simplest and most natural interpretation, then, is here, as elsewhere in the Bible, the best; and following this, we must conclude that, at the time of Christ's appearing in our world as the Redeemer of men, with credentials of divine power, the kingdom of darkness was also permitted to put forth its malign but extraordinary energy in the opposite direction, and that Jesus here, in a concrete and typical manner, showed not only his antagonism to wicked spirits but his complete and ready mastery of them.

Matt. iv. 18—20; vii. 28, 29; viii. 14—17. Mark I. 16—34. Luke iv. 32—41; v. 1—11.

1. Jesus being on the shore of the Sea of Galilee, and a crowd of people gathering about him, he enters a boat belonging to one of his friends and addresses them. Lu. v. 1—3; Matt. iv. 18; Mark i. 16.

2. Miraculous draught of fishes. Lu. v. 4—7. (a) Improbability of success, but obedient disposition. (b) Have we previously met those to whom this direction was given? (c) Result of the venture. (d) What practical lesson do we learn?

3. The effect on Peter. 8, 9. What conviction was wrought in his mind concerning Jesus?

4. How many disciples were together at this time, and what appears to have been their vocation? Had any others been called by Jesus, up to this time?

5. Jesus' answer to Peter, and his promise to them all. Lu. v. 10; Matt. iv. 19. What did they do? Matt. iv. 20; Lu. v. 11; Mark i. 20.

6. His visit to Capernaum, and his preaching there. Mark i. 21. The effect of his preaching on the people. 22; Matt. vii. 28, 29; Lu. iv. 32. Can you give any characteristics of Christ's teaching? Did he reason much, or quote authorities?

7. Cure of the demoniac. Mark i. 23—28; Lu. iv. 33—37. (a) The nature of the malady. (b) Source of the utterance, "Let us alone," and the cause of the antagonism to Jesus? (c) The word and power of Jesus,—to what addressed? (d) Effect upon the afflicted man? Effect upon the people? (e) What did this power indicate upon the part of Jesus? (f) Effect on the inhabitants of the neighboring regions?

8. Miraculous healing of Peter's mother-in-law. Mark i. 29—31. Matt. viii. 14, 15; Lu. iv. 38, 39. What visible means were used for the restoration? Was there any natural efficacy in these?

9. Effect of these events upon the inhabitants of Capernaum? Mark i. 32—34. Matt. viii. 16; Lu. iv. 40, 41. What did Jesus do to the gathering multitudes? What injunction did he lay upon the evil spirits? What testimony did these attempt to give? Why should he rebuke them?

10. What messianic prophecy was here fulfilled? Matt. viii. 17. Where is it found in its original form?

X.

Continued Travels and Ministering throughout Galilee.

Matt. iv. 23—25; viii. 2—4; ix. 2—9. Mark i. 35—45; ii. 1—14. Lu. iv. 42—44; v. 12—28.

1. The early rising and retirement for devotion. Mark i. 35; Lu. iv. 42. Was this an exceptional act? Can you mention other instances?

2. The disciples, seeking him, urge the desire of the people to see and hear him. Mark i. 36, 37. What does he propose, and what does he do? 38, 39; Lu. iv. 43, 44.

3. Extensive journeys and labors. His work and its consequences. Matt. iv. 23—25. How far did his fame extend and what was the result?

4. Healing of the leper. Mark i. 40—45; Matt. viii. 2—4; Lu. v. 12—15. (a) Nature of this disease? How was it regarded under the Levitical law? Lev. xiii. and xiv. (b) What does the leper ask of Jesus, and what does the expression show as to the way in which the disease was regarded among the Jews? Mark i. 40. (c) How was the cure effected? 41, 42. (d) What charge did Jesus give and why? (e) What ceremony and offering of cleansing was required in such a case? Lev. xiv. 2—20. In case of poverty, what modification? 21—32. (f) What did the man do who had been healed? The effect on the work of Jesus? Mark i. 45.

5. Where do we next find Jesus and under what conditions? Mark ii. 1. Distinguished visitors present, and their purpose? Lu. v. 17.

6. Cure of the paralytic. Lu. v. 18—26; Matt. ix. 2—7; Mark ii. 3—12. (a) Action of the sick man's friends. What did it indicate? (b) Startling announcement. Effect on the religious teachers present? What was their reasoning? Was it sound reasoning? (c) Reply of Jesus, and the sequence. What powerful and conclusive argument was implied in this? Was it supposed that any being could give the power to work miracles, who could not also forgive sins? (d) Effect on the convictions and views of the people.

7. The call of Levi. Mark ii. 13, 14; Matt. ix. 9; Lu. v. 27, 28. (a) By what other name was this disciple known? What important position did he fill in relation to Christianity? (b) What had been the office and occupation of this new disciple? What was its reputation among the Jews? Did Jesus know of the character of the employment? (c) What did the man thus called do? The practical lesson? (d) Did Jesus choose his special disciples, or did they choose him?

XI.

Beginning of the Second Year of Christ's More Public Ministry. His Second Public Visit to Jerusalem.—The Ordaining of the Apostles.

We find occasional allusions in the Evangelists to a party designated as Herodians. There is also very frequent mention of the Scribes. The former comprised those among the Jews who were in favor of securing the title of king to Herod Antipas, the tetrarch of Galilee. This prince was the son of Herod the Great, and is the same one who imprisoned John the Baptist at the instigation of his unlawful wife, and afterward put him to death under the same influence. He himself and his adherents doubtless had some hope that in some way the extensive dominions and power of his father, of which only a small fraction had fallen to him, might be restored. But of this there was never any even moderate prospect, as the Roman government had already reduced the whole region to the condition of a province, and the efforts made by Herod Antipas to enlarge his power ignominiously failed.

But this party during the life of Christ were very active, and owing to the intimations and mysterious outgivings which were prevalent concerning the new teacher, they manifested an intense antipathy to Christ. The growing interest in the character and teaching of Jesus, the extraordinary deeds which he did, the messianic hopes excited every-where, the fear that he might become the leader of a great popular party the influence of which must be adverse to the claims of Herod, made it for their interest to create a hostile public sentiment by whatever means lay in their power. As the same kind of feeling prevailed in the Pharisaic party, which also was bitterly jealous of the increasing influence of Jesus, a coalition for the common purpose of bringing Christ into disrepute was readily effected,—though the two parties were, for other reasons, antagonistic to each other.

The *Scribes*, as the name implies, were originally mere writers or copyists of the law. Gradually, and not unnaturally, they came to have such familiarity with it that they were often called upon for information or interpretation, and so in time to be teachers and to have authority. In the time of Christ, they constituted a kind of professional order similar to that of lawyers. They had, so far as popular respect and reverence were concerned, come to take the place of the priests, though the chief of the latter still maintained an official dignity. The scribes were principally of the Pharisaic party, and, as such, were hostile to Jesus, whose natural yet spiritual interpretation of the Scriptures was utterly opposed to their technical, formal and baldly literal notions. We find them frequently approaching him with puzzling questions, and misleading and entangling forms of statement, hoping to expose him in some way to contempt. We all know how, at almost every point, he met them with so much ease, and disposed of their objections with so much wisdom, that we almost overlook the fact that there had been any difficulty at all. It became necessary for them, and for the whole party to which most of them belonged, if they would make any headway against Jesus, to resort to other methods.

John v. 1—47.   Matt. xii. 1—21.   Mark ii. 23—28; iii. 1—19.   Luke vi. 1—16.

1. Jesus goes to Jerusalem to attend a feast. Jno. v. 1.
2. The impotent man healed. 2—9. (a) The pool of Bethesda, and the popular belief concerning it. (b) The infirm man, the length of his sickness and the reason why he had not been cured. (c) Jesus' inquiry, and the answer. (d) The word of Jesus and the effect.
3. Rebuke of the man by the Jews, and the ground of it? 10. His reply. What was the force of the argument?
4. Did the restored man recognize Jesus, when he healed him? 13. How did he find him out? The advice given. 14. What does this seem to imply?
5. How did the knowledge that it was Jesus who had cured him affect the Jews? What fault did they find? 16.
6. Reply of Jesus. What additional offense did they see in this? 17, 18.
7. He discourses of his relation to the Father, and the assurance of more marvelous things to come. 19, 20. Assertion of his participation, as the Son of God, in the power and honor of the Father. 21—23.
8. Solemn assertion that faith in him is essential to salvation from eternal condemnation. 24.
9. Explicit announcement of the *Resurrection* and the *Judgment*,—their relation to Christ, and the alternative result. 25—29.
10. The judgment and witness of Christ not in his human personality, but in his divine. 30—32. Testimony of John the Baptist, and his character. A higher testimony found in Jesus' works. 33—36.
11. What does he say to the Jews respecting their rejection of evidence?

The character of the Scriptures? The selfish greed of their worldly life? 37—44.

12. Reference to Moses and his testimony. 45—47. What did Moses say? Gen. xxii. 18; Deut. xviii. 15 and 18.

13. The disciples pluck and eat the corn by the wayside on the Sabbath. The Pharisees criticise. Matt. xii. 1, 2; Mark ii. 23, 24; Lu. vi. 1, 2. Did they object to the taking of the grain, or to the violation of the Sabbath? Was it lawful for them to take the corn of another in this way? Deut. xxiii. 25. What indication do we have as to the worldly condition of the disciples?

14. Examples cited in justification of the disciples. Matt. xii. 3—5. (Also Luke and Mark.) What was the case of David referred to? I. Sam. xxi. 6.

15. Further fundamental and spiritual principles adduced. 6—8. Mark ii. 27, 28.

16. Cure of the man with a withered hand. Mark iii. 1—5. Matt. xii. 9—13; Lu. vi. 6—10. (a) Who were the scribes? (b) Their cavilings about the Sabbath. (c) The Lord's answer. (See Matthew.) Had they any reply to this, or was any possible? How did their conduct affect Jesus? Mark iii. 5. What did he do? (d) What effect did this have upon the caviling scribes? What did they do? Why were they angry? (e) Who were the Herodians? (See Introduction.)

17. Jesus' withdrawal to the sea-coast, and the occasion of it. Resort of multitudes to him, from great distances. Mark iii. 7, 8; Matt. xii. 15.

18. Inconvenient experience, and how remedied. Mark iii. 9, 10. The effect of his presence upon the evil spirits. Why did he forbid their testimony? 11, 12. Where, in the Old Testament, do you find the prophecy quoted in Matt. xii. 18—21? What remarkable intimation in the last clause? What is meant by the statements in 19 and 20?

19. The night of prayer and solemn preparation. Lu. vi. 12. What special importance was involved in the action about to take place?

20. The twelve apostles selected. 13—16. Mark iii. 13—19; Matt x. 2—4. Give the names. Meaning of the word? Can you think of any reason why *twelve* were chosen?

21. Continuation of his ministry. Extraordinary power and efficacy. Lu. vi. 17—19.

XII.

The Sermon on the Mount.

Matt. v., vi. and vii. Lu. vi. 20—38.

1. The Beatitudes. Matt. v. 1—10. (Commit.) Special blessings to persecuted believers. 11, 12. Woes upon the self-complacent and greedy of worldly flattery. Lu. vi. 24—26.

2. Believers described as salt of the earth and light of the world. Matt. v. 13—16. Meaning of these metaphors.

3. He rebukes the low, mechanical morality of the Jews of that age. 17—48. (a) Divine character and perpetuity of the moral law of the Old Testament. 17—19. (b) Insufficiency of the formal righteousness of the Pharisees. Murder, adultery and such sins not merely in the outward act, but in the hatred and lust of the heart. The crime of easy divorce. 20—32. (c) Profanity more extensive than verbal utterance of oaths. Simplicity of speech enjoined. 33—37. (d) Retaliation forbidden; concession to foes recommended. 38—42. (e) Enemies, as well as friends, to be loved. 43—47. (f) A purpose of perfect assimilation to the divine character, required. 48.

4. Unostentatious performance of religious duties. (a) Benevolent deeds should be quiet and private. vi. 1—4. Individual prayer to be offered secretly, and with simple sincerity and directness. The MODEL PRAYER. The spirit in which we are to pray. 5—15. (c) Fasting private, and between the individual and God. 16—18.

5. Treasure in heaven and not on earth. Singleness of purpose indispensable. 19—24.

6. Reliance on God to supply all our wants. All real needs providentially met. Illustrated by the feeding of the birds, and the array of the grass and the flowers. Man far dearer to God than any of these. 25—32. The true method of life. 33, 34.

7. Charity and carefulness in condemning others. We are to scrutinize our own character first. vii. 1—5. Circumspection in counseling others. 6.

8. The assured effectiveness of prayer. God's affection prompts him to give what is needed. 7—11.

9. THE GOLDEN RULE. Necessity of intense diligence in seeking the way of truth. Definiteness and exclusiveness of this way. False teachers to be avoided. 12—15.

10. A good character to be known by its effects. A good heart incompatible with bad actions. Profession *versus* practice, and the result. 21—23.

11. Christ's words the only foundation. They must, however, enter into the life, and not merely the intelligence. 24—27.

12. Effect of this teaching upon the populace. 28, 29.

XIII.

Continuance of Christ's Galilean Ministry.—Miracles and Teaching.

Matt. viii. 5–13; xi. 2–19; xii. 22–50. Mark iii. 19—25; 28—30. Luke vii. 1—50; viii. 1–3, 20, 21; xi. 15, 24—28; 37—54.

1. Cure of the centurion's servant. Lu. vii. 1—10; Matt. viii. 5—13. (a) Meaning of the word, "centurion?" (b) Character of the officer? Was he a Jew? (c) Why did he not himself come to Jesus? (d) Why did not

Jesus go to the man's house? What was implied in the message? (e) How did Jesus regard the message and the state of the centurion's mind? (f) What did he say concerning the extension of his kingdom beyond the limits of the Jewish nation? (g) Remarkable feature of this cure?

2. Raising of the widow's son at Nain. Lu. vii. 11—17. (a) How far, and in what direction, was this from Capernaum? (b) Give the particulars. (c) Effect on the people?

3. John the Baptist sends to Jesus to inquire more particularly concerning his messiahship. Lu. vii. 18—20. Where was John, at this time? Matt. xi. 2.

4. The evidence furnished. Lu. vii. 21—23. Is it probable that John was familiar with any prophecy which applied these marks to the Messiah? Isa. xxxv. 5, 6; lxi. 1.

5. Jesus' testimony concerning John. Lu. vii. 24—28; Matt. xi. 7—12. (a) How did John's character differ from that implied in the question of Jesus? Matt. iii. 4. (b) Identification of John with the Elias prophesied of as the forerunner. (c) John's greatness as a prophet and preacher, and his influence. Lu. xvi. 16; Matt. xi. 12. (d) Inconsistency of the people, in their judgment of John and of Christ. Matt. xi. 16—19. (e) The class of people that accepted John, and the class that rejected him. Lu. vii. 29, 30.

6. Jesus dines at a Pharisee's house. Remarkable occurrence there. Lu. vii. 36—38. (a) The character of this woman. Did she give evidence of penitence? 38. (b) The evil thought of the Pharisee. How did Jesus know it, and what did he reply? 40—42. The host's answer. (c) Jesus contrasts the Pharisee's want of courtesy, and scant hospitality, with the conduct of the woman. 44—46. (d) His bold declaration concerning her. 47, 48. (e) Further cavil, and renewed assurance to the woman. 49, 50.

7. Who accompanied Jesus, from this time, in his further travels? What remarkable woman do we first meet here? Did these women, in any way, aid in his work? Lu. viii. 1—3.

8. Apprehensions of Jesus' friends, because of the vast multitudes thronging about the house where he lodged. Mark iii. 19—21.

9. Exorcism of a demon which had made the victim blind and dumb. Conviction of the people concerning Christ. Matt. xii. 22, 23.

10. The Pharisaic party, troubled at the growth of this conviction, resort to a singular expedient to diminish it. 24; Mark iii. 22; Lu. xi. 15.

11. How does he confute this reasoning? Matt. xii. 25—28. What is the inference concerning himself?

12. The strong man's house and the robber. Jesus and Satan,—the antagonism. 29, 30. The unpardonable sin. 31, 32. Mark iii. 28—30.

13. The tree and its fruit,—men's moral condition and their acts. Character of the Pharisees. Human accountability. Matt. xii. 34—37.

14. Desire of the Pharisees for a sign. 38. Was it sincere? Reply of Jesus? 39—42.

15. Case of the man from whom the spirit of evil has been expelled, but who has not received the Spirit of God. 43—45; Lu. xi. 24—26.

16. Admiration of a woman in the audience, and the reply of Jesus. Lu. xi. 27, 28.

17. Visit of his mother and brothers. Spiritual relationship placed above temporal. Matt. xii. 46—50; Lu. viii. 20, 21; Mark iii. 21—25.

18. Another invitation to dine with a Pharisee. Marvel of the host at the neglect of a ceremonial custom. Lu. xi. 37, 38. Jesus discourses on inward and outward purity, and rebukes the practice of the Pharisees. 39—44. (Also, Matt. xxiii. 25—28.)

19. The lawyer reproved. Plots of the Pharisees. Lu. xi. 45—54.

XIV.

Continued Teaching and Working in Galilee.—He Begins to Make More Constant Use of Parables.

We note about this time, a change in our Lord's method of teaching. Heretofore, it is true, his discourses and conversations have abounded in figurative expressions, similes, metaphors, and various apt comparisons. The terms, *parable* and *parabolic*, have often been applied to these; but the parable proper seldom appears in the portion of the narrative over which we have now gone. The full meaning of the parable implies that it is a story, in which imaginary or fictitious incidents are made to illustrate moral and religious truth. It differs from simile and metaphor, in that these merely suggest the comparison or analogy, without embodying it in a narrative. It differs from a fable, in that the latter teaches some homely prudential maxim by attributing to lower animals and inanimate objects the qualities and properties of rational beings, and so far forth, though attractive and entertaining, they are not and do not pretend to be true to nature; while the parable is used to convey moral and spiritual truth by a higher order of figures, in stories which, though fictitious, are always true to nature, it differs from the allegory in the narrower sense of the latter, in the fact that the allegory is the offspring of a poetical imagination, while the parable is conversant with the actual relations of life.*

"The parables uttered by our Saviour claim preëminence over all others, on account of their number, variety, appositeness and beauty. Indeed, it is impossible to conceive of a mode of instruction better fitted to engage the attention, interest the feelings, and impress the conscience, than that which our Lord adopted."† Of these parables of Christ, there are some fifty in all, and most of them were uttered by him after the middle of the second year of his public ministry.

In the interpretation of a parable, it is not necessary to find a figurative meaning for every expression or every phase in the story. Something doubtless, in most cases, belongs to the filling up of the narrative, or to the dress and decoration which is designed to make it presentable and attractive. There is always one main thought or principle to be conveyed, and this should

---

* See McClintock & Strong's Cyclopædia,—article, "Parable."   † Ibid.

be first sought. Not unfrequently there are subordinate and incidental lessons which may be deduced; but, in looking for these, care should be taken not to produce confusion in respect to the main object.

The chief motive of Jesus, in speaking in parables, is obvious from what has been already said. To the people to whom he primarily addressed himself, it was both a most attractive and effective method of conveying truth, and, in some instances, no doubt, truth was presented in this way which could not be in any other. But there was another reason which he himself avers, and which has been widely misunderstood. He says, Matt. xiii. 13, 14, that he speaks to the Jews in parables, "because they, seeing, see not, and hearing, they hear not, neither do they understand," thus fulfilling the prediction of Isaiah. It was not that the truth was ever hidden from those sincerely desirous of knowing it; but doubtless it was not intended to be revealed to those who, through obstinacy and perverseness, were indisposed to receive it. There was light enough in these parables, so that all candid and sincere souls would follow it up and seek the full meaning, as did the disciples of Jesus, while "those who had pleasure in unrighteousness" would not "come to the light, lest their deeds should be reproved." To such, the clear revelation of truth would be "the casting of pearls before swine."

Luke xii. 1—21; xiii. 1—9, 18, 19; viii. 4—12, 22—56; ix. 57—62; v. 33—38. Matt. x. 26—31; xiii. 1—23, 31—52; viii. 21—34. Mark iv. 1—41; v. 1—43; ii. 18—20.

1. Jesus rebukes the hypocrisy of the Pharisees. Concealment and deception only temporary. Lu. xii. 1—3; Matt. x. 26, 27; Mark iv. 22.

2. The only proper object of fear. God's careful and particular providence. He takes care of sparrows,—how much more of men! Lu. xii. 4—6; Matt. x. 28—31.

3. Consequences of confessing and denying Christ. The Holy Spirit will give aid in all trying exigencies of Christ's disciples. Lu. xii. 7—12.

4. Requested to arbitrate between two brothers. Parable of the rich man and his meditation, illustrating the folly of covetousness. 13—21.

5. Calamities not proportioned to the particular sins of the victims. Illustrations. xiii. 1—5.

6. Parable of the barren fig-tree. 6—9. Danger of unbelief and impenitence.

7. Preaching to the assembled multitudes, from a boat near the shore. Parable of the sower. Matt. xiii. 1—9; Mark iv. 1—9; Lu. viii. 4—8.

8. Objection to the parables, and the answer of Jesus. Matt. xiii. 10—15; Lu. viii. 9—12; Mark iv. 10—12. Was there any thing arbitrary or unjust in this? (See Introduction,—last part.) How do men become keen to perceive and quick to learn truth, and how do they grow dull and obtuse and undiscerning?

9. Interpretation of the parable. Matt. xiii. 18—23. (Also, Mark and Luke.)

10. Parable of the tares and the wheat. Matt. xii. 24—30. Of the husbandman's seed sown. The power of truth to produce effect. Mark iv. 26—29.

11. Of the *mustard seed*. The *extensive* development of God's king-

dom from small beginnings. Of the *leaven in the dough.* *Intensive* development. Matt. xiii. 31—33; Lu. xiii. 18, 19; Mark iv. 30—32.

12. Characteristics of Christ's teaching, from this time. Matt. xiii. 34, 35. What is a parable? How does it differ from a fable? What noteworthy features in Christ's parables? (See Introduction.)

13. Interpretation of the parable of the tares and the wheat. 36—43. What is the lesson taught?

14. Treasure hid in the field, and pearl of great price. Supreme value of religion. 44—46. The well furnished householder. Varied methods of teaching truth. 51, 52.

15. Parable of the net and the fishes. Mixed character of the church on earth. 47—50.

16. Going to the other side of the lake, a scribe comes to Jesus, volunteering to be his disciple. He is taught that, to do this, he must be prepared to sacrifice all worldly considerations. Matt. viii. 18—20; Lu. ix. 57, 58. Another, also, instructed that there must be no conditions in his discipleship. Matt. viii. 21, 22; Lu. ix. 59—62.

17. Jesus on the sea asleep in the storm. The terrified disciples awake him. He rebukes the storm and makes a calm. Their astonishment. Matt. viii. 23—27; Mark iv. 38—41; Lu. viii. 22—25.

18. Cure of the demoniacs. Matt. viii. 28—34; Mark v. 1—20; Lu. viii. 26—39. (a) How do the Evangelists differ in their statements? (b) How did the evil spirit affect the victim? (c) Effect of the sight of Jesus? (d) Conversation with the man. (e) Request of the evil spirits. (f) The permission and the consequences. (g) Effect on the people? On the man healed?

19. Feast at Levi's house. Who was Levi? The kind of people present. Cavils of the Pharisees, and Jesus' reply. Matt. ix. 10—13; Mark ii. 15—17; Lu. v. 29—32.

20. The Pharisees find fault with the disciples for not fasting. Reply of Jesus. Matt. ix. 14, 15; Mark ii. 18—20; Lu. v. 33—35.

21. Parables of patched garments, and new wine in old bottles. Actions must be adapted to circumstances. Matt. ix. 16, 17; Mark ii. 21, 22; Lu. v. 36—38.

22. Jesus summoned to the daughter of Jairus. Faith of a woman on the way, and her marvelous cure. Death of the ruler's daughter, and her miraculous restoration. Mark v. 22—43; Matt. ix. 18—26; Lu. viii. 41—56.

XV.

Jesus Continues to Teach in Galilee and to Manifest his Divine Power.

Matt. ix. 27—38; xiii. 54—58; x. 1—14, 40—42; xiv. 6—36; Mark vi. 7—56; Lu. ix. 1—17; John vi. 1—71.

1. Cure of the two blind men. Matt. ix. 27—31. What is implied here and elsewhere by the title, "Son of David," as applied to Jesus?

2. A dumb man under the dominion of an evil spirit dispossessed, and his speech restored. Effect on the people; on the Pharisees. 32—34.

3. Jesus revisits Nazareth, and teaches in the synagogue. Astonishment and questionings of the inhabitants. What is implied in their utterances? The effect of the state of their minds on the work of Jesus. Mark vi. 1, 6; Matt. xiii. 54—58.

4. Jesus, in his travels, is greatly affected at the condition and wants of the masses of the people. Laments the fewness of workers. Matt. ix. 35—38; Lu. x. 2.

5. The apostles sent on their first mission, and their directions. Matt. x. 1—14; Mark vi. 7—11; Lu. ix. 1—5. (a) To whom sent. Matt. x. 5, 6. (b) Their message. 7. (c) Their work. 1 and 8. (d) Provision for their journey. 9, 10. (e) Support among the people, and what they have a right to expect. (f) Rule in case of rejection.

6. What is implied in the acceptance or rejection of Christ's ambassadors? Matt. x. 40; Lu. ix. 16. A reward for any service, however simple, if rendered in the name of Jesus. Matt. x. 41, 42.

7. The apostles depart to do the work assigned them. Jesus, also, goes on with his own work. Mark vi. 12; Matt. xi. 1.

8. John the Baptist put to death by Herod Antipas, at the instigation of Herodias. The festival; the dance; Herod's rash oath; the atrocious and unexpected demand; the judicial murder; the action of John's disciples. Mark vi. 21—28; Matt. xiv. 6—12.

9. Herod alarmed at the fame of Jesus. His fear and perplexity as he remembers his flagrant guilt concerning John. Mark vi. 14—16. (Also, Matt. and Luke.)

10. Return and report of the apostles. They retire to recuperate at a distance from the throngs coming and going. But the multitude still eagerly following, Jesus, in his compassion for them, continues his instruction. Mark vi. 30—34; Lu. ix. 10, 11; Jno. vi. 1—9. Another reason why Jesus deemed it advisable to leave the more central parts of Galilee. Matt. xiv. 13, 14.

11. Miraculous feeding of the five thousand. Give the particulars. How did the fragments remaining at the close of the meal compare with the original amount? Mark vi. 35—44; Matt. xiv. 15—21; Lu. ix. 12—17; Jno. vi. 5—13.

12. Effect of this miracle on the people, and their disposition towards Jesus. How did he act? Jno. vi. 15.

13. The disciples, leaving Jesus to dismiss the multitudes, embark to cross the sea, and are troubled with a rough wind. Jesus, after spending a part of the night in prayer, comes to them, walking on the water. Their fright. He allays it. Peter's impulsive request granted. His failure and rescue. Jesus enters the ship, and the storm ceases. Amazement of the disciples. Matt. xiv. 22—31; Mark vi. 45—56; Jno. vi. 15—21.

14. Arrival in Gennesaret, and miraculous work there. Matt. xiv. 34—36; Mark vi. 53—56. Return to Capernaum, and the people follow and seek him. Jno. vi. 22—24.

15. His discourse. 25—65. Give some of the principal points of this conversation.

16. Some of the disciples withdrawing on account of the smallness of their faith, he asks the Twelve whether they will also leave him. The reply of Peter. Christ's prediction of the treachery of one of them. 66—71.

XVI.

Beginning of the Third Year of Christ's Public Ministry.—Continues his Labors in Galilee.—The Pharisaic Party still Watch, Cavil and Plot to Entangle Him.—Begins gradually to Unfold to his Immediate Disciples what the Tragical Outcome of his Mission will be.

John vii. 1. Mark vii. and viii. Matt. xv. and xvi. Lu. xii. 54—57; ix. 18—27.

1. On account of the animosity of the Jews, Jesus does not go up as usual to the Passover at Jerusalem. Jno. vii. 1. Pharisees and scribes come from Jerusalem to watch him. They find fault with the disciples for not observing the traditional washings. What were some of these? Mark vii. 1—5; Matt. xv. 1, 2.

2. Jesus rebukes this undue stress on mere outward forms, and so little on inward purity; and this scrupulousness towards human traditions, while neglecting divine injunctions. Instances. Mark vii. 6—13; Matt. xv. 3—6. The real source of defilement. Mark vii. 14, 15; Matt. xv. 10, 11.

3. The Pharisees offended. Jesus' remarks thereat. 12—14. The matter further explained to the disciples. 15—20; Mark vii. 17—23.

4. Jesus going to the border of Phœnicia to seek retirement, is eagerly sought by a Gentile woman, who beseeches him to relieve her afflicted daughter. Jesus intimates that his work is among the Israelites. But this only emphasises her faith and humble devotion. This faith honored, and her child healed. Matt. xv. 21—28; Mark vii. 24—30.

5. Returning near the Sea of Galilee, Jesus cures a deaf man with an impediment in his speech. The charge not to publish it. The charge disregarded. Mark vii. 31—37.

6. Great numbers resort to Jesus to be healed. Four thousand miraculously fed. He recrosses the sea. Matt. xv. 30—38; Mark viii. 1—10.

7. The caviling Pharisees demand a sign in the heavens. He refuses the sign, and shows them their insincerity and inconsistency. Matt. xvi. 1—4; Mark viii. 11, 12; Lu. xii. 54—57.

8. The disciples, in returning, forget to take bread. They are cautioned concerning the leaven of the Pharisees, etc. They misunderstand, and are rebuked for the spiritual dullness. The explanation. Matt. xvi. 5—12; Mark viii. 13—21.

9. Cure of the blind man at Bethsaida. Method of the restoration. Gradual restoration. Mark viii. 22—26.

10. In the neighborhood of Cæsarea-Philippi. Where was this? Inquiry as to the popular opinion concerning Christ. Reply of the disciples. Inquiry as to their own belief. Peter's declaration. Christ's approval and grand announcement. Silence enjoined for the present concerning their faith in his Messiahship. Matt. xvi. 13—20; Mark viii. 27—30; Lu. ix. 18—21.

11. Jesus begins to show his disciples what must be the issue of his earthly mission. Matt. xvi. 21; Mark viii. 31, 32; Lu. xvii. 22.

12. Peter's ardent remonstrance. Jesus rebukes him for his worldly conceptions. Matt. xvi. 22, 23; Mark viii. 32, 33.

13. The great condition of Christian discipleship. Loss and gain of soul and life. The great problem; Matt. xvi. 24—26; Mark. viii. 34—36; Lu. ix. 23—25.

14. Confessing and denying Christ. His coming kingdom and judgment. Matt. xvi. 27, 28; Mark viii. 38; Lu. ix. 26, 27, and xii. 8.

XVII.

The Transfiguration.—Instructions to the Disciples.—Sending Out of the Seventy.

Matt. xvii.; xviii. 2—25; x. 23—26. Mark ix. 2—50. Lu. ix. 28—56; x. 1—11. Jno. vii. 2—10.

1. THE TRANSFIGURATION. Matt. xvii. 1—8; Mark ix. 2—8; Lu. ix. 28—30. (a) The three special friends of Jesus chosen to accompany him to the mountain. (b) Jesus at prayer, and the sudden strange radiance of his countenance, and the brilliant appearance of his raiment. (c) The manifestation of Moses and Elias conversing with Jesus. (d) Effect on the disciples. Peter's wish. (e) The bright cloud and the supernatural voice.

2. The disciples charged not to divulge the vision till after Christ's resurrection. The questioning as to the meaning of this resurrection. Matt. xvii. 9; Mark ix. 9, 10; Lu. ix. 30.

3. Inquiry concerning the prophecy of Elias' coming. Where is this prophecy? How does Jesus explain it? He again instructs them that his life will end in persecution and violence. Matt. xvii. 10—13; Mark ix. 11—13.

4. Cure of the demoniac, whose case was too obdurate for the disciples. Characteristics of this possession. Terrible convulsions at the exorcism. Mark ix. 14—27; Matt. xvii. and Lu. ix.

5. The disciples inquire concerning their inability to effect this cure. The Lord's reply, and mild rebuke. Mark ix. 28, 29. What illustration is given of the power of faith? Matt. xvii. 20; Lu. xvii. 5, 6.

6. Jesus, for the present, avoids public notice, and privately instructs his disciples. He still urges upon their reluctant minds the facts of his coming sufferings and sacrifice and subsequent triumph. Mark ix. 30—32. Matt. xvii. 22, 23; Lu. ix. 43—45

7. Return to Capernaum. The tribute money, and the coin in the fish's mouth. Matt. xvii. 24—27.

8. Dispute among the disciples about precedence in the coming kingdom. Why were they silent when Jesus questioned them? What did he say? Mark ix. 33—35; Lu. ix. 46, 47.

9. Illustration of the nature of conversion. What are the qualities essential to Christian discipleship? What further is said concerning the relation of childlike character to himself? Mark ix. 36, 37; Matt. xviii. 2—5. Lu. ix. 46—50.

10. How are we to regard persons doing good, but who are not full believers, or are possibly unbelievers? Mark ix. 38, 39; Lu. ix. 49, 50.

11. The guilt and doom of those who make others to fall. The grace of God in the soul like salt in its conserving power. Mark ix. 42—50.

12. Caution against thinking lightly of the humblest of Christ's real followers. Matt. xviii. 10.

13. How to act in case of a difficulty with a Christian brother. Power and authority of the Christian body. Power of united faith. 15—20.

14. Forbearance, charity, repeated forgiveness to an offending brother. Parable of the servant whose great debt was forgiven, but who forgave not the most trifling debt of a fellow-servant. What is the application? 21—35.

15. Jesus appoints and commissions seventy additional disciples for evangelistic work. Instructions to them, as also to the apostles. Lu. x. 1—11. Matt x. 23—26.

16. Jesus urged by some to go to Jerusalem to the Feast of Tabernacles. Their professed reasons. His reasons for not going immediately. He afterwards goes up privately. Jno. vii. 2—10.

17. The journey through Samaria. Inhospitality of the people. Indignation of James and John. The rebuke. Lu. ix. 51—56.

18. Healing of the ten lepers. What direction was given, and the result? Thoughtful gratitude of one, and the unappreciativeness of the others. What made it more singular in the case of this one? Lu. xvii. 11—19.

XVIII.

Jesus at the Feast of Tabernacles.—The Pharisees Dispute with Him.—His Discourses and Works.

John vii. 11—53; viii.; Matt. xi. 25—30; Lu. x. 17—42; xi. 5—8.

1. The people inquire for Jesus at the feast, and discuss his character. His arrival among them. He teaches in the Temple, and the people wonder at his ability, as he had not been a scholar in any of the great schools. Jno. vii. 11—15.

2. Jesus, answering their thought, assures them that he receives his doctrine from God. 16. Lays down the grand, simple, comprehensive method

by which all essential, saving truth may be ascertained by each man for himself. 17. Consider its full meaning.

3. Difference between the man who speaks in his own name and him who speaks in God's name. 18. Men not made righteous by the law. Why? Reproaches the leaders with the intent to put him to death. 19.

4. They accuse him of having a devil, and deny their intent. He shows their inconsistency. 20—26.

5. His boldness and ready mastery of his foes excites anew the wonder of the people, who also wonder that the leaders do not carry out their hostile purpose. They stifle the conviction that this is the Messiah, by a popular fallacy. 25—27.

6. Their cavils answered. Their convictions shown to be strong enough. The desire to put him to death still thwarted by fear. The Pharisees, alarmed at the inclination of the people towards him, attempt and again fail to cause his arrest. 28—32.

7. The Jews puzzled at his discourse of his personal presence and his future going away. 33—36.

8. He is declared as the source and inspiration of life to believers. 37—39. How does he put this thought elsewhere? Matt. xi. 28—30.

9. Deepening conviction, opposition and dispute. Jno. vii. 40—44. Singular report of officers sent to arrest him. Ill-natured rebuke of the council. Protest of Nicodemus. Persistence of the opposition, which is still futile. 45—53.

10. A night out of the city. Return to the Temple. The adulterous woman. Jesus' marvelous judgment, and the discomfiture of the accusers. viii. 1—11.

11. Continued discourse. "The Light of the world." Dispute of the Pharisees, as to his record and testimony, and Jesus' reply. Intimate divine relationship. The Pharisees ignorant because of the state of their hearts. 12—20. Their great destroying sin. Replies to their oft-repeated question who he is, by referring to his previous answer and to his mission from the Father. "Lifted up" and thus revealed. Perpetual acceptance with the Father. 21—29.

12. Freedom by the truth, and truth through obedience. The Jewish claim of freedom as a birthright refuted. The only genuine freedom. Inconsistency of claiming righteousness through descent from Abraham, and then seeking to murder him who was speaking the truth in Abraham's spirit. The children of Satan rather than Abraham. 30—45.

13. Challenges proof of any wrong in himself. Accused of being a Samaritan and a demoniac. He calmly denies this. Startles them by announcing that those who obey him shall never see death. Jews ask, Was he greater than Abraham? He refers to the honor which the Father puts upon him. 46—55.

14. Jesus declares his antecedence and consequent superiority to Abraham. The rage of the zealots impel them to stone him, but he passes out unharmed. 56—59.

15. Return and report of the seventy. The true ground of rejoicing. Lu. x. 17—20. Thanks that the simple may understand that at which the wise stumble. 21, 22; Matt. xi. 25—27.

16. The lawyer's question and the answer. "Who is my neighbor?" Parable of the man falling among thieves. Lu. x. 25—37.

17. Visit to Mary and Martha. Characteristics of the sisters. Jesus' discrimination. 38—42.

18. Importunacy in prayer illustrated. Lu. xi. 5—8.

XIX.

Continued Teaching at Jerusalem.—Extraordinary Miracles. Increasing Bitterness of the Pharisaic Party.

The careful observer can hardly fail to see that, as Jesus approaches the end of his earthly career, his discourses become more profoundly spiritual. It is to the period with which we are now dealing that most of the extended discourses in John's Gospel are to be referred. That these, together with the startling miracles of this period, greatly affected the masses of the people and tended to draw them to him, is evinced not only by the record but also by the fact that the growing malignity of the Pharisees and their extraordinary efforts to destroy his popularity barely succeeded, notwithstanding the powerful influence which they had, and the machinery at their command. We are now in the last six months of Christ's public ministry. The time occupied in the present study extends from November to January of our time. Most of this was spent in Jerusalem and the vicinity, though there appear to have been two excursions to the neighborhood of the Jordan and to the country beyond. Some of his most remarkable miracles were now performed right here at Jerusalem, and in the most public manner possible, so that there was no disputing them except by resort to the most shallow sophistry. Indeed, in spite of the powerful partisan and malicious motives to the contrary, there appears to have been an almost universal belief, even among the priests and scribes and Pharisees, that the miracles performed by Jesus were genuine. The force of these could only be broken or minified by the pretense that they were wrought by diabolical rather than divine power. Yet this opinion could have had but little weight among the people, as the prevalent doctrine did not allow of such a supposition. Accordingly, we see that the most desperate measures were necessary, in order to prevail against Jesus. Even these would have doubtless been unavailable, but for the fact that it was our Lord's purpose *to lay down his life*, in execution of his grand scheme of redemption.

John ix.; x.; xi. 1—54; Mark x. 1; Matt. xix. 1, 2.

1. Cure of the man blind from his birth. Jno. ix. 1—7. Astonishment and questionings of the people. Statement of the man. 8—12.

2. The man brought to the Pharisees, who examine him closely. The

simple story of the cure. The enemies of Jesus, having no other ground of fault, denounce the deed because done on the Sabbath. The common sense of the people revolts from the notion that such a deed can be sinful. 13—16. The malignants ask the opinion of the cured man, but immediately reject it and pretend to suspect him of imposture. They inquire of his parents who confirm the story of his congenital blindness, but warily refrain from expressing an opinion. 17—23.

3. The man being exhorted to reject his deliverer, makes a memorable answer. 24, 25. Questioned again, he answers somewhat sharply. Vexed that they can find no ground of accusation, they use invective, to which he replies with keen sarcasm. They reproach him, and expel him from the synagogue. 26—34.

4. Jesus finds him. He becomes spiritually as well as physically healed. 35—38. The Pharisees rebuked and condemned. 39—41.

5. Parable of the shepherd and sheep. Jesus both a shepherd and a door to his flock. x. 1—5. Explanation. 6—9. Difference between real and false leaders and guides. The love of Christ for his people evinced by his giving his life for them, thus again showing his divine character and relationship. 10—15.

6. He desires to save *all*, and for this voluntarily suffers death, having so covenanted with the Father. The people divided; some malign, others favor him. 16—21.

7. Some proof, which shall compel belief, demanded. He refers to his works as sufficient evidence, and rebukes the moral perversity which rejects it. 22—26. Where and when was this? Does God compel religious faith?

8. Reverts to the sheep and shepherd. Christ's infinite saving power. The same as that of the Father, with whom he claims to be one. 28—30.

9. The Jews, astonished and enraged at his words, threaten to stone him. He calmly reasons with them, and appeals to his works, which, by their own doctrine, could only be wrought by the power of God, and which no bad man could do. Confounded by his unanswerable words they seek to arrest him, but are not able. 31—39.

10. The difference between him and John the Baptist. 40—42.

11. Sickness of Lazarus announced. Relation of Jesus to the family. How he regarded this sickness. His delay. xi. 1—6.

12. Return to Judea. Conversation by the way. Announcement concerning Lazarus misunderstood, and explained. Special design in the circumstances, the end of which will be the increase of the disciples' faith. 7—15.

13. Arrival at Bethany. Distance from Jerusalem? Mourning and sympathy. Martha's partial faith. Jesus' assurance of Lazarus' restoration referred by her to the general resurrection. Grand announcement of Christ's relation to the resurrection. 17—28.

14. Mary meets Jesus. Resort to the grave. The Jews sympathize but question. The command of Jesus, and astonishment of Martha. Jesus prays. Lazarus called, and comes forth from the tomb. 29—44.

15. Some Jews convinced by this astounding event. Others report to

the Pharisees. Their consternation. Uuconscious prophecy of the High Priest. 42—52.

16. The still more settled purpose to effect Christ's death. His withdrawal to another place. 53—54. What effect does more than sufficient evidence have on those that reject that? Goes beyond Jordan, and again teaches the multitudes who gather to him there. Mark xli.; Matt. xix. 1, 2.

XX.

Traveling and Laboring in the Country North-East of Jerusalem and on the East of the Jordan.—Parables and Miracles.

Luke xiii. 10—33; xiv.; xv.; xvi.; xvii. 20, 21. Matt. vii. 13, 14; xxii. 5—14; xviii. 11—14.

1. The woman afflicted eighteen years healed on the Sabbath. The synagogue ruler indignant at this profanation of the day. Discomfited by Jesus' reply. Lu. xiii. 10—17.

2. Disciples' inquiry concerning the number of the saved. They are advised that it is a more important question to determine their own salvation. A mere profession not enough to save a man. Desperate condition of those who have only this to plead. 22—27; Matt. vii. 13, 14.

3. Descent from the patriarchs gives the Jews no claim to the kingdom of God. May be excluded for unbelief, while Gentiles are admitted through faith. Lu. xiii. 28—30.

4. The Pharisees attempt to intimidate him, by showing Herod's hostility. His reply. 31—33.

5. Enemies watch his action in respect to a case of healing on the Sabbath. He asks a question which they dare not answer. The cure performed. xiv. 1—6.

6. Parable of guests at supper, and the assumption of positions of honor. Propriety of humility in self-estimation. Givers of feasts exhorted to invite the poor instead of the rich. A more unmistakable and genuine hospitality. 7—14.

7. Parable of the Wedding Supper. Invitation to men universally to partake of the provisions of grace. Matt. xxii. 1—4; Lu. xiv. 16, 17. Excuses made and the rejection by those to whom the invitation primarily comes. These often perish while the despised and outcast are brought in. The Jews, and the highly-favored in Christian lands, in the former class. Matt. xxii. 5—10; Lu. xiv. 18—23.

8. The guest without the wedding-garment. Matt. xxii. 11—14. What does it symbolize?

9. The multitude instructed that Christian discipleship implies sacrifices and self-denial. They are exhorted to count the whole cost before pledging themselves to him. Does this apply now as well as then? Lu. xiv. 25—33.

10. Jesus' association with the wicked and despised people censured. Lu. xv. 1, 2. What utterance of his, elsewhere, explains this? Lu. xix. 10.

Matt. xviii. 11. Further illustrated by parables. (a) The rejoicing of the finding of the lost sheep. (b) The lost piece of silver. Lu. xv. 3—10; Matt. xviii. 12—14.

11. Parable of the Prodigal Son. Much greater joy over the return of a lost soul, than over those who have not apostatized. Give the story, and show its application. Lu. xv. 11—32.

12. Parable of the dishonest steward. We may make such use of those temporal advantages which are a snare to selfish and worldly men as to make them of great spiritual advantage. Lu. xvi. 1—9.

13. Faithfulness in temporal things essential to spiritual excellence. Singleness of purpose necessary. 10—13.

14. Covetous Pharisees offended at his discourse. Parable of the Rich Man and Lazarus. The best conditioned in this world often totally unprepared for eternity; while those who are destitute here, may be abundantly provided for there, through faith and faithfulness. Permanency of the future state. 14—26.

15. Extraordinary and astonishing evidence of no value to those who already are convinced by the ordinary means. 27—31.

16. The kingdom of God not outward and temporal, but inward and spiritual. Lu. xvii. 20, 21.

XXI.

His Labors in Perea, and Between the Jordan and Jerusalem.

Luke xviii.; xvii. 7—10; xix. 2—27. Matt. xix. 3—29; xx.; xxv. 14—30; xxvi. 6—13. Mark x.; xiv. 2—8. John xi. 55—57; xii. 1—8.

1. Parable of the unjust magistrate and the widow. Value of persistent prayer. Lu. xviii. 1—8.

2. Parable of the Pharisee and the publican at prayer. Self-righteousness and genuine humility contrasted. 9—14.

3. The Pharisees still ply him with questions intended to embarrass. The subject of divorce. His clear statement of the true doctrine. A definite moral rule. The sacredness of marriage, and the sin of its violation. Matt. xix. 3—9; Mark x. 2—12.

4. Disciples dejected at the severity of the doctrine. Jesus' reply. Matt. xix. 10—12.

5. Blessing little children. Objection of the disciples. He rebukes them and receives the children. Mark x. 12, 13; Matt. xix. 13—15; Lu. xviii. 15—17.

6. How to be saved. Conversation with the rich young ruler. Mark x. 17—22; Matt. xix. 16—22; Lu. xviii. 18—24. (a) The earnest inquiry. (b) Direction to observe the commandments. (c) Profession of entire legal obedience. (d) "ONE THING THOU LACKEST." Inordinate love of wealth must be crucified. (e) Mortification and sorrow at the discovery.

7. Jesus' view of the perilous character of the love of wealth. The

disciples astonished. The principle enforced by a striking simile. The disciples reassured. Mark x. 23—27; Matt. xix. 23—26; Lu. xviii. 24—27.

8. Peter's profession, and Christ's reply. The vast compensations. Matt. xix. 27—29. (Also, Mark and Luke.)

9. Parable of the servant's relation to the master. Man's obedience not meritorious. Lu. xvii. 7—10.

10. Parable of the Laborers in the Vineyard. The laborers of an hour receive the same as the toilers of a day. God's bestowment not according to merit, as we merit nothing; but on other grounds. Matt. xx. 1—18.

11. On the way towards Jerusalem. Feeling of fear and dread falling upon the disciples. Jesus again instructs them concerning his coming arrest, prosecution, maltreatment and death. Their slowness to apprehend the case. Mark x. 32—34; Matt. xx. 17—19; Lu. xviii. 31—34.

12. Ambitious request of James and John, through their mother. Misapprehension of the nature of Christ's kingdom. Jesus' remonstrance and mild rebuke. Matt. xx. 20—23; Mark x. 35—40.

13. Jealousy of the other disciples. Reproof and instruction of the Master. Matt. xx. 24—28; Mark x. 41—45.

14. Healing of Bartimeus and another of their blindness. Where was this? The multitude rebuke the afflicted as they cry for help. But Jesus invites them to him, and makes them whole. Mark x. 46—52; Matt. xx. 29—34; Lu. xviii. 35—43.

15. The story of Zaccheus. Lu. xix. 2—9. (a) What was Zaccheus' office? Was it a popular one? Why? (b) His eagerness to see Jesus, and his device. (c) The Saviour's recognition of his sincerity, and the honor bestowed on him. (d) Zaccheus' practical penitence and proposed righteousness. (e) His acceptance by Christ.

16. Parable of the Talents. Our responsibility in proportion to our abilities. Doom of unfaithful servants. 11—27; Matt. xxv. 14—30.

17. The enemies of Jesus inquire about his coming to the Passover. Jno. xi. 55—57. Their malevolent purpose.

18. The anointing with the precious ointment. (a) The feast, the host and the guests. (b) Mary's costly offering. (c) The censure of the expensiveness of the offering. Who made this objection? Was there a reason? (d) Mary justified by the Master. The action anticipatory of his near decease. Jno. xii. 1—8; Matt. xxvi. 6—13; Mark xiv. 2—8. What prediction concerning this act of Mary's is still being fulfilled?

XXII.

Christ's Public Entry into Jerusalem in Fulfillment of Messianic Prophecy, and Subsequent Events.

We now come to the last week of Christ's public ministry. It was a week voluminous in the number and weight of the incidents which belong to it. In the record are found some of the most remarkable instances of the utter discomfiture and humiliation of his foes by the ready replies of Jesus to their most skillfully devised and ingeniously complicated questions. So complete was this defeat, even in the estimation of the populace, that the most ordinary worldly prudence might have turned it into a permanent triumph, and have made Jesus the enthroned leader of the people to the utter overthrow of the power of the Pharisaic and priestly party. It was the very event which this party had wrought so desperately and unscrupulously to prevent,—a position which Jesus, at the moment when it was within his easy reach, resolutely but calmly declined to accept; since he had come forth, not for the purpose of worldly dominion and triumph, but to die a cruel and ignominious death. He had "power to lay down his life," and this power, instead of the other, he accepted and exercised.

This was the period, too, of several of those most powerful and marvelous discourses of Christ, chiefly to his disciples, recorded in the last part of Matthew's and John's Gospels.

The week began with the Sunday before the Passover, commemorated since by the Christian Church as "Palm Sunday." Jesus had been journeying from the Jordan with his disciples, and had just arrived in the vicinity of Jerusalem when he made preparation for this prophetically predicted public entry, as the Messiah,—the anointed Prince of Israel, of David's line,—into the capital city of his nation. It was the only public official demonstration that he made. And what a strange demonstration it was! It was one of mingled grandeur and simplicity, of exulting triumph and genuine humility. There was no military display, no magnificent civic procession, no chariots or horsemen, no even moderate elaborate previous preparation. Simply himself, in his ordinary garb, surrounded by his few humble companions, who, instead of more gaudy trappings, had spread their outer garments upon the young ass on which the Master rode. But the progress and the entry were triumphant, nevertheless. The multitude, moved as by one mighty impulse, hailed him with hosannas as David's royal heir, divinely designated, and coming to assume his throne. Nor was Jesus for a moment deceived by this universal popular acclamation. He knew that, ere the week would end, all this enthusiasm would cease; that a disastrous revulsion would come; and that the same lips that now shouted, "Hosanna," would cry: "Away with him! Crucify him!" Nevertheless, it became him thus to present himself to his nation, and to enter in this kingly way into the sacred city.

Matt. xxi.; xxii. 15—46. Mark xi.; xii. Lu. xix. 29—48; xx. John xii. 12—19.

1. The preparation for the official entry. Matt. xx. 1—9; Mark xi. 1—10; Lu. xix. 29—38; Jno. xii. 12—18. (a) The two disciples sent to secure the young ass. (b) They find it according to the prediction, and, having explained to the owner what was wanted, bring it to Jesus. (c) He rides upon the beast, with no other trappings but the disciples' raiment. (d) The prophetic declaration. Where is it found? (e) Greeting of the people, and their joyful acclamations acknowledging him as the Messiah. What event had enhanced this enthusiasm? Was it lasting?

2. Depression of the Pharisees. Jno. xii. 19. They, with unconcealed disgust, ask him to rebuke his friends. His remarkable reply. Lu. xix. 39, 40.

3. The pathetic lamentation over Jerusalem. Its grand rejected opportunity about to cease forever. The appalling consequences. Lu. xix. 41—44.

4. Excitement in the city at Christ's entrance. Inquiry and answer. Matt. xxi. 10, 11.

5. Jesus in the Temple. Expulsion again of the traffickers. How does his denunciation of their conduct differ from that uttered on the former occasion? 12, 13; Mark xi. 15—17; Lu. xix. 45, 46. (See, also, John ii. 16.)

6. He exercises his healing power upon those who come to him in the Temple. Laudation and joy of the people, and even of the children. Displeasure of the Pharisees who surlily call his attention to this. The striking reply. Matt. xxi. 14—16.

7. Lodging at Bethany on Sunday night, he returns in the morning to Jerusalem. The Barren Fig-Tree cursed. The moral and spiritual lesson implied. 17—19.

8. Teaches in the Temple. Eagerness of the people to hear him, and the growing malice of the Pharisees seeking for pretexts to destroy him. Lu. xix. 47, 48; also, xxi. 37, 38.

9. Tuesday morning, returning from Bethany, the disciples marvel at what had befallen the fig-tree. Jesus makes it the occasion of teaching the power of real faith. Matt. xxi. 20, 22; Mark xi. 20—24.

10. The Pharisees demanding of him the authority for his assumptions, Jesus, in turn, demands of them their opinion concerning John's mission. Their painful dilemma, and humiliating and cowardly answer. Matt. xxi. 23—27; Mark xi. 27—33; Lu. xx. 1—8.

11. Parable of the two sons. Obedience better than profession. Applied to self-righteous Pharisees, and penitent publicans and harlots. Also, of universal application; Matt. xxi. 28—32.

12. Parable of the murderous tenant husbandmen. The atrocious guilt and final rejection of the Jewish church. Matt. xxi. 33—41; Mark xii. 1—9. Lu. xx. 9—16.

13. The rejected stone. Anger of the Pharisees at the application of these parables. Their plotting still baffled. Matt. xxi. 42—46; Mark xii. 10—12.

14. The Pharisees unite with the Herodian party in an attempt by hypocritical words to entrap him into some dangerous statement. The question of the lawfulness of the Roman tax. Their easy and palpable discomfiture. Matt. xxii. 15, 22; Mark xii. 13—17; Lu. xx. 20—26.

15. The Sadducees attempt to puzzle him with a question pertaining to the future state. He rebukes their ignorance of spiritual things, and asserts, and briefly cites authority for, the doctrine of the resurrection. Matt. xxii. 22—32; also, Mark and Luke. Verdict of both people and scribes. 33; Lu. xx. 39.

16. A scribe and lawyer sent with the device of drawing him out to make invidious distinctions between the precepts of the Decalogue. Discomfiture of the questioner. Mark xii. 28—34; Matt. xxii. 34—40.

17. Jesus, in turn, confounds the Pharisees by questioning them as to the descent of the Messiah from David, who yet calls him Lord. The effect on the people. Matt. xxii. 41—46; Mark xii. 34—37; Lu. xx. 41—44.

XXIII.

Conclusion of the Last Day of Christ's Public Ministry.—Prophetic Discourses and Conversations.

Matt. xxiii.; xxiv.; xxv. 1—13, 31—46; xxvi. 1—16. Mark xii. 38—44; xiii. 1, 2; xiv. 1, 2. Luke xx. 45—47; xiii. 34, 35; xxi. 1—6; xxii. 1—6.

1. His indignant exposure of the character of the Jewish religious leaders. Matt. xxiii. 1—36; Mark xii. 38—40; Lu. xx. 45—47. (a) Ostentatious in their religion. Matt. xxiii. 1—6. (b) Eager for popular approbation, contrary to the spirit of true religion. 7—12. (c) Hypocritical in their prayers and proselytism. 13—15. (d) Corrupt in their teachings, making fanciful distinctions where none exists. 16—22. (e) Their religion outward. Particular to practice the cheap virtues, but disregarding the more costly. 23—28. (f) Worshipers of the past; building monuments to the memory of those whom they themselves would have slain. 29—32. (g) Deadly and poisonous in their influence. Wicked and cruel towards the divine messengers. 33—39.

2. Lamentation over Jerusalem, on account of the sins of its leaders. 37—39; Lu. xiii. 34, 35.

3. The small contribution of the poor widow. Such offerings more valuable, in God's sight, than the treasures of the rich. Mark xii. 41—44; Lu. xxi. 1—4.

4. Greek proselytes ask an introduction to Jesus. He shows them that there is no worldly advantage to be expected by accepting him. The spiritual benefit great and glorious, must come, if at all, through his own death and the self-renunciation of his followers. Jno. xii. 20—26.

5. Jesus, oppressed in spirit, cries out in prayer. The heavenly voice, and the effect on the people. 27—30.

6. The great crisis at hand. Christ to be lifted up, in order that he may draw all men to him. Questionings of the people as to his meaning. Jesus' parting exhortation to accept him as the Light of the world, lest they stumble. 31—36.

7. The close of his public teaching, and his final withdrawal from the Temple. Rejected of his own people. Fulfillment of prophecy. 36—41.

8. He reproves the moral timidity of those chief men who were convinced of his real character, but were afraid to acknowledge him. In rejecting him, they denied God, loving the praise of men instead. 42—50.

9. He retires with his disciples. They call his attention to the magnificent architecture of the Temple, and its splendid adornments. He predicts the utter overthrow of all these. Matt. xxiv. 1, 2; Mark xiii. 1, 2; Lu. xxi. 5, 6.

10. The threefold inquiry of the disciples as he sat down with them on

the Mount of Olives. He enjoins upon them sobriety of judgment. Rumors of extraordinary events, great excitements and fierce wars, not necessarily precursors of the final catastrophe. Matt. xxiv. 3—8.

11. Fierce persecutions to befall his followers, and they are to be hated even to death. In these, many will lose faith and apostatize. Endurance and salvation. 9—13.

12. General spread of the gospel, before the final destruction of Jerusalem. The awful calamities attending this destruction. Christians, warned by indications which he now suggests, to flee from the city. 14—22.

13. They are not to be imposed upon by rumors of extraordinary occurrences and of Christ's reappearance. Attempted deception. When Christ comes, his coming will be palpable to all. 23—28.

14. Second advent described. Natural signs of its proximity. The time unknown to all men and angels. The event analogous to that of the Flood. Duty of watchfulness. 36—51.

15. Parable of the Ten Virgins. Necessity of perpetual vigilance. xxv. 1—13. Same thought illustrated by parable of servants waiting for their Master. Lu. xii. 36—38.

16. Illustration of the character of the General Judgment. Separation of the good and the bad. The principles which determine this separation and destiny. Eternal reward and punishment. Matt. xxv. 31—46.

17. The disciples reminded that the Passover is at hand, and that it is to be accompanied by his own betrayal. Matt. xxvi. 1, 2; Mark xiv. 1; Lu. xxii. 1.

18. Priests and scribes plot for his arrest, but are fearful of taking any open action. Judas yields to the temptation of Satan, and offers, for a sum of money, to betray the Lord. They eagerly accept his proposition. Matt. xxvi. 3—16; Mark xiv. 1, 2, and 10, 11; Lu. xxii. 2—6; Jno. xiii. 2.

XXIV.

The Passover Feast.—Conversation and Discourse.—Institution of the Lord's Supper.—The Betrayal and Arrest.

After the previous remarkable discourse with his disciples, at the close of that last great day of his public ministry, Jesus appears to have retired to Bethany, and to have remained in seclusion and solemn silence from Tuesday evening till the afternoon of Thursday. That was the day of the preparation for the Passover, the great national and religious feast of the Jews, which had been observed for nearly fifteen hundred years in commemoration of the deliverance from Egyptian bondage; also in typical anticipation of the immeasurably greater deliverance now about to be achieved by the offering of the "Lamb slain from the foundation of the world." It was meet that he, who had come to be the infinite paschal victim, should fulfill all righteousness by observing to the very last this typical and ceremonial feast,—that up to the very hour when the "eternal victim slain" should be ready for the sacrifice, that which had been its foreshadowing and prophecy should be scrupulously maintained.

There is some dispute as to just what time in the day the paschal lamb was to be slain; but probably it was between the hour of the evening sacrifice and sunset of Thursday,—that is, soon after the ninth hour, or about three o'clock in the afternoon. The Jewish day began at sunset, and the supper lasted till evening. It was to this feast, prepared especially for them in Jerusalem, that Jesus came with his chosen Twelve. Here, in the brief period which by the greatness of the events seems almost to have occupied days rather than hours, occurred not only the simple ceremonies pertaining to the occasion, but also the affectionate, familiar conversation; the calm but startling announcement of the traitor in their midst; the lesson of humility; the prediction of defection in which they would all be involved; the institution of a new, solemn and sacred memorial service, to continue till the second advent, and which is observed by millions of Christ's followers still; the profounder discourse with which he comforted and encouraged the hearts of his friends, and left on record for all the generations of those who were to believe on his name; and the wonderful intercessory prayer. From this feast, too, he went out to the appalling agony of the garden, the betrayal, the arrest, the foretold trial and condemnation.

Lu. xxii. 7—54. Matt. xxvi. 17—56. Mark xiv. 22—51. John xiii.; xiv.; xv.; xvi.; xvii. xviii. 1—11.

1. Peter and John sent to prepare the Passover Feast for Jesus and the Twelve. Directions for finding a place. They make the requisite preparations. Lu. xxii. 7—13; Matt. xxvi. 17—19; Mark xiv. 12—16.

2. The feast, and the words of Jesus. Give some account of the character and signification of the feast, both in its commemorative and in its typical aspects. Lu. xxii. 14—17; Matt. xxvi. 20; Mark xiv. 17.

3. The discussion as to who should be greatest in the new kingdom. Lu. xxii. 24. The great, memorable lesson of humility. *The washing of the disciples' feet*, and instruction. Peter's objection. The disposition enjoined upon them towards one another. Jno. xiii. 3—15. Jesus repeats some former words on *service*, not *lordship*, as the distinguishing trait of Christian discipleship. Lu. xxii. 25—30.

4. Jesus, greatly distressed, divulges his knowledge that one of them would betray him. Their consternation. The anxious inquiry, the answer, and the sign. Jno. xiii. 17—26. Judas goes out on his errand, though unsuspected by the others, yet indicated by Jesus. 27—30.

5. Jesus speaks of his departure and his glorification. They still fail to apprehend him, and Peter resolutely purposes to follow him even to death. Jesus foretells to the astonished disciples his denial of him that very night. Jno. xiii. 31—38.

6. The defection of them all predicted. Peter warmly asserts his constancy, even if all alone. The Lord's further warning, and Peter's emphatic reässertion. Matt. xxvi. 31—35; Mark xiv. 27—31; Lu. xxii. 31—34.

7. Modified instructions to the disciples concerning the conduct of their future mission. Lu. xxii. 35—38.

8. INSTITUTION OF THE LORD'S SUPPER. Matt. xxvi. 26—29; Mark xiv. 22—25; Lu. xxii. 18—20.

9. The consequences to them of his going from them. Thomas' question, and Jesus' answer. Philip's request. Christ's union with the Father. The resources of real believers. Jno. xiv. 1—14.

10. Effect of loving Christ. His absence implies the presence of the Comforter, the Holy Ghost. His peace. His departure and future coming. 15—31.

11. Love to Christ the spring of Love. The Vine and the branches. Mutual love of Christians. *The new commandment.* The world's hatred. Testimony of the Comforter. xv.

12. Persecutions, fierce and bitter, foretold. But though he leaves them to this bitter experience, they will not be as orphans or comfortless. The divine support. The Spirit's office. Christ will return. The interval to them. The disciples seem to apprehend him, and express unbounded confidence; but he sees that, even immediately, their faith will fail. xvi.

13. *The great Intercessory Prayer.* (a) For himself. xvii. 1—5. (b) For the apostles. 6—19. (c) For all believers. 20—26.

14. The company sing a hymn,—probably the "Great Hallel." (Ps. cxv.—cxviii.) This closes the feast, and they go out toward the Mount of Olives. Jno. xviii. 1; Matt. xxvi. 30; Mark xiv. 26; Lu. xxii. 39.

15. THE AGONY IN GETHSEMANE. (a) Arrival at the garden. Leaving the disciples, except Peter, James and John. (b) The profound and crushing sorrow. He goes alone to pray. (c) The cry of intense anguish, yet resolute submission. (d) The return to his companions, to find them asleep. (e) He goes and prays the second and third time, in the same awful agony. The intensity of suffering; the bloody sweat. Exhausted nature succored by the ministry of an angel. His return to his still sleeping friends. Matt. xxvi. 36—44; Mark xiv. 32—40; Lu. xxii. 40—44.

16. He announces his instant betrayal. The immediate arrival of Judas, with a large company, sent by the priestly party to arrest him. Matt. xxvi. 47; Mark xiv. 43; Lu. xxii. 47; Jno. xviii. 2, 3.

17. THE BETRAYAL. The traitor's kiss. Christ's gentle but severe reproach. Matt. xxvi. 48—50. (See, also, Mark, Luke and John, following above.)

18. Jesus' voluntary presentation of himself to the company. The marvelous effect of his presence and words. Jno. xviii. 4—9.

19. The disciples disposed to repel the assault. Peter's impulsive attack, and the rebuke of Jesus, who also miraculously repairs the mischief done by the sword. Matt. xxvi. 51—56; Mark xiv. 47; Lu. xxii. 50—54; Jno. xvii. 10, 11.

20. Jesus, while yielding himself a prisoner, reproaches the band for their manner of arrest. Matt. xxv. 55, 56. (Also, Mark and Luke.) What was the probable reason of this nocturnal and strategic method? The disciples, terrified and panic-stricken, forsake him and flee. Matt. xxvi. 56; Mark xiv. 50, 51.

XXV.

The Trial and the Condemnation.

It was probably about midnight between Thursday and Friday, when the arrest of Jesus was made. There appears to have been still among the leaders a great fear of a popular uprising in favor of Jesus, if they proceeded at once publicly against him. They therefore took him first to the house of Annas, who seems to have been a man of great authority in religious matters. He was the father-in-law of the high priest, and is reported by some reputable writers as having previously been the high priest himself, but deposed by the Roman government. The proceedings here were doubtless informal and tentative, rather than judicial. The leaders were still in doubt as to how far they might safely go. But it was determined to go on with the prosecution, and he was taken to the high priest, the highest judicial functionary of the Jews. The brief examination by the high priest, perhaps, indicates a desire to ascertain how far the rulers themselves had become infected with the conviction of his Messiahship. The Sanhedrim, or great council, was called together at early dawn, and, in unseemly haste, they proceeded to the formal trial. There was a remarkable lack of testimony against Jesus. It was only at the last that two false witnesses were found, who, on the slight cross-examination which some fair-minded members of the council seem to have made, so contradicted one another that their testimony, not very important even if true, was quite annihilated. Jesus made no defense, called no witnesses, asked no questions. They, at last, called him to testify concerning himself. He calmly expressed his confident conviction that nothing which he could say would avail any thing with them; that the result was a foregone conclusion, and that his condemnation was determined. But he boldly assured them of his future appearance on the throne of the world's judgment, at God's right hand. He was then directly asked, under the form of solemn oath, to declare whether he were the Messiah and Son of God. He, with equal directness, with simplicity and solemnity, affirmed that he was. This was instantly seized upon as satisfactory evidence against him, and, in token of this, the high priest gave the usual sign of distress and horror by rending his clothes. It needs to be said that this fully sustained the charge of blasphemy, unless there was also evidence that Jesus was what he professed to be. But this evidence had been furnished, in great abundance, before the eyes of all of them; and to this, Christ had constantly appealed, and, in view of it, had already pronounced their condemnation. They had willfully, wickedly and obstinately rejected the most palpable evidence of their own Messiah.

The next step, in accordance with simple Jewish law, would have been to conduct Jesus outside of the city, and then for the people to stone him to death. But there were two reasons for not doing this. One was, that Judea was now a Roman province, and Jewish tribunals had not the power to inflict the punishment of death. That must be left to the imperial authorities. Very likely, however, this of itself would not have prevented that result, as we find there were previous occasions on which they would have resorted to this method, even without form of trial, had not Jesus disappeared from the midst of his foes. The other reason probably was, that, in the light of the recent popular enthusiasm for Jesus, it was not deemed entirely safe to risk it. In this, too, was the fulfillment of his own prediction, that he should be delivered to the hands of the gentiles, and be crucified. For both the reasons assigned, it was desirable that there should be a formal condemnation of Jesus by the Roman authority; and yet it was only by the utmost urgency and clamor that Pilate, who was fully disposed to acquit him, could be persuaded to condemn him.

John xviii. 13; xix. 4—17. Matt. xxvi. 57—75; xxvii. 1—34. Mark xiv. 53—72; xv. 1—24. Luke xxii. 4—7, 54—71; xxiii. 1—32.

1. Jesus brought to Annas. Jno. xviii. 13, 14. Who was he? (See Introduction.)

2. Peter follows, is accused of being Jesus' disciple, and denies, repeating his denial once and again, as Jesus had foretold. Jesus' look at Peter, and Peter's remorse. Matt. xxvi. 58, and 69—75; Mark xiv. 54, and 66—72; Lu. xxii. 54—62; Jno. xviii. 15—18.

3. The preliminary examination. Jesus' answer. The smiting. The remonstrance. Jno. xviii. 19—23.

4. Jesus sent to Caiaphas. Gathering of the council. Attempt to bring testimony. The evidence meager, trivial, and contradictory. Though urged to reply, he makes no defense. Jno. xviii. 24; Matt. xxvi. 57—65; Mark xiv. 53—61; Lu. xxii. 66.

5. Jesus himself questioned and adjured. His bold, dignified and majestic reply; his calm assumption of Messiahship and Divinity. Lu. xxii. 66—70; Matt. xxvi. 63, 64; Mark xiv. 61, 62.

6. Excitement and indignation of the council, who, on this profession, summarily condemn him. Contemptuous and insulting treatment. Lu. xxii. 63—65 and 71; Matt. xxvi. 65—68. Mark xiv. 63—65.

7. What would be the usual course after the condemnation? Why was it not pursued? (Introduction.) Jesus before the Roman governor. The accusation called for by Pilate. What reply was made? What did Pilate wish them to do, and what did they answer? Jno. xviii. 28—32; Matt. xxvii. 1, 2; Mark xv. 1; Lu. xxiii. 1.

8. New accusations. Was there any evidence? Lu. xxiii. 2. Pilate examines him as to the charge of setting himself up for a king. What does Jesus say as to his kingship and his kingdom? Jno. xviii. 33—38. The impression left on Pilate's mind. 39.

9. Christ's silence at the accusations, and Pilate's wonder. Matt. xxvii. 12—14; Mark xv. 3—5. The disposition of Pilate toward Jesus at this point, and its reception by the people. Lu. xxiii. 4, 5. The mention of Galilee, and what occurred. 6, 7.

10. Reception by Herod. His motive. What Herod was this? The conduct of Jesus here. Insulted by Herod and his attendants. Effect on the relations between Pilate and Herod. Lu. xxiii. 6—12.

11. Pilate's decision. The custom of release. Jesus or Barrabbas? Pilate's wife's entreaty. Matt. xxvii. 15—21; Mark xv. 6—11; Lu. xxiii. 13—19; Jno. xviii. 39, 40.

12. Pilate's continued disposition to release Jesus. Overcome by the fury of the mob, he yields, but washes his hands of the crime. Did this exculpate Pilate? Matt. xxvii. 22—26; Mark xv. 12—15; Lu. xxiii. 20—24.

13. Jesus delivered to the Roman soldiers. Their maltreatment of him. Matt. xxvii. 27—30; Mark and Luke.

14. John's account of Pilate's final action. Further conversation with Jesus. Fear, perplexity, vacillation, and final consent. Jno. xix. 4—16.

15. Remorse of Judas. Futile attempt to repair his error. His despair and suicide. Use made of the returned bribe. Matt. xxvii. 3—10.

16. Jesus carrying the cross on which he was to suffer. Another compelled to help. Matt. xxvii. 31, 32; Mark xv. 20, 21; Lu. xxiii. 26; Jno. xix. 16, 17.

17. Great concourse of people. Weeping women. Words of Jesus to them. Lu. xxiii. 27—31.

18. Arrival at Golgotha or Calvary. The customary stupefying draught offered and declined. Mark xv. 22, 23; Matt. xxvii. 33, 34; Lu. xxiii. 33. Jno. xix. 17.

XXVI.

The Crucifixion and the Burial.

Matt. xxvii. 35—66; Mark xv. 25—46; Luke xxiii. 33—56; Jno. xix. 19—42.

1. The two malefactors. Fulfillment of prophecy. Prayer of Jesus. Mark xv. 25—28; Matt. xxvii. 35—38; Lu. xxiii. 32—34.

2. *Title of the accusation*, in the three languages of the three great civilizations. Chagrin of the Jews, and Pilate's mockery. Jno. xix. 19—22; Matt. xxvii. 37; Mark xv. 26; Lu. xxiii. 38.

3. Distribution of Christ's garments, and lottery for the outer robe. Revilings of the people, and tauntings of scribes and priests. What great truth did they unconsciously utter? Jno. xix. 20—24; Matt. xxvii. 35—37. Mark xv. 24—32; Lu. xxiii. 24—37.

4. Conduct of the malefactors. Penitence and salvation of one. Lu. xxiii. 39—43. Matt. and Mark.

5. The women at the cross. Jesus commends his mother to the care of John. Jno. xix. 25—27; Matt. xxvii. 35; Mark xv. 40, 41.

6. The great darkness at noonday. The terrible cry of Jesus. Response of the by-standers. The thirst; the sponge and the vinegar. "IT IS FINISHED." Final utterance and death. Matt. xxvii. 45—50; Mark xv. 36, 37; Jno. xix. 28—30; Lu. xxiii. 44—46.

7. Rending of the sacred veil, convulsions of nature, and other extra-

ordinary phenomena. Conviction of the centurion, and alarm of the people. Matt. xxvii. 51—54; Mark xv. 38, 39; Lu. xxii. 45—48; Jno. xix. 30.

8. What was the Jewish law concerning the bodies of criminals who had been put to death? Deut. xxi. 22, 23. What special reason why this should be observed in the case of Christ and the malefactors? Jno. xix. 31.

9. Measures taken that they might be dead, in order to burial. How was it that Jesus had died sooner than usual? Precaution of the centurion. Fulfillment of prophecy. 32—36. What was the rule in the offering of the paschal lamb, the type of Christ? Ex. xii. 46; Num. ix. 12; I. Cor. v. 7.

10. The burial by Joseph of Arimathea, a wealthy counselor. Assistance and offering of Nicodemus. Mark xv. 42—46; Matt. xxvii. 57—60; Lu. xxiii. 50—54; Jno. xix. 38—42. What prophecy was thus fulfilled? Isa. liii. 9.

11. The women watching and preparing to embalm the body. Lu. xxiii. 55, 56.

12. Fear and precaution of the Pharisees, lest the prediction of Jesus' resurrection should be verified. The heavy stone, the government seal, the military guard. Matt. xxvii. 62—66.

XXVII.

The Resurrection and the Ascension.

Matt. xxviii. 1—20. Mark xvi. 1—19. Luke xxiv. 1—53. Jno. xx. 1—29; xxi. 1—23. Acts i. 1—12.

1. THE RESURRECTION. Matt. xxviii. 1—7; Mark xvi. 1—7; Lu. xxiv. 1—8; Jno. xx. 1—10. (a) The earthquake,—the angel,—the terror and swoon of the soldiers. (b) The early coming of the women to embalm the body. (c) Fear that the stone can not be moved from the door of the sepulchre. Their astonishment to find it rolled away. (d) The hastening of Mary Magdalene to find Peter and John. (e) Discovery by the other women that the body was gone (f) Announcement by the angels that *Jesus was risen*. (g) Peter and John visit the sepulchre. Their experience.

2. The manifestation. (a) The women, going to tell the disciples, meet Jesus in the way. (b) Mary Magdalene returns and weeps at the sepulchre. She suddenly discovers Jesus, who talks with her. (c) These things announced to the disciples, who are still incredulous; Matt. xxviii. 8—10; Mark xvi. 8—10; Lu. xxiv. 9—12; Jno. xx. 11—18.

3. Walk of the two disciples to Emmaus, and conversation on the recent events. Jesus joins them, but does not manifest himself. Instructs them that what has taken place was just what was to be expected, according to the Scriptures. Reveals himself as they are at the table. They return, and report to the other disciples. Lu. xxiv. 13—35.

4. What measures were taken by the Pharisees, when the soldiers reported the occurrences at the sepulchre? What was the penalty when a Ro-

man soldier slept on guard? Is the testimony of what was done when the witness was asleep regarded as good evidence? How, then, does this whole story appear? Matt. xxviii. 11—15.

5. The disciples being assembled together in a room with closed doors, Jesus appears in the midst of them. Their fright and Jesus' assuring. He convinces them of his identity, and they rejoice. Gives them further instruction concerning the correspondence of the events with the Scriptures and with his own previous teachings. Lu. xxiv. 36—49; Jno. xx. 19—21.

6. Commissions them anew to preach and establish this gospel of his every-where. His promise and assurance of aid. The special endowment of the Holy Ghost. Mark xvi. 15—18; Jno. xx. 22, 23.

7. Doubting Thomas. His reässurance and Jesus' gentle rebuke. Jno. xx. 24—29.

8. The disciples return to Galilee, and meet again with Jesus there. At work in their vocation on the sea. The toilsome and fruitless night. Jesus seen on the shore in the morning, but not recognized. The conversation and revelation. Jno. xxi. 1—14.

9. Tender, suggestive and effective conversation with Peter. Peter's grief and contrition. Allusion to John and his future. Jno. xxi. 15—23.

10. Another meeting, probably with other disciples, on a mountain in Galilee. Renews their commission, and promises power for all their future needs. Matt. xxviii. 16—20.

11. THE ASCENSION. (a) The apostles meet him in Jerusalem, and accompany him as far as Bethany on the Mount of Olives. (b) He gives them his final benediction. (c) He disappears from their sight, and departs from the earth, a cloud receiving him. (d) Two angels appear, and assure the disciples that as Jesus has gone into heaven, so he shall return again. Mark xvi. 19; Lu. xxiv. 50—52; Acts i. 1—12.

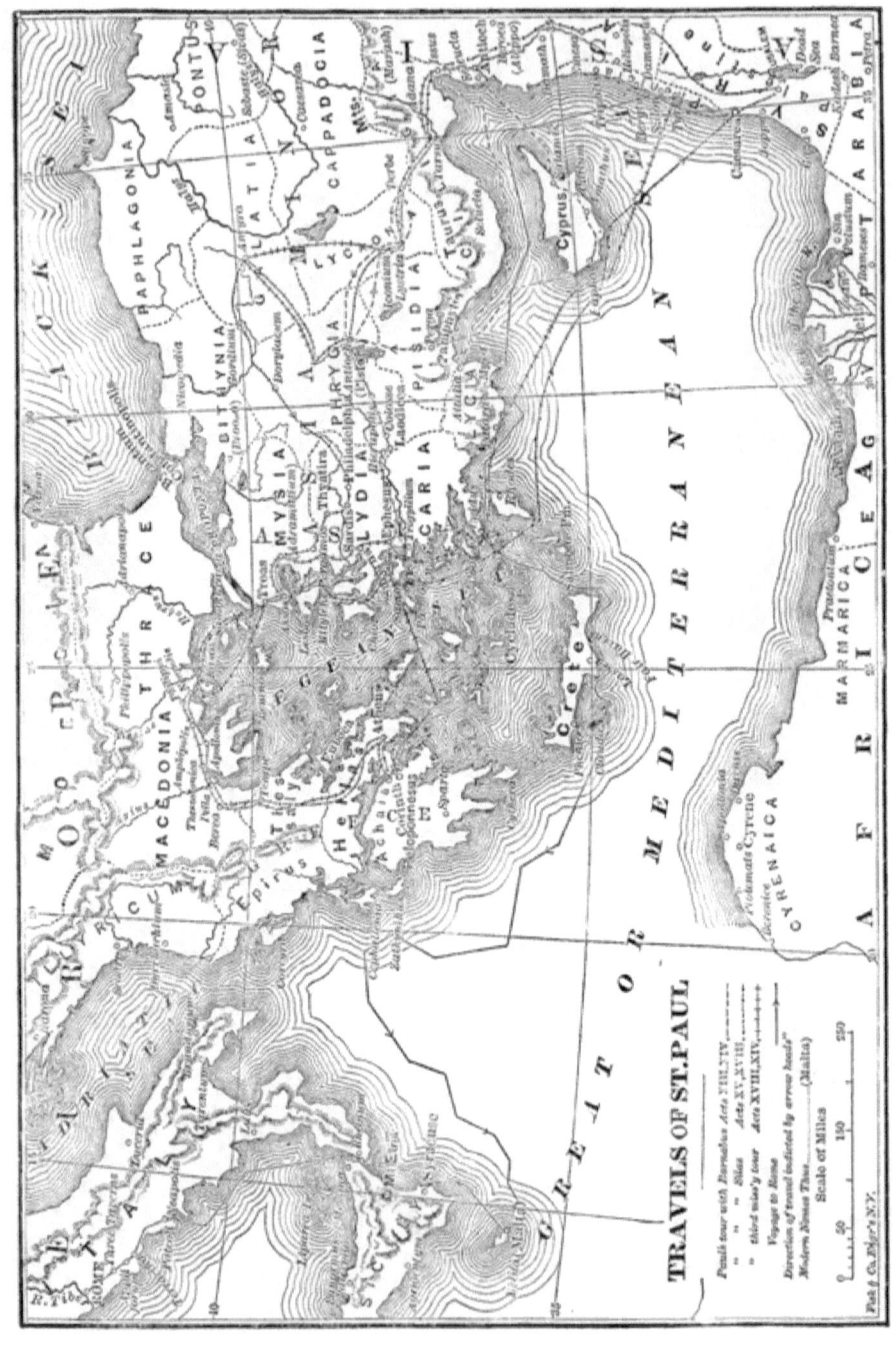

FOURTH YEAR'S COURSE.

THE PROPAGATION OF THE GOSPEL.

BOOKS OF REFERENCE.
FOURTH YEAR.

McClintock's and Strong's CYCLOPÆDIA.
Kitto's CYCLOPÆDIA.
Conybeare and Howson's ST. PAUL.
Farrar's LIFE AND WORK OF ST. PAUL.
Stalker's LIFE OF ST. PAUL.
Taylor's PAUL THE MISSIONARY.
Macduff's FOOTSTEPS OF ST. PAUL.
Thomas Lewin's LIFE AND EPISTLES OF PAUL.
Neander's PLANTING AND TRAINING OF THE CHRISTIAN CHURCH.
Farrar's EARLY DAYS OF CHRISTIANITY.
Fisher's BEGINNINGS OF CHRISTIANITY.
Uhlhorn's CONFLICT OF CHRISTIANITY WITH HEATHENISM.
Schaff's HISTORY OF THE APOSTOLIC CHURCH.
Vaughn's CHURCH OF THE FIRST DAYS.
Geikie's HOURS WITH THE BIBLE.
Smith's BIBLE DICTIONARY.
Kitto's DAILY BIBLE ILLUSTRATIONS.
Smith's NEW TESTAMENT HISTORY.
F. W. Robertson's LECTURES ON CORINTHIANS.
Farrar's MESSAGES OF THE BOOKS.
Lewin's FASTI SACRI (for dates, and corresponding secular history).
Arnot's CHURCH IN THE HOUSE.
Bernard's PROGRESS OF DOCTRINE.
Green's THE APOSTLE PETER.
Taylor's PETER THE APOSTLE.
Howson's EVIDENTIAL VALUE OF THE ACTS.
Paley's HORAE PAULINAE.
Eugene Stock's LESSONS ON THE ACTS.
Joseph Parker's APOSTOLIC LIFE, AS REVEALED IN THE ACTS.

The Propagation of the Gospel.

I.

The Disciples Waiting for the Gift of Power.

THE scriptural history of the planting of the Christian Church, is found in the book of the Acts of the Apostles, and in the letters to societies, to individuals, and to scattered classes of believers. The title of the first of these, as Dr. Smith has well observed, is misleading. The "acts" or works of only a few of the apostles are alluded to, at all. Only four of them are in any way prominent; and most of the treatise is occupied with the missionary labors of Paul, who, at the beginning of the history, was not even a disciple.

But while, like the narratives of the life of Christ, this book is free from any appearance of literary intention on the part of the writer, and while it is also somewhat fragmentary and not altogether connected and chronological, it gives just what the Church in subsequent ages has needed, a simple, definite and impressive account of the manner in which the religion of Jesus was propagated after his departure, and how it was received by the people to whom it was first preached. It is a wonderful story, abounding in marvelous facts, yet one in which the writer is free from self-consciousness, with no trace of sensationalism,—bound only to give a plain, simple and natural narrative of the events as they transpired. We are to remember that this whole New Testament history, including the fragmentary allusions and statements in the epistles, covers scarcely so much as forty years from the death of Jesus, while yet the events were distributed over a vast territory, and many of them took place in some of the most important cities of either the ancient or modern world.

Jesus had commanded the disciples to remain at Jerusalem till they should receive the promised baptism of the Holy Ghost, which was to especially qualify them for their work. After his ascension, ten days had elapsed, during which they continued closely united in prayer for the fulfillment of the promise. At the end of this time, occurred the wonderful event, when they were not only filled with the Spirit, but gave palpable evidence of it both physically and in its convincing energy upon the people.

The time was remarkably favorable to the event. It was the feast of Pentecost, which, as the name implies, was fifty days after the Passover. It was the great national festival of first-fruits, which had been kept from the earliest period of the nation, and was wont to be more numerously attended than even the Passover itself. Hence the vast multitudes that were now present, embracing not only visitors from every part of Palestine, but also great numbers of Israelites scattered abroad in almost all nations of the known world. Hence, too, this first powerful impression of the gospel of Jesus was likely to be felt, to some extent, in the most distant places.

Acts i.; ii. Tiberius, Emperor, A. D. 14—37. Pentecost, May 27th, A. D. 30.

1. The writer alludes to a former narrative of his. i. 1—2. What was this? Rehearsal of the events between the resurrection of Jesus and his ascension. The commission to the apostles. (a) Manifestation of Christ and personal intercourse with the disciples. 3. (b) Injunction to wait at Jerusalem. 4—5. (c) Inquiry of the disciples respecting the restoration of the Israelitish kingdom, and the answer. 6—8. (d) The ascension. The astonished gaze of the disciples, and the appearance and assurance of the angels. 9—11.

2. The return to Jerusalem, and the constant meeting for prayer. Names of the apostles. 12—14.

3. Peter rehearses the story of the treachery of Judas, showing in it the fulfillment of prophecy, and an allusion to Judas' death. 15—20. He proposes that some one be chosen in the place of the apostate apostle. Condition of apostleship? Manner of the choice? The election? 21—26.

4. Pentecost and meeting of the disciples. ii. 1. Meaning of "Pentecost?" What is the name of this feast in the Old Testament, and the order for its observance? Lev. xxiii. 15, 16. To about what time does it correspond in our calendar? How long was this after the crucifixion? How long after the ascension?

5. What occurred at this time? 2, 3. The effect upon the disciples? 4. What is meant by "other tongues?"

6. The multitudes of Jews present from remote countries, their amazement, and the cause of it. 5—12. Why were so many present? Give the geographical situation of the countries referred to. What does this indicate concerning the state of the Jewish people?

7. What reason was assigned by certain persons for this remarkable phenomenon? 13. Peter's answer? 14, 15.

8. Peter's address,—give an outline. 16—36. How would you characterize some of his declarations concerning Jesus, and the conduct of the people toward him? What bold avowal was made concerning Christ's present state?

9. Effect upon the people. Exhortation and direction. 38—40. What intimation here that the Gentiles were to share in the benefits of the Messiah's advent? 39. The result of the demonstration? 41, 42.

10. What power came to the apostles? 43. Beginning of the Christian *Community*, and its character. 41—46.

II.

Rapid Progress of the New Faith. The Beginning of Opposition and Persecution.

Acts iii.; iv.; v.; vi. 1—7. Tiberius, Emperor, A. D. 14—37. Events of Lesson, A. D. 30.

1. Healing of the cripple at one of the chief gateways of the Temple. iii. 1—10. What time in the day was this, and what service always took place at this time? 1. How old was the man? Also, iv. 22.

2. Effect on the people. 11. Peter's address. 12—26. How did the miracles of the apostles differ from those of Jesus? (Examples of the latter, as compared with this.) How does Peter explain the phenomenon? 12 and 16. What does he declare concerning Christ, and how does he speak of the Jews' treatment of him? 13—15. Mitigation of their crime, and exhortation to repentance, with a glance at the future. 17—21. Testimony of the prophets; promises to those to whom he spoke. 22—26.

3. Interruption of the discourse. The immediate cause of it? iv. 1, 2. Who were the Sadducees? What effect was the preaching of the apostles likely to have on the popular estimate of their creed?

4. Imprisonment of the apostles. 3. Did this destroy the effect of the sermon? The number of converts by this time? 4.

5. Arraignment of the apostles. Does the examination appear to have been thoroughly judicial, and were there any definite charges? 5—7.

6. Peter's answer. Does he speak in his own wisdom? 8. How does he meet the inquiry? 9—12. What do you think of the character of the reply? What great doctrine was laid down? 12.

7. How did this speech affect the leaders? 13. Conference and perplexity of the latter. Why perplexed? Their determination. 14—17. Was this candid and honest?

8. Communication of the decision to Peter and John, and their answer. 18—20. Why did not the rulers punish or detain them? 21, 22.

9. The return and report of the apostles. 23. Effect on the company. Their thanksgiving and praise. 24—30. The divine answer, and the result. 31.

10. What remarkable disposition manifested itself among the believers? 32—37. Was there any command or positive obligation that the disciples should dispossess themselves of property?

11. Story of Ananias and Sapphira. v. 1—11. Lesson of the divine abhorrence of false-heartedness and hypocrisy, at the very beginning of the history of the Church. Is it probable that there had been any *uttered* lie? What is meant by "Thou hast not lied unto man, but unto God"?

12. Indications of divine power in the apostles. Wholesome fear on the multitude. Effects of the fame of these facts. 12—16.

13. Effect of the apostle's success on the rulers? Their action. 17, 18. The sequence. 19—21. Report of the officers; perplexity of the council. The apostles heard from. Their re-arrest and careful treatment, and reappearance in the council. 22—27.

14. Renewal of charges. What great fear seems to have affected the

rulers? 28. Why had they no reason to complain? (See Matt. xxvii. 25.) Peter's courageous answer. What grand principle does he lay down concerning the relation of moral to civil obligations? His repeated assertions concerning Christ. 29—32.

15. Effect on the Sanhedrim. Give the outline of Gamaliel's speech. 34—39. Who was he, and what important position did he hold?

16. What influence did this speech have on the council? 40. What were they previously disposed to do? 33. Effect on the apostles? 41, 42.

17. The Hellenistic* Jews complain of favoritism. The occasion of the first institution of offices in the Church. Seven men chosen to attend to the temporalities, that the apostles might not be diverted from their special work. vi. 1—6. Character of the men. Increase of the reformation. 7.

III.

From the Martyrdom of Stephen to the Conversion of Saul

It is a matter of interest to observe the difference between the discourses in support of the religion of Jesus addressed by the apostles to the Jews, and those addressed to the Gentiles. Of the former, we have a complete type in the speech of Stephen before the Sanhedrim. It is, perhaps, the longest discourse on this subject in the New Testament, or at least more fully reported; for we can hardly think that, of most of the addresses, we have more than a brief epitome or outline. The great characteristic of this, as well as of the others addressed to Jewish audiences, is that it reasons with entire exclusiveness from the Old Testament Scriptures. The whole argument is, granting what no one in such an audience disputed, that the whole Patriarchal, Hebrew and Jewish history implied the coming of a Messiah, and that types, ceremonies and explicit predictions had unmistakably foretold such a one as the Deliverer of the people, then Jesus is that Messiah. Even the fact of his rejection by the very nation which had for ages expected him, the humiliation to which he was subjected, the ignominious death visited upon him, all became evidence in his favor, and were abundantly indicated in prophecies concerning him. This general characteristic we find in Peter's addresses at the very opening of the work in Jerusalem, as also in Paul's discourses to the Jews everywhere. So we learn that whenever any of the apostles or disciples, in their missionary journeys, went into the synagogues, they preached first to the Jews; out of their own Scriptures " opening and alleging that this is the very Christ." In the speech of Stephen, however, there is this peculiarity, that he charges upon the Jews and sustains his charge with most palpable evidence, that the nation has always resisted any new revelation of the divine will, or any demand for moral reformation. This rejection of Christ, there-

---

* The term " Grecians," in the text, refers to the Jews who were scattered throughout the Gentile world, and who had come under the influence of the Greek culture and used the Greek language. They were called " Hellenistic," in distinction from the Hebrews who dwelt in Palestine.

fore, by the elders and the people, argued nothing against the genuineness of his Messiahship, as it was in perfect keeping with the character of the nation in its whole history to discard and repudiate the highest and most essential truth.

The speech of Paul, on Mars' Hill in Athens, is a type of the reasoning used with the Gentiles. There, he begins with what may be known of God by the teachings of nature, and from these principles of natural religion proceeds to show the necessity of a new revelation both of his will and of himself. The latter condition leads easily to Christ, the facts of whose life and works and character, we may suppose, would be set forth. It is true we have no complete discourse in which this is done, but there are many intimations of this general method.

Acts vi. 8—15; vii.; viii.; ix. 1—30. Tiberius, Emperor, A. D. 14—37. Stephen, Martyr, A. D. 36. Saul's Conversion, A. D. 37.

1. Faith and power of Stephen. Opposition aroused by his preaching. vi. 8, 9. Arrest and persecution. False charges and false witnesses. Stephen's appearance. 10—15.

2. Stephen's defense and remarkable discourse. vii. 1—53. What is the main argument of his address? Of what does he accuse his nation, in its whole history? Does the fact that the nation had rejected Jesus and condemned him to death and treated him with ignominy, make against the truth of his Messiahship? Why? (Introduction.)

3. How did this powerful presentation of the case against the nation affect the people? What was Stephen's condition amid the excitement? His ecstatic vision. His startling declaration, and its effect on the mob. The violent assault. Stephen's prayer and death. 59, 60. What remarkable character first comes to light here? 58.

4. Fierce persecution of the Christians. Saul conspicuous. viii. 1 and 3. What incidental advantage to the cause from this persecution? 4.

5. Philip preaching to the Samaritans. 5—8. Simon Magus and his pretensions and influence. 9—11. Difference between his tricks and Philip's miracles. Have we any thing like this in modern times?

6. Effect of Philip's preaching. 12. Simon's apparent conversion. 13. What was Philip's office? vi. 5.

7. Action of the Church at Jerusalem, when they heard of the work in Samaria. 14. Special effect of the coming of Peter and John. 15—17. Had the baptism of the Spirit been given, except through the apostles' instrumentality?

8. Effect of this manifestation on Simon. What kind of a character is indicated? What English word do we have from this occurrence. Its meaning? Peter's terrible rebuke and Simon's professed penitence. 18—24.

9. Philip and the eunuch. 26—38. Who was this eunuch? Where was the kingdom of Ethiopia? What was the religious condition of the eunuch? How did Philip explain the passage which he read? 35. What was the result? 36—38. What occurred to Philip? 39, 40.

10. Saul's mission to Damascus. Where was this city, and how far from Jerusalem? Saul's business there? ix. 1, 2.

11. The vision, the voice, the revelation, the conviction and inquiry. 3—6. Effect on Saul's companions? Physical effect on Saul? 7—9.

12. Ananias sent to him. His reluctance and the reason. How was it overcome? The errand and the result? 10—18. Was it Saul's *conviction* or his *conversion* that was miraculous?

13. What did he do? Effect on the Damascene Jews? Plot to kill him. His escape and subsequent return to Jerusalem. Was this return immediate? What occurred meantime? Gal. i. 17, 18. Alarm of the disciples. Re-assured by Barnabas. Paul's powerful preaching and the persecution aroused. Escape to Tarsus. 19—30.

IV.

From the Conversion of Saul to the Death of Herod Agrippa I.

The city of Antioch deserves attention as being, next to Jerusalem, the most important center for the diffusion of the Christian faith. It was situated near the north-eastern corner of the Mediterranean Sea, and was about three hundred miles north of the Jewish capital. It was founded about 300 B. C. by one of the Seleucid kings, and became the capital of the territory ruled by that dynasty. At the time with which we are now engaged, it was the capital of the Roman province in Asia, and was a city of probably 200,000 or 300,000 inhabitants. It was a place of great wealth, culture and refinement.

Many Jews resided in the city, and enjoyed both great privileges as citizens, and a large degree of political liberty, not a few of them being Roman citizens. It was not strange that, in the "scattering abroad" which took place because of the persecution at Jerusalem, some of the disciples should have been found at Antioch; nor was it strange that they should have found a degree of readiness there to receive the gospel, inasmuch as there were doubtless many from this city present on the day of Pentecost.

It is probable that the number of converts there was second only to that at Jerusalem. Thither came Saul, under the escort of Barnabas, after his escape from Jerusalem to Tarsus. There he labored with Barnabas for a year, and thence he departed on his great missionary journeys. Here, too, was the first great strife in the Church as to the status of the Gentiles, which was settled by an appeal to the brethren at Jerusalem. The name of "Christians" was first applied at Antioch. By some, it is supposed to have been a nick-name and given in derision. If so, it was not the last time in which a term, intended for reproach, has become a name of honor and renown.

Acts ix. 30—43; x.; xi.; xii. 1—25.   Claudius, Emperor, A. D. 41—54. Caligula, Emperor, A. D. 37—41. Conversion of Cornelius, A. D. 40.

1. Cessation of persecution, and prosperity of the churches. ix. 31. Visitation by Peter. Cure of the paralytic Æneas. Popular effect. 32—35.

2. Peter at Joppa, and the occasion of his coming. Character of Dorcas. The mourning and the mourners. Peter's action. Restoration and its influence. Peter's abode there. 36—43.

3. Cornelius; his character and office. x. 1, 2. The vision and instruction. 2—6. Peter sent for. 7, 8.

4. Peter's vision and its significance. 9—16. What was the Jewish law concerning some of the animals presented in the vision? Lev. xi.

5. Arrival of the messenger from Cornelius. 17, 18. The divine announcement and direction. Introduction and statement of the errand. Peter's ready compliance. 19—23. Can you think of any reason why Peter might have hesitated? Why did he not?

6. The meeting with Cornelius and the gathering. Peter's introduction and inquiry, and the explanation of Cornelius. 24—33.

7. Peter's discourse. Announcement of his conviction of the error of Jewish exclusiveness. His brief and simple statement of the substance of the gospel facts and doctrines. Give this. 34—43.

8. What followed the preaching? Surprise of the Jews who were present, and the reason of it. Baptism of the first Gentile converts. 44—48.

9. Report of these facts at Jerusalem. Peter's conduct criticised. His plain account of the matter. His own doubts—how they were resolved—and the confirmation of his convictions by the events at Cæsarea. The conclusion to which the council came. xi. 1—18.

10. Disciples, scattered from Jerusalem, preach in other cities to the Jews, and gather congregations of believers. The work at Antioch among the Hellenistic ("Grecian") Jews. 19—21.

11. Barnabas sent from Jerusalem to superintend the work. His character. 22—24. What did he do soon after his arrival? 25. How long did Paul and Barnabas labor together at Antioch? What name was first applied here? 26.

12. The prophets. Prediction of Agabus, and action of the Church at Antioch. Barnabas and Saul go to Jerusalem. 27—30.

13. Persecution under Herod Agrippa I. Who was he, and what relation to Herod the Great? What was his territory? Martyrdom of James, and imprisonment of Peter. Precautions concerning him. Prayer of the Church. xii. 1—5.

14. Peter's deliverance by the angel. 6—11. His coming to the house where the prayer-meeting was held. Astonishment of the brethren and his statement to them. James notified. Who was this James? 11—17.

15. The excitement occasioned by Peter's disappearance. Action of Herod. 18, 19. Circumstances of the king's death. 20—23. Progress of the cause. Return of Barnabas and Saul from Jerusalem to Antioch. 24, 25.

V.

Paul's First Missionary Journey.

Henceforth, in this history, by far the most conspicuous and commanding figure is Saul of Tarsus,—afterwards known as Paul the Apostle. He is one of the most powerful characters in the history of the world, and probably more of history has been affected by his influence than by that of any other one man. Though not one of the original apostles, yet all "the signs of an apostle" were manifest in his work, and he doubtless does not exaggerate when he says that he "labored more abundantly than they all."

He was born at Tarsus, near the north-eastern corner of the Mediterranean Sea, not more than a hundred miles from Antioch. It was the capital of the province of Cilicia, and had been for several centuries a city of much distinction. At the time of Paul, Strabo says that, in all that relates to philosophy and general education, it was even more illustrious than Athens and Alexandria. It was, so far as culture and the character of its educated classes was concerned, a Greek city.

For some time previous to Paul's birth, the province had been under the Roman government. About fifty years before the birth of Paul, Cicero, as proconsul, had this as his assigned province, with his official residence at Tarsus. Tarsus was a "free city,"—that is, it had the privilege of being governed by its own magistrates, and many other franchises, but that of Roman citizenship was not one of these. There were many Roman citizens there, but they had received this privilege by some special favor of the government. Paul's father, though a Jew, was a citizen, and Paul himself was thus "free-born."

Paul was thus a Hellenistic Jew,—that is, he was a Jew speaking the Greek language and having the Greek culture to a certain extent, at least. But neither he nor his family appear to have ranked themselves as belonging to the Hellenistic party, according to the divisions between that party and the Asmonean or Hebrew party. They rather held more closely to the Jerusalem traditions and the more exclusive faith. Paul regarded himself as a "Hebrew of the Hebrews," and preserved his family lineage and tribal descent, as he also bore the name of the most illustrious of that tribe. After his general education at Tarsus, he went in his later youth or early manhood to Jerusalem; and there, under the direction of the most famous rabbi of his time, the celebrated Gamaliel, he became familiar with all the learning of the Jews. He adopted the tenets of the Pharisaic party, and became a bigoted enthusiast in their defense. Of his bitter and fierce opposition to Christianity, we have already had evidence.

The conversion of such a man was a remarkable event to the struggling young Church, and a terrible shock to its Jewish opposers. A more powerful human instrumentality for the establishment and diffusion of the faith, can scarcely be conceived. In him were combined results of the three great civilizations, which, meeting at that time in history and at that geographical point, met also in this one man. He was, both by birth and by the most thorough and determined training, a *Jew*, giving promise of becoming perhaps the ablest defender of that faith. He was a *Greek* by language and by culture, thus coming into communication with the whole learned world. He was a *Roman citizen*, and entitled to a degree of protection and consideration which was denied to most of his countrymen. Such a man was eminently fit to be, not merely the scholar among the apostles, but, more especially, to be the APOSTLE TO THE GENTILES.

Dr. Smith gives the following table of the chief epochs of Paul's life:
I. His *First Appearance* at Jerusalem as a *Persecutor*.

II. His *Conversion* on the way to Damascus.

III. His *Introduction to the Apostles* at Jerusalem, and retirement for a time to Tarsus.

IV. His *Labors at Antioch* and visit to Jerusalem, A. D. 44.

V. His *First Missionary Journey* in Asia Minor.

VI. His *Visit to Jerusalem* about the Gentiles.

VII. His *Second Missionary Journey*, and *Introduction of the Gospel into Europe*.

VIII. His *Third Missionary Journey*, and long *stay at Ephesus*.

IX. His *Seizure at Jerusalem*, and *Imprisonment at Cæsarea*.

X. His *Voyage to Rome*, and *First Imprisonment*.

XI. His *Release*, and subsequent labors.

XII. His *Second Imprisonment*, and *Martydom*.

Acts xiii.; xiv. Claudius, Emperor, A. D. 41—54. Events of Lesson, A. D. 45—48.

1. Give an account of the relation of Paul to the early propagation of Christianity. His birthplace, character of the city, and his early culture. His religious and national relations before conversion? What three great characteristics united in him gave him special human fitness for his work?

2. Conference at Antioch. Direction of the Holy Ghost. xiii. 1—3.

3. Departure of Barnabas and Saul to Seleucia and Cyprus. Preaching in the synagogue at Salamis. Adventure at Paphos. Elymas the sorcerer, and the Roman proconsul. Miraculous judgment on the former, and conversion of the latter. Saul henceforth known by a Latin instead of his Hebrew name. 4—12.

4. Paul's company continue their tour. Mark, who had been with them hitherto, returns to Jerusalem. 13. What was a subsequent effect of this departure? xv. 37—40.

5. Arrival at Antioch in Pisidia. Attendance upon the synagogue service. Paul's address. 16—41. Outline of the argument that Jesus was the Messiah. Why does he dwell so much upon Christ's humiliation? What false ideas had the Jews acquired on the subject? What warning does he give them?

6. Desire of the Jews. 42. Candid and serious-minded Jews exhorted. Vast multitudes of Gentiles and Jews drawn to hear Paul. Envy of the latter and their opposition. 43—45.

7. The rebuke administered. What was the regular order of presenting the Gospel? 46. The Gentiles invited. Greatness of the work. 47—49.

8. Persecution and expulsion of the apostles. 50. How does their conduct agree with the direction of their Master? 51, and Mark vi. 11. Their departure to Iconium, and their state of mind. 51, 52.

9. The apostles at Iconium. Preaching to the Jews first. Conversion of Gentiles. xiv. 1. Persecution incited by hostile Jews. Progress of the work nevertheless. Combination of Jews and heathen, and flight of the apostles to Lystra and Derbe. 2—7.

10. Miracle at Lystra. Compare it with the first apostolic miracle at Jerusalem. Effect on the people. Attempt to offer sacrifice to Barnabas and Paul as gods. Action and address of the apostles. Give the line of the

argument. 8—17. Difference between the method of their argument and that usually addressed to Jews. The sacrifices prevented. 18.

11. Jews from Antioch and Iconium instigate persecution. Paul nearly killed. They go to Derbe. Return to the cities recently visited, organizing the churches and encouraging believers to persist even through tribulation and persecution. 19—23.

12. Continued journey and preaching. Return to Antioch. They make report of their mission and abide for a time. 24—28.

VI.

The Council at Jerusalem. Second Missionary Journey, and Introduction of the Gospel into Europe.

The first marked division of sentiment in the infant Church was concerning the relation of the converted Gentiles to the Jewish ceremonial law. The controversy appears to have broken out at Antioch, where the Jewish element of the population was large, and great numbers, both of Jews and Gentiles, had been converted. The more rigid Jews among the converts held, not only that all the converted Jews should carefully continue to observe the Mosaic ceremonial ordinances, but that the Gentile converts should also be required to conform to them,—doubtless regarding Christianity only as a development of Judaism, in which nothing of the latter was to be abrogated. To this the converted Gentiles would naturally object, and with them Paul and Barnabas and the more liberal and spiritual of the Jews held. The controversy seems to have reached a stage of grave importance soon after the return of the two apostles to Antioch from their first missionary journey. The situation involved was so serious that Paul and Barnabas were sent with a deputation to Jerusalem to consult the apostles and leaders there. The result of the deliberations there is given in the history. It evidently was not perfectly satisfactory to the extremists of the Jewish party, and there are symptoms of disturbance on this account at subsequent points in the scriptural narrative. Still it was a substantial general settlement of the question.

The city of Philippi, distinguished by being the first point in Europe at which the Gospel of Christ was preached, was also noted for several other things. It had been founded or rebuilt by Philip, king of Macedon, and father of Alexander the Great. It was doubtless the birthplace of the latter, and the capital of his hereditary domains. It was also in the immediate vicinity that were fought the decisive battles between the imperialists and republicans of Rome, in which Octavius and Antony triumphed over Brutus and Cassius. At the time of Paul, it was under Roman dominion, and belonged to the class of cities designated as "colonies." By this term was meant something different from the modern signification attached to that word. It had a peculiar form of government under its own magistrates, and the governing element of the inhabitants were Roman citizens.

There were only a few resident Jews, as it was rather a military than a commercial city; and they had no synagogues, only a slighter structure where they met for prayer.

Acts xv.; xvi. Claudius, Emperor, A. D. 41—54. Events of Lesson, A. D. 50—51.

1. Controversy concerning the relation of the converted Gentiles to the Mosaic law. Paul and Barnabas resist the demands of the Jewish party. A deputation sent to Jerusalem to consult the leaders there. xv. 1, 2.

2. Their journey, and events by the way. Arrival at Jerusalem, and report to the authorities. Opinion of the Pharisaic party in the council. Peter's argument against their demand. Paul and Barnabas show that God had wrought salvation obviously among the Gentiles, in the absence of the condition supposed to be required. 3—12.

3. James's statement of the case, and decision against the Judaizing plan, and in favor of simple moral and spiritual conditions. His views accepted, and a deputation appointed to bear a letter embodying them to Antioch. 13—29.

4. The arrival at Antioch, and the meeting of the believers. Delivery of the message, and joy of the Church. Silas remains with Paul and Barnabas, who go on with their work. 30—35.

5. Preparation for another missionary tour. Dissension of Paul and Barnabas. The cause of it. 36—38. When did the desertion referred to occur? xiii. 13.

6. Result of the controversy. What are the probabilities of the amount of the good and evil growing out of this difference? Does it prove that either was right? Paul's course. 39—41.

7. Paul at Derbe and Lystra. Conversion of Timothy. His family connections and character, and Paul's purpose concerning him. Why does Paul circumcise Timothy, when he generally opposes the subjection of Gentile converts to the ceremonial law? xvi. 1—3. Do we hear much of Timothy after this?

8. Visitation of the churches, and communication to them of the regulation adopted at Jerusalem. 4. Condition of the churches and the work. 5.

9. Through what parts did they travel, and where were they forbidden to go?* 6, 7. Describe the situation of the regions and the cities named. Arrival at Troas. 8. Where was this, and what famous events of classic interest took place in this vicinity?

10. Paul's vision and call to go over into Europe. The call accepted, and the voyage to Philippi. Trace out the course on the map. First preaching of the Gospel in Europe. Paul and Silas at Philippi. Labors among the Jews. A notable convert and her hospitality. 9—15. What is indicated by the change of the narrative here to the first person? 13. Give some account of Philippi.

11. The demoniac young woman. Her conduct. The demon exorcised in the name of Christ. 16—18.

---

*The "Asia" mentioned in the text and elsewhere in this history, was simply a proconsular Roman province of no very great extent, embracing the western part of Asia Minor, and having Ephesus for its capital.

12. Resentment of her employers, and the reason for it. The malicious prosecution; the accusation and condemnation. The punishment. 19—24. How did Paul and Silas act? 25.

13. What occurred in the night? Its effect on the prison? On the jailer? Why this desperation? Paul's re-assurance. Inquiry of the officer, and his conversion. What did he do further? 26—34.

14. Action of the magistrates the next day. Paul's dignified attitude. How did this affect the magistrates, and why? 35—39. Can you state some of the privileges of a Roman citizen? Were most of the apostles or the Jews generally or a very large proportion of the inhabitants of the empire entitled to these privileges?

VII.

Continuation of the Second Missionary Journey.

Thessalonica, which was the first city in which Paul made any considerable stay after leaving Philippi, was, at that time, the chief city of Macedonia, as well as the most populous and wealthy. It was, also, the seat of the Roman government for that province. It was situated at the head of the Thermaic Gulf or inlet of the Ægean Sea, and was favorably located both for commerce and for military purposes. It was of no small note in the ancient world for a long time previous to the Christian Era, and has several times been of great importance in the subsequent ages. The Jewish population, at the time of Paul's visit was very great, and it appears to have had the only synagogue in all that region of country. It became an important center for the diffusion of Christianity, and an active and vigorous church was formed there at Paul's first visit, notwithstanding the storm of persecution that so soon greeted him. The two epistles to the Thessalonians, written not very long after Paul's visit, are probably the earliest of his letters to the churches.

Athens is the next of the great cities visited by Paul on this missionary tour. Of it little need be said here, since all students of Ancient History are supposed to be somewhat familiar with the character of this, in many respects, the most noted city of the ancient world. Perhaps no city in any period has ever attained to such eminence in the arts, in letters, in philosophy and in the general culture of society as this. Probably there never were found within the time of a single century so many men of brilliant intellect and great power grouped in one city, as were found in Athens between 350 and 450 B. C. The time of Paul's visit was several centuries after that, and it had fallen far below the standard of its highest fame. It was not now even the capital of the Roman province of which it was a part. It was, however, a "free city," under the general government of the empire, and, as such, had many privileges.

Yet, even now, it was a wonderful city, crowded with temples, palaces, and statues and other marvelous works of art. "We go through the gate: and immediately the eye is attracted by the sculptured forms of Minerva, Jupiter, and Apollo, of Mercury, and the Muses, standing near a sanctuary of Bacchus. We are already in the midst of an animated scene, where temples, statues, and altars are on every side, and where the Athenians, fond of publicity and the open air, fond of hearing and telling what is curious and strange, are enjoying the climate and enquiring for news. . . . . If we look up to Areopagus, we see the temple of that deity from whom the eminence had received the name of 'Mars' Hill.' . . . . If we look forward to the Acropolis, we behold there, closing the long perspective, a series of little sanctuaries on the very ledges of the rock,—shrines of Bacchus and Æsculapius, Venus, Earth, and Ceres, ending with that lovely form of that Temple of Unwinged Victory which glittered by the entrance of Propylaea. . . . . Thus every god in Olympus found a place in the Agora. But the religiousness of the Athenians went even further. For every public place and building was likewise a sanctuary. . . . . The Council-House held statues of Apollo and Jupiter, with an altar of Vesta. . . . . The Pnyx, near which we entered, on whose elevated platform they listened in breathless attention to their orators, was dedicated to Jupiter on High, with whose name those of the Nymphs of the Demus were gracefully associated. And as if the imagination of the Attic mind knew no bounds in this direction, abstractions were deified and publicly honored. Altars were erected to Fame, to Modesty, to Energy, to Persuasion and to Pity. . . . . It is needless to show how the enumeration . . . . . (which is no more than a selection from what is described by Pausanias) throws light on the works of St. Luke and St. Paul; and especially how the groping after the abstract and invisible, applied in the altar alluded to last, illustrates the inscription 'To the Unknown God' which was used by the apostolic wisdom to point the way to the highest truth."*

We have hinted at only a very small fraction of the works of art and the religious memorials in this wilderness of beauty, into the midst of which this apostolic missionary of the cross of Jesus Christ had come. But he felt his spirit "stirred within him" as he saw the whole city given to idolatry. He visited the synagogue of his Jewish brethren, and made known both to them and the people of the city his mission. The latter were attracted by the novelty of his views, and determined, without much serious intent doubtless, to give him a public hearing. Then he began that wonderful oration worthy of the place and subject, which, as he touched upon the doctrine of the resurrection, appeared so like "foolishness to the Greeks" that they jeeringly interrupted him, and he was not permitted to finish. Only a few were convinced, and there appears to have been no organized body of believers formed there.

Another scarcely less important city, visited by Paul at this time, was Corinth. In its relation to Christianity, it was indeed vastly more important. Even in its political relations, it was, just at this time, much superior to Athens. It was the capital of the Roman province of Achaia, which now embraced nearly the whole of ancient Greece, and was under the government of the proconsul Gallio, a brother of the celebrated philosopher Seneca. This man has become famous and his name proverbial, from his relation to and because of his treatment of the case in which the Jewish opposers of Paul

---

*Conybeare and Howson. "Life and Epistles of St. Paul."

brought the latter before him for trial, and which he somewhat contemptuously but not without good reason dismissed.

The situation of Corinth was about thirty miles west of Athens, on the famous isthmus which connects ancient Peloponnesus,—the modern Morea,—with the main land. It was here that the great contests of racing, wrestling, and other games were celebrated, and to witness which, multitudes assembled from all parts of Greece. To these, as was not unnatural, Paul in his epistle to the Corinthian church refers, and from them draws some of his most effective illustrations. No more eligible spot could have been chosen for a commercial city than this, where a harbor could be found on each side, and ships through different waters approach from opposite directions. Hence the wealth and luxury of the city were very great. It was a place, it is true, of much culture and refinement,—second, perhaps, in this respect, only to Athens. The arts flourished here and the city gave a name to an order of architecture perhaps the most elegant of any age, and which continues to exist and be admired even now. But the abundance of wealth had its not unusual effect of breeding self-indulgence, low worldliness, sensuality and carnal corruption of the most offensive character;—these were among the chief obstacles to the prosperity of the Christian Church there. It forms one of the prominent topics in both of the apostle's letters to the converts, and it is evident that they had suffered severely from these causes.

Hither Paul came from Athens; and here, after having first declared his message to his own countrymen, and by the majority of them being rejected, he turned to the Gentiles, among whom he made many converts. It is a remarkable fact that though Paul always maintained the doctrine that it was the duty of the churches to support those who preached the Word to them, yet in this wealthy city where evidently there were many Christian converts, for some reason, he chose to waive this claim, and supported himself by daily labor as a mechanic, with some assistance received from places previously visited. Fortunately, he had not only, like the children of the Jews generally, learned a trade in his youth, but here at Corinth he had met and formed the acquaintance of two persons of the same trade, whom he joined in industrial labor, and who became also his efficient fellow-workers in spiritual things. For a year and a half, he continued here, pursuing his secular occupation, and at the same time laying the foundations of a powerful Christian church.

Acts xvii; xviii. 1-22. Claudius, Emperor, A. D. 41—54. Events of Lesson, A. D. 52-54.

1. The rest at the house of Lydia, and the departure from Philippi. xvi. 40. The journey to and arrival at Thessalonica. xvii. 1. Give some account of this city. State what Paul and Silas did in Thessalonica, and the result. 2—4.

2. Conduct of the unbelieving Jews. What social element did they make use of, and what did they do? In the accusation made, do you discern any important but unintended truth? 5—7.

3. Action of the city authorities. The apostle's party sent away privately to Berea. Character of the Berean Jews, and their sensible conduct. The consequence. 10—12. What class is particularly mentioned, both here and at Thessalonica, as among believers? 4 and 12.

4. Emissaries from Thessalonica, and their malign influence. Departure of Paul, and arrival at Athens. 13—15. Give some account of this city. Can you mention any of the eminent men among its citizens? What was its religious character?

5. How was Paul affected, as he looked about the city? What did he do? What schools of philosophers did he encounter? What did these schools generally believe? What impression did Paul make on them? 16—18.

6. Paul on Mars' Hill. What was this place? The object of his being there — a judicial trial, or merely a public hearing? What was a noted characteristic of the people? 19—21.

7. The speech. Was the opening remark a compliment or reproof? To what might the phrase "too superstitious" (far better and more literal, "your carefulness in religion,") have reference? Does he propose to introduce any new deity among them? How is this skillfully avoided, without in the least compromising his own faith? Give the line of argument, and the main points. 22—31.

8. At what point was his discourse interrupted? With what disposition did the hearers treat this doctrine of the *resurrection?* Were there any converts? 32—34. Do we ever hear of a church at Athens?

9. Paul at Corinth. Give some account of this city, — its geographical situation, — its political, intellectual, social and moral condition. What new acquaintances does the apostle make, and what glimpses do we get of his condition in life and of the independence of his character? xviii. 1—3.

10. Labors on the Sabbath among the Jews. Arrival of Silas and Timothy, and the putting forth of more vigorous efforts. Rejection of the Gospel by many of the Jews, though some believe. The Gentiles addressed, many of whom are converted. Paul's vision and encouragement. How long was this ministry among the Corinthians? 4—11.

11. Disturbance and persecution by unbelieving Jews. Paul's arrest and accusation before the proconsul. How did Gallio treat the case? The conduct of the Jews provokes the violence of the Greeks. Gallio's indifference. 12—17.

12. Paul's subsequent course. Who accompanied him in his journey, and whither did he go? What was his ultimate destination, and his object? Return to Antioch. 18—22.

VIII.

The Epistles to the Thessalonians.

Though the writing affixed at the end of these epistles names Athens as the place where they were sent, a careful examination of all the data makes it evident that the apostle wrote them sometime during his residence at Corinth. Though in the order of their arrangement they are among the last of Paul's letters to the general churches, yet in the order of time they are regarded by competent critics as the earliest of all his communications of this kind. The First Epistle was doubtless written during the earlier part of Paul's residence in Corinth. Silas and Timothy had been left in charge of the work at Thessalonica when Paul departed to go to Athens, but they were expected to join him soon after. We have already seen that they arrived at Corinth just at the time when Paul was most severely pressed in his contests with the unbelieving Jews. The intelligence which they brought was doubtless the occasion of the first letter. The other epistle seems to have been written something like a year later. Each of the epistles of Paul appears to have some one especial characteristic. That of the letters to the Thessalonians, is the subject of the Second Coming of Christ,—to which some allusion is made in nearly every chapter, though, for the most part, only casually in the First Epistle. This subject had engaged the attention of the members of the church in Thessalonica to an unusual degree, and many of the brethren were morbidly affected by it. Misinterpreting certain expressions in the first letter, some appear to have regarded the event as so near, that they were neglecting their business, and were falling into fanatical ways concerning it. It was, in part, to correct these evils that the Second Epistle was written. But both abound in affectionate counsels and wholesome suggestions to the persecuted and otherwise afflicted band of believers.

FIRST EPISTLE.

Claudius, Emperor, A. D. 41—54. Date of Epistles, A. D. 52 or 53.

1. Where was this Epistle probably written? Who are joined with Paul in the salutation? Can you think of any reason for this? (See Acts xvii. 10; also, I. Thess. iii. 2).

2. What are some of the things concerning this church, for which the apostle gives thanks? i. 2—6. What important position did this church occupy and what had been the effect? 7 and 8. What evidence is there that these Christians had formerly been heathen instead of Jews? 9, 10.

3. Paul reminds them of the circumstances under which he came to them. What were some of these? ii. 2, and Acts xvi. 12—xvii. 14. How is Paul's sincerity evinced? ii. 1—5. What do you gather respecting his dependence upon them for support, and his reasons for this? 6—9. (See, also, II. Thess. iii. 8 and 9; also his action at Corinth).

4. What was Paul's method among them? ii. 10—12. The effect of it? 13. What were some of the conditions which made their state similar to that of Jewish converts? What Jewish opposition does he refer to? What opposition had the Thessalonians encountered? 14—16.

5. What had Paul's longing to know about them, while he was in Athens, resulted in? What was the effect? iii. 1—9. What did he still desire? 10—13.

6. Some instructions on practical morals. Give the principal duties enjoined. iv. 1—12.

7. What statements does he make concerning the second advent and the resurrection? 13—17. What fears appear to have been entertained by the Thessalonians? 13. How does he allay them? 14, etc. Does he give any intimation concerning the exact time? What does he teach? v. 1—3. How

are Christians to be prepared for the great day? 4—10. What other allusions to this event are found in this epistle? (See last verses of Chaps. i., ii. and iii.)

8. Special brief exhortations. Give them in order. 12—22.

SECOND EPISTLE.

9. Where and when was this probably written? What appears to have been the character of the church at Thessalonica at this time? i. 3 and 4. What would be the consequences to persecutors and persecuted?

10. What great event does he describe? 5—10. What erroneous impressions does he correct? ii. 1, 2. What are to be the conditions precedent to this event? 3, 4, 8—10. When are men in danger of being left to believe in lies and delusions, and the destruction consequent? 11, 12. How did these Christians stand in this respect? 13, 14.

11. What are some of the things for which the apostle asks the prayers of these brethren? iii. 1, 2. What confidence is expressed? 3—5. What command does he lay upon them? 6. What right had he to give this order? Was there reason for it? 12, 13.

12. What was the general principle of the relation of the apostles to the churches in respect of support? I. Corinth. ix. 13 and 14. Why did he not claim this right? 7—9. What is the general benediction? 16. What the personal? Why two?

IX.

The Third Missionary Journey. Residence at Ephesus and Journey to Jerusalem.

The eastern coast of the Ægean Sea opposite Achaia was early settled by colonies from Greece. They gave the name of "Asia" to this region, and it gradually came to characterize a considerable extent of territory in that neighborhood. After some time, the name attached itself to the whole peninsula between the Mediterranean and the Euxine, and finally to the whole continent. Thus, what was primarily the designation of only a diminutive region, became the name of the largest of the grand divisions of the earth.

In the time of our history, Asia proper was as yet only the Roman province embracing about one-third of what is known in modern times as Asia Minor. It is interesting to Christian students from the fact that the Gospel was here widely disseminated at an early day, and that here were situated all of the *Seven Churches* to which special revelations were made through St. John, — the last of the prophets, the mysterious seer of the new dispensation.

Of this Roman province, Ephesus was the capital; and as this was for a longer period than perhaps any other the residence of Paul, and at a later period for some years the home of John, and as it was a most influential center from which the Gospel was propagated, it is proper that we have some brief account of it. Its situation was most favorable for commerce both by sea and by land. It consequently became a large, populous and very wealthy city, long before the Christian Era. In the time of Paul, it was probably as flourishing as at any previous period, and its influence was felt far and near. It had many distinguished and costly buildings. Prominent among these, was the theater,—the ruins of which are with difficulty traced, but which is doubtless the same in which the Ephesian populace assembled in the excitement caused by the outcry of Demetrius and his fellow-silversmiths against Paul, whose successful preaching of Christ was likely to interfere with their trade in the shrines of the chief deity of their city. But the most famous of its edifices, was that of the Temple of Diana, the tutelary goddess of the Ephesians. This was so magnificent and costly as to be accounted one of the seven wonders of the world. It was several times rebuilt, each time doubtless with increased splendor. The edifice before that of the time of which we are now speaking, had been destroyed by fire on the very night of the birth of Alexander the Great, being set on fire by a certain Erostratus who confessed that he had no other motive but to immortalize his name. Such immortality as it is he seems to have achieved.

The new temple was 220 years in building, and was the largest of all the Greek temples, being about four times the size of the Parthenon at Athens. "It was magnificently decorated with sculptures by Praxiteles, and a great painting by Appelles. The statue of Diana was of ivory, furnished with exquisitely wrought golden ornaments." A considerable part of the trade of the city was concerned with the manufacture and sale of silver miniature images or models of the statue of the idol. Hence the purely secular motive of Demetrius and his fellow-tradesmen is evident. It is also evident that Paul's preaching had been very successful, when such numbers were converted from idolatry as to endanger the business of producing these shrines of the goddess.

Acts xviii. 23—26; xix.; xx.   Nero, Emperor, A. D. 54—68.   Events of Lesson, A. D. 55—57.

1. Beginning of the Third Missionary Journey. Tour of Galatia and Phrygia. xviii. 23. Where were these regions?

2. Apollos at Ephesus. What was his character and his religious relations? What did he need in order to profitable preaching? How was this supplied? 24—26.

3. Whither did he go after this? How was he introduced to the brethren there, and what was the effect of his ministry among them? 27, 28. Do we find any incidental confirmation of Apollos' ministry at Corinth, in Paul's writings? I. Cor. iii. 4—6 and 22.

4. Paul again at Ephesus. What singular facts are here mentioned? xix. 1—3. How do you connect it with xviii. 24, 25. Paul's instruction of these disciples and the result. 4—7.

5. How long did Paul continue to present the Gospel in the Jewish synagogue? 8. What was the consequence of his preaching to his countrymen, and what did he do on this account? 9. How long did he continue to preach in this Gentile locality, and with what success? What is meant by "Asia" here? What powerful manifestations accompanied his preaching? 11, 12.

6. Attempted imitations of Paul's miraculous power, and the result. 13—16. Effect upon the people. 17.

7. Evidences of religious reformation in the converts. 18—20. The value of the magical books destroyed? (A silver piece or *denarius* was worth about fifteen cents, our money). What did this indicate? 20.

8. Paul's purpose. What preparation did he make towards carrying it out? 21, 22. Disturbance excited by Demetrius. What was the real motive? What does it indicate as to the success of Christianity in Ephesus? What was the most notable edifice in Ephesus? Can you give any account of it? Relate any remarkable incident connected with its history. 23—27.

9. The result of the harangue of Demetrius? Effect on the disciples? Meeting in the theater, and Paul's bold venture kindly prevented. The confusion and uproar, and the futile attempt of Alexander to speak. What possible reference is made to this person, in Paul's writings? (See II. Tim. iv. 14, 15). Why would not the multitude hear him? 28—34. Cry and uproar. Appeal of the magistrate. His argument and advice. 35—41.

10. Paul's departure to Macedonia. What were some of the places he would be likely to visit there? Arrival in Greece. What city would he probably make his headquarters there, and how long did he stay? What occurred to change his mind as to his journey to Syria? xx. 1—3.

11. Companions of his journey. 4. What reason have we to suppose that Luke was of this party? 5. Philippi to Troas, and conference with the disciples at Troas. Protracted address, and one of the consequences. The restoration. Further conference and departure. 6—12.

12. Further incidents of the journey. Arrival at Miletus. 13—15. Where was Miletus? In the neighborhood of what important city? Paul's haste and the reason of it? 16. What took place at Miletus? Give the main points of Paul's address. 17—35. What expectation does he utter concerning himself? 22—25. What warning does he give the Ephesian brethren? 29, 30. What elements of character are manifest in this address? 19, 20, 24, 27, 33—35. Effect on the Ephesian disciples? 36—38.

X.

The First Epistle to the Corinthians.

Within the period covered by the previous study, at least four of Paul's Epistles to particular churches appear to have been written; viz., the two Epistles to the Corinthians, the one to the Galatians, and the one to the Romans.

The first to the Corinthians was probably written during the third year of the apostle's residence at Ephesus, about A. D. 56 or 57. There are some allusions in the epistles to a brief visit to Corinth during the ministry at Ephesus, but there is no record of it in the narrative by Luke. He had heard reports of certain disorders and irregularities in the church, and probably his visit was intended to rectify them. These evils continuing, there are indications that he wrote them a letter which is not now extant. In this letter he had evidently written (for one thing) requiring them to separate themselves from certain impure and profligate persons of their number. This they failed to understand fully, and wrote for an explanation. In the letter now known as the "First Epistle to the Corinthians," he states his meaning more explicitly. (See v. 9—13.)

Among the evils which had sprung up in the Corinthian Church, was, first and foremost, that sensual immorality which was characteristic of the city, and which it was difficult to overcome among the Gentile converts. Upon this, Paul was especially severe, and with reference to it exercised his apostolic authority to its utmost extent. Then closely connected perhaps with this, was a kind of Antinomianism—a sentiment that trust in Christ was sufficient to save the soul; and that moral conduct was not essential, omitting the important fact that faith in Christ implies obedience to him. There were also divisions into parties. Four of these are referred to as the parties "of Apollos," "of Paul," "of Peter," and, singularly, "of Christ." Neither of the apostles were leaders of these parties, or lent the least countenance to them. Probably there was some prejudice against Paul on the part of the more worldly and profligate members, on account of his thoroughness of discipline. There would also be an ultra Jewish party, which perhaps was substantially one with those who are called the party of Cephas, who would be prejudiced against Paul on account of his catholic disposition towards the Gentile converts and his opposition to the Jewish exclusiveness. Then, too, very likely, Apollos, who appears to have been a man of great rhetorical powers and perhaps learned in Greek philosophy, may have been a favorite with certain of the philosophizing Greeks, and he may thus have unwittingly aided in building up a sentiment against Paul. Of the party "of Christ" it is difficult to determine the basis. Probably this was a self-assumed title, like that of the Jesuits or "Society of Jesus" in modern times.

We get in both these epistles, and especially in the first, many historical intimations, and much light is thrown on the condition of the early Church.

Analysis of the Epistle. I. Salutation and Introduction. i. 1—9. II. Exhortations relative to their dissensions. i. 10—iv. 21. III. Concerning the person guilty of incest; the purity of marriage; and warnings against sensuality. v.—vii. IV. Concerning the eating of things offered to idols; law and liberty in respect to Christian conduct. viii.—x. V. Certain ecclesiastical regulations, orderly action in the congregations, and the exercise of right dispositions. xi.—xiv. VI. Concerning the Resurrection. xv. VII. Concerning collections for the poor of other churches; miscellaneous exhortations; salutations, etc. xvi.

Chapters i.; ii.; iii.; iv.   Nero, Emperor, A. D. 54—68.   Date of Epistle, A. D. 56 or 57.

1. When and where was this letter probably written? What reason have we for supposing that a previous letter not now extant had been written? v. 9. A prominent object of that letter?

2. What were some of the evils which had sprung up in the Church at

Corinth? What parties had been formed, and under what names? i. 12. What were some of the causes of opposition to Paul?

3. Give the chief topical divisions of the Epistle.

4. How does Paul describe the people to whom he writes. i. 2. For what particular things does he give thanks? 4—7. Is this description of the Corinthian Church consistent with some characteristics set forth in this epistle?

5. How does the apostle meet the case of their dissensions and partisan divisions? 13—17. What appears from this to have been Paul's chief work?

6. What do we learn concerning the philosophy and wisdom of this world as compared with the simplicity of the Gospel? 18—21. What did the Jews demand, and what the Greeks, and what did the apostle present in place of these? 22—25.

7. From what classes have the great majority of Christ's followers usually come? 26—29. Lady Huntington, a pious woman of the nobility of England, thanked God for one letter in this description. What was it? 26. What does Christ become to those who trust in him? 30.

8. The fundamental principle and purpose of Paul's ministry among them? ii. 1—3. The effect of it? 4. How does he describe the greatness and grandeur of what is implied in spiritual wisdom and wealth? 7—9. How revealed and discerned? 10—16.

9. What condition of the Corinthian brethren prevented their spiritual discernment? iii. 1 and 2. What evil grew out of this condition? 3, 4. How does the apostle treat these divisions? 5—10. What is the sole basis and foundation of all Christian character and Christian work? 11—13. What is the grand final exhortation, and the basis of it? 21—23.

10. What position do ministers hold in relation to the sacred things of religion? iv. 1. To whom are they accountable? 2—4. What rule is laid down concerning criticism and fault-finding? 5. What tendency does Paul here wish to correct? 6.

11. What contrast is made between those who set themselves up as philosophizing Christians, and the apostle? 7—13. Are the differences among men always and altogether matters of praise or blame? 7. Are there any instances in Paul's experience verifying the description in 11—13?

12. What had been said about Paul's visit by those opposed to him? 18. How does he meet it and how assert his authority? 19—21.

XI.

Continuation of the First Epistle to the Corinthians.

Chapters v.; vi.; vii.; viii.; ix.; x.

1. What is the subject of the Third Division of the book? What was the moral reputation of the city of Corinth? How did the evils implied affect the Christian community?

2. What rebuke does the apostle administer, because a member had been allowed to marry his step-mother? What does he say of the moral

flagrancy of this act? What had the church done in regard to it, and what should have been done? What direction does Paul give? Had he authority to thus order? v. 1—5.

3. What further direction is given, and for what reason? 6—8. What is meant by the "old leaven?" What is the lesson taught concerning our associations in the world and in the Church? 9—11.

4. What practice respecting the settlement of controversies among Christians, and on what grounds? vi. 1—7. What practices does he rebuke? 8—10. Were these vices probably generally prevalent among Christians? 11. What rule is laid down concerning the use of the body? 12, 19, 20.

5. Was there any reason why those who were already married should separate and families be broken up? vii. 10, 11. The rule concerning the Christians who had unbelieving wives or husbands? 12—17.

6. What was there in the condition of Christians, and especially of Christian ministers, in those times, in some respects unfavorable to marriage? What tendency was possible in the married life, which was not as likely to be in the unmarried? 26—34.

7. What is the main subject of the *Fourth Division* of the epistle? Was the flesh of an animal that had been offered in sacrifice to an idol any worse on that account? viii. 8. Was it not possible nevertheless that in the estimation of some, the eating of such flesh might sanction idolatry? 7. What damage may be done by thus using one's liberty, even where it is not against one's own conscience, and what rule is laid down? 9—13.

8. What were some of the things which Paul and other apostles were at liberty to do, but from which, for the sake of others, they abstained? ix. 1—13. The reasons for this? 14—23. What figure does he use here, and why would it be familiar to the people of Corinth? 24—27.

9. What examples of warning are given to the Corinthian Christians? x. 1—11. What privileges and advantages did God's ancient people enjoy? What sins did they commit, and what punishments were consequent? Can you find in the Old Testament the instances referred to? Is any temptation to sin irresistible? 12, 13.

10. How were the Corinthian brethren to regard idolatry? 14—22. Was it a sufficient argument in favor of indifference to say "the idol is nothing," and why? 20, 21. What final rule is laid down respecting the eating of things offered to idols? What are some points of the argument? 23—33.

XII.

First Epistle to the Corinthians—continued.

Chapters xi.; xii.; xiii.; xiv.; xv.; xvi.

1. What is the subject of the *Fifth Division?* What are some of the directions concerning the conduct of women in religious assemblies? xi. 2—16. Was there any condition of the times and the places which rendered these directions more applicable than to modern society?

2. What great religious ordinance does the writer next speak of? 17—34.

What abuses had crept into this solemn service? What scene does he describe? 23—25. The object of this ordinance? 26. What dreadful crime is committed by participating unworthily in this? 27, 29. What difference is there between partaking *unworthily* and being *unworthy to partake.*

3. What is said concerning the diversity of ability among men and among Christians? xii. 1—10. Is this opposed to unity? Wherein does the latter consist? 11, 13. How is it illustrated? 12, 14—26. The application? 27—31.

4. What is the subject of Chapter xiii.? How does the writer compare it with other virtues? 1—3. How many distinct characteristics does he give of charity or love? 4—8. How does it differ from certain special gifts or abilities? 8—12. In what respect is it greater than *faith* and *hope*? 13.

5. To what spiritual *gift* does the apostle give the pre-eminence? xiv. 1. To what modern vocation was this similar or equivalent? (See i. 17, 21, 23, etc.) What special gift does he speak of at length, and what restrictions does he lay upon it? 2—28. What are some of these regulations? What directions concerning prophesying, preaching or exhortation? 29—33. What directions concerning the speaking of women? 34, 35. Is this direction of universal and perpetual application, or only designed for that time and place? The final, comprehensive charge? 40.

6. What heresy had been disseminated by certain persons at Corinth as well as elsewhere? xv. 12. What proofs of Christ's resurrection were common to the preaching of all the apostles? 3—7. What additional evidence did Paul have? 8.

7. The argument from Christ's resurrection to that of men generally? 13—23. What consequences would come to Christianity and Christians if this doctrine were false? 17, 19, 30—32. What caviling question was sometimes asked? 35. What relation is the resurrected body to have to the present body? 36—38, 42—50.

8. What general and awful event is portrayed? 51, 52. The nature of the change? 53, 54. The triumphant conclusion? 55—58.

9. What directions concerning benevolent collections are given? xvi. 2. For what purpose were these taken, and what was to be done with them? 3, 4. What is indicated concerning his future movements? 5—9. Whom will he send in the meantime? 10.

10. Of what special friends does the apostle make particular mention? 15—18. The final salutation and benediction? 21—24.

XIII.

The Second Epistle to the Corinthians.

After writing the First Epistle to the Corinthians, Paul probably remained only a few months at Ephesus. It was not long after, that the riot and tumult excited by Demetrius took place. He had intended, as we have seen in the closing part of the First Epistle, very soon to make a journey through

Macedonia, visiting the churches there, and to come to Corinth. Whether his departure was hastened by the tumult referred to, is not known, though probably he did not leave much earlier than he had intended. We find in the Epistles many incidents alluded to, of which we have no other account. It appears that he spent some time at Troas, waiting for the return of Titus, who had been sent on an embassy to Corinth, and who for some reason was long in coming. But the apostle found a large opening for the exercise of his calling in that neighborhood, and appears to have preached very effectually and to have gathered a good company, and perhaps several companies, of believers.

We learn further by the general tone of this epistle as well as by specific allusions, that Paul was, during the whole interval and up to the time of his writing this letter, suffering severe afflictions. These appear to have been partly of the nature of physical disease; and partly in consequence of the state of the churches, and especially that of Corinth, in which much mischief was being wrought, both in opposition to Paul's authority, and through this and other means by the demoralization of brethren and the damage to the cause generally. There was the "thorn in the flesh;" "without were fightings, within were fears." After his arrival at Philippi, Titus' long deferred coming took place. He brought him the good news that the apostle's directions had been obeyed, and the most prominent offender in the church had been brought to trial, and excluded for his immorality. But there were other items of intelligence less encouraging, to the effect that false disciples had come to Corinth, and had stirred up among the very members of the church an opposition to Paul, thus aggravating the divisions previously mentioned. This opposition appears to have been of a bitter and malignant kind, and was both unjust and cruel. This faction, though a minority doubtless of the church, appears to have been led by a certain person or persons bearing "letters of commendation" from Judea, who questioned Paul's authority as an apostle, and otherwise calumniated him, to the detriment of the cause. This was an additional grief to Paul. But, though cast down by all these things, yet we find him rejoicing in the midst of his distresses. The present letter was written, in part, to meet these calumnies, and to induce in the Corinthians a better mind. It was probably written within a year after the sending of the first epistle.

The following are the prominent divisions of the epistle:

I. The apostle's account of the character of his spiritual labors, accompanied with notices of his affectionate feeling towards his converts. i.—vii.

II. Directions about the collections for the poor Christians in Judea. viii.—ix.

III. A defense of his own apostolical character against those who were impeaching him in this respect. x.—xiii.

Chapters i.; ii.; iii.; iv.; v.

1. Where was Paul when the former letter to the Corinthians was written? What took place between the writing of the First and Second Epistles? How long after the former was the latter written? Where was Paul when he wrote it?

THE PROPAGATION OF THE GOSPEL.   153

2. What experiences had he been subject to, in the interval? (See Introduction; also i. 8; ii. 12, 13; vii. 5). What effect did the return of Titus and his report have? Was there any unfavorable intelligence mixed with the favorable? What was the character of the opposition to Paul in the church?

3. Give the prominent divisions of the book. Are these very clearly defined?

4. With what assertion concerning Paul's apostleship does the epistle open? i. 1. Was there any special occasion for this?

5. What may we infer from the apostle's language concerning his state of mind? 4, 6, 9. What compensation did he find? 3, 4, 5, 10, 12.

6. What purpose had Paul originally formed concerning a visit to them? 15, 16. Why had he changed his mind? 23. Was the state of things in Corinth at the time of writing his former epistle a good reason why he should wait to see the effect of that appeal? ii. 1—4. Of what had some accused him when he failed to come, and how does he vindicate himself? i. 17—23.

7. What had evidently been the consequence of the discipline of the offending member, and what does Paul further counsel concerning his treatment? ii. 5—11.

8. What marked change in Paul's feelings is manifest on his going from Asia to Macedonia? 12—14. What had transpired to produce this effect? vii. 5, 6, 13. Different effects of the Gospel on believers and unbelievers? ii. 15, 16.

9. How does he compare his authority and standing among them with one who had come with "letters of commendation" and was endeavoring to disparage Paul? iii. 1—3. Is there any conceit or self-sufficiency in this? 4—7.

10. How does he compare the old with the new dispensation, and what apt illustration does he use? 8—17. What is the historical incident to which he refers? What grand sentiment is here uttered, and what is its import? 18.

11. How does he further vindicate himself and his cause? iv. 1—7. What is the Christian preacher's business? 5, 6.

12. What antithesis of experience does he present? 8—16. What great hopes buoy him up, and more than compensate his distresses? 10, 14, 17, 18.

13. What glorious expectation does he cherish? v. 1—4. The doctrine of the general judgment? 10. The great motive of the apostle's preaching? 11—13.

14. What radical change of purpose is implied in and essential to conversion or regeneration? 14—17. Paul's theory of the atonement, and his office as a minister? 18—21. What is implied concerning the costliness of this redemption? Can you find other expressions in the Bible implying this?

XIV.

The Conclusion of the Second Epistle to the Corinthians.

Chapters vi.; vii.; viii.; ix.; x.; xi.; xii.; xiii.

1. The costliness of the divine offering for man's redemption has been spoken of; does it also involve any sacrifice on the human side? What was

involved in the publishing of it by the apostles and early Christians? vi. 1—9. Were there any, even temporal, compensations? 9, 10.

2. In view of all this, what affectionate injunction does the apostle lay upon the members of the Church? 11—18. How should Christians live in relation to those who are not Christians? Was it more necessary then than now?

3. What general exhortation of high import does the writer base on this foundation? vii. 1. What personal entreaty is made, and what allusion to his relation to them? 2—4. How had his former letter affected them? Was the grief occasioned by it salutary? 8—11. How did this react on Paul? 12—16.

4. The subject of the Second Division of the Epistle? viii., ix. Meaning of "we do you to wit?" viii. 1. What example of liberality is cited, and the character of it? 1—5. The object of these contributions? (I. Cor. xvi. 3.) What exhortation to the Corinthian brethren, under the stimulus of this example? 6—8. What grand example of divine offering? 9.

5. What further advice is given? 10—15. What provision had been made for collecting and forwarding this offering? 16—24. What had Paul said then concerning the Corinthian liberality, and what did he fear on account of it? What precautions did he take? ix. 1—5.

6. What does he show as to effect of generous charities? What quotations are made? 6—15.

7. The Third Division of the epistle? x., xiii. What insinuations had some of Paul's enemies made as to his personal appearance and address? x. 1, 10. How does he defend himself from the carnal motives imputed to him? 2—7. How does he assert his authority? 8, 9, 11. What was Paul's assertion concerning his work as a pioneer? And what his conclusion concerning self-glorying and self-commendation? 12—18.

8. Some one or more had come to Corinth endeavoring to alienate the converts from Paul, and bringing in new religious tests. How does Paul speak of them? xi. 1—4. How does he assert himself? (a) as to his apostleship? (b) his competence? (c) his self-denying interest for them? 5—8.

9. For what reason did he decline to receive support from them while their minister? 9—12. Were the opponents of Paul probably honest and honorable men, or were they insincere? 13—15.

10. They had boasted of their Judaism. What could Paul say on that point? 18, 22. What concerning his devotion to Christ? 23—33. Was this a vain boast, or was it a necessary reminder?

11. What other evidence of his apostleship and special divine commission does he give? xii. 1—6. What humiliation was given, lest he should unduly exult in the extraordinary honor bestowed? 7. What lesson do we learn concerning Paul's prayer and the effect of it concerning his affliction? 8—10.

12. How does he again state his disinterestedness in their behalf? 12—21.

13. What does he give them to understand as to the exercise of his authority in matters of discipline, when he shall come to them again? xiii. 1, 2. What mingling of weakness and power does he point out in the gospel, and how does he apply the principle to himself? 3, 4. What final exhortations does he offer? 5—14.

XV.

The Epistle to the Galatians.

After writing the Second Epistle to the Corinthians, Paul tarried for some time longer in Macedonia. But not wishing to hasten his journey to Corinth in the then condition of the church there, he appears to have spent some time in the regions north of Greece, visiting new fields, and establishing churches where none had been founded before. It is likely that it was at this time that he extended his apostolic labors "around about unto Illyricum," according to the allusion in Romans xv. 19. We have no account of this in the history contained in the book of the Acts; but we are to remember that this does not profess to give a complete history, and that there are many labors and experiences of Paul alluded to in his epistles, to which there is no reference in the narrative of Luke.

How long he continued in this region we do not know, but evidently not a very long time. When matters were in a suitable state, he made his contemplated visit to Corinth, where he remained about three months. It was during this time that, according to some of the best authorities, the Epistle to the Galatians was written. There are others who place it earlier, namely, before his departure from Ephesus; and some, though on quite insufficient grounds, place it still earlier, making it the first of his epistles to the churches.

Galatia was a region in the central part of Asia Minor. It was a rough, mountainous region, and contained no large towns or cities. It was inhabited by a simple, hardy race of men, who had come to this territory from the northern part of Greece, but whose ancestors had emigrated some ages previously from Germany. As the name implies, they were evidently of the Gallic stock, and related to the Gauls and Celts of western Europe, whom, also, they resembled in many respects both in character and in certain elements of their language.

It was among the scattered villages and hamlets of this region that Paul had gone, preaching the gospel, during his second missionary journey. We have no details of this work, and no account of the particular churches gathered, except what is implied in this epistle. The epistle itself differs from all others of Paul's epistles to the churches, in that it is addressed not to a particular church, but to "the churches"—a group of churches—in Galatia.

The occasion of the communication appears to have been this: After Paul had left this people, certain of the Judaizing teachers came among them, endeavoring to modify the doctrine which Paul uniformly proclaimed to the Gentile converts concerning their relation to the Mosaic dispensation. This was, substantially, that it was unnecessary for them to obey the cermonial law. This had been only preparatory to the coming of Christ, and was not intended by itself to be a means of salvation; and that to trust in it after the coming of Christ, to lead to whom was its sole use, was to make Christ of no avail. While he did not object to the present observance of these ceremonies by the Jews who had been brought up in them, and while he himself observed them, he evidently anticipated the time when they would be regarded as of no account by both Jews and Gentiles.

But the more rigid of the Jewish converts, aided doubtless by emissaries from abroad, antagonized Paul in this respect, and, as we have seen, formed a party hostile to him. They went so far as to cherish a prejudice against him, and to belittle his authority and cast suspicion upon his apostleship; and some of the more bitter partisans, to malign his character. We have had an account of the opposition at Corinth, which was partly incited by this party. In Galatia, the emissaries of this sect had scattered the seeds of doubt and dissension among a warm-hearted, simple-minded and impulsive people. Paul evidently was very tenderly attached to them, and he was overwhelmed with distress at the mischief that had been wrought among them. This letter was written to remonstrate with them, and to endeavor to correct their false notions. It is energetic, direct and unsparing, but at the same time tenderly affectionate. He finds it necessary, not only to correct the views which had been imposed upon them, but also to vindicate himself from the aspersions cast upon his office and teaching.

Nero, Emperor, A. D. 54—68. Date of Epistle, A. D. 56 or 57.

1. What was the situation of Galatia, and the origin and character of the Galatians? How does this epistle differ from others in its address? i. 2. Where do we find the account of Paul's first visit to this region?

2. What was the particular occasion of this communication? Have we seen any hostility to Paul of similar character elsewhere? (Introduction to Epistles to Corinthians). What were some of the intimations concerning Paul? What allusions to this in the epistle? i. 7; ii. 4; iii. 1; iv. 17; vi. 12, 13.

3. What feeling was excited against the apostle? How does he vindicate his apostleship? i. 1; ii. 12. What narrative does he give in support of this? 13—24. What particular event subsequent to his conversion does he give, not elsewhere found? 17.

4. What confirmation of his divine call did the church at Jerusalem and the apostles give him? ii. 1—10. Had there been any opposition to him at this time? 3, 4. What influence had these opponents afterwards on Peter at Antioch, and what was the effect on the relations of the two apostles? 11—14. Is it probable that there was any permanent estrangement? II. Peter iii. 15.

5. What evidences have we of the warm-heartedness of the Galatians, and the affectionate relations existing between Paul and them? iv. 13, 14, 15, 19, 20. Was it their personal estrangement that pained him, or something else? i. 6, 8; iii. 1.

6. What was the position taken by Paul concerning the relations of converted Gentiles to the Jewish or Mosaic law? What the position taken by his opponents? (See introduction). What is the main question discussed in chapters iii. and iv.? Under the Jewish dispensation, what was deemed necessary to salvation? Under the Christian, what? iii. 2.

7. What is meant here by "the Law?" Could the law really save any one? Was Abraham, or any of the good men anterior to him, considered righteous because of their relation to the law? Why? iii. 6, 15—17. Is the

"faith" that saves, simply believing the truth about a person? Does it imply any purpose and determination; and if so, what?

8. What, then, was the design of the law? 23, 24, 25. How did a godly man under the law differ from one under faith? iv. 1, 3—7.

9. What allegorical illustration of his doctrine does he give? 21—31. What is the condition of the man of faith as distinguished from the man under the law? v. 1. What argument is made concerning the uselessness of the sacrifice and atonement of Christ, if men could be saved by obedience to the law? 2—4.

10. What is the great, essential thing in religion? 6; vi. 15. What caution is given concerning the use of liberty? 13. What is the one great key-word of the religion of Christ? 14. Is it good doctrine that, if we have the right belief, the way we live is of little consequence? If men do not discipline their carnal impulses, what effects will ensue? 19—21. What will the discipline of a soul really trusting in Christ, lead to? 22—24. Do you notice the difference in the number of virtues and that of the vices?

11. What is the general rule for our treatment of one another? 26. What, in case of a brother's fault? vi. 1. What particular rules of mutual spiritual relationship? 2—6, 10. What important doctrine as well of practical philosophy as of spiritual and moral conduct? 7, 8.

XVI.
The Epistle to the Romans.

Paul's three months' visit to Corinth must have been a time of much labor and many cares. It was not a small undertaking to restore order and harmony among the factions which were injuring the church, and to exercise the needful discipline upon the members guilty of immorality. There were also parties, as we have seen, which were bitterly antagonistic to Paul, and that, too, because of his condemnation of the false doctrines which they were disseminating to the hurt of the cause. Two of these were in diametrical opposition to each other, and had no band of unity except hostility to the apostle. One of these was the Judaizing party, who insisted that all Christians were bound to obey the *whole ceremonial law*. The other was the Antinomian party, who held that even the observance of the *moral law* was not implied in faith in Christ, and that the latter liberated the believer from all moral obligation. Doubtless, out of this teaching had come much of the immorality which called for the exercise of apostolic authority. Though there is no detailed account of Paul's action during this visit, there is good reason to believe that he excommunicated the immoral members, that he gave proofs through the miracles he was permitted to work, of his apostleship which had been impeached, that his maligners were discomfited and rendered powerless, and that order and harmony were restored.

This work, the attention to the collection for the indigent Christians in Judea, visits to the churches in the vicinity and the epistle to the Galatians, would occupy his time. The letter to the Romans was probably written just before his departure on the journey to Jerusalem. There is this peculiarity about this epistle, that it was written to a church he had never visited. Still as an important church, occupying a position in the metropolis of the civilized world, a place to and from which there would be many comers and goers of all classes, and especially, as we see from the great number of salutations at the close of the epistle, a church in which Paul must have had many personal acquaintances, he felt desirous to communicate with them.

Concerning the establishment of Christianity in Rome, we have no certain account. The Roman Catholics claim that it was founded by Peter, but there is no reliable proof of this, and it is even disputed by some, that Peter ever was at Rome. Yet it is easy to see that in the constant and abundant communication of Rome with all parts of the vast empire of which it was the capital, some Christians would inevitably find their way thither. We read that among the multitude present on the day of Pentecost, "strangers of Rome" are mentioned. It is probable that Jewish Christians here as well as elsewhere formed the nucleus of the church, but we judge that there was a large proportion of Gentiles in the body of believers. There do not appear to have been any such antagonisms between the two elements here as at Corinth and in some other places, and the impression we get from this epistle is of a united, devoted and energetic church, having in it many men and women of ability and some distinction.

The epistle, while in many respects, and especially in the particular subjects discussed, similar to that to the Galatians written not long before, differs from it in this respect, that the latter was designed to correct erroneous views and perversions of doctrine, and was therefore highly polemical; this has no such object to accomplish, and therefore, while being thoroughly doctrinal, is also almost purely didactic. It is a profound and masterly setting forth of the fundamental doctrine of salvation by faith in Jesus Christ. One leading part of this is the *relations of the Law to the Gospel*, while the preliminary showing of the universal sinfulness, the insufficiency of ceremonial and moral observance to remedy this, the method of righteousness by faith, the existence of which had been indicated in the case of Abraham, and through him had become the inheritance not of the Jews only but also of the Gentiles, with the bearings of this doctrine on all the interests of humanity, with practical and hortatory directions, complete this masterly treatise.

Chapters i.; ii.; iii.; iv.; v.; vi.   Nero, Emperor, A. D. 54—68.   Date of Epistle, A. D. 57 or 58.

1. Where was Paul when the epistle was written? What matters occupied his attention mainly while there? What trials did he have at this time?

2. What importance did the church at Rome have? What was there peculiar about Paul's writing to them? How is it supposed that Christianity was first introduced into Rome? Of whom was the church composed? The character of the church?

3. To what other epistle is this similar? How does it differ from that? What is the main subject? What is one of the principal topics? What are some of the subjects preliminary and subsidiary to this?

4. To what authority does the apostle appeal in proof of the truth of

the Gospel? 1, 2. To what fact in relation to Christ, here and elsewhere, is reference made as certifying to his divine character and mission? 4.

5. What commendation of the church at Rome is made? 8. The feeling of Paul towards them? 9—11.

6. What does he announce and make the grand, paramount subject of his letter? 16, 17.

7. Are the heathen who have not the Bible wholly excusable on that account? 18—20. By refusing to obey the light they had, what followed? 21—25. What dark picture does the writer draw of the heathen world? 26—32.

8. If the Gentiles who had no direct revelation were to be condemned, how was it with the Jews? ii. 1, 3, 5. If the latter with all their light still sinned, how would their condemnation compare with that of the former? What is the general doctrine comprehending both those who have and those who have not a revelation? 12, 13—15.

9. What is the teaching concerning unapplied knowledge? 17—24. Would an outward observance of the ceremonial law among the Jews render them really the people of God? 25—29. How does this apply to Christians?

10. What advantage had the Jews over the Gentiles? iii. 1—4. Did this necessarily save them? 5—9. What terrible indictment does the apostle bring against the human race as a whole? 10—20.

11. If then men are not saved by the law, what is the remedy? 21—26. Is "the righteousness of God" something to be substituted for our righteousness, or is it a method by which we are to be made righteous? What is the conclusion, then, concerning the relations of the Jews and Gentiles as regards the Gospel dispensation? 27—31.

12. What example does the apostle cite to prove that this very idea of justification by faith is anterior to the giving of the law? iv. 1—3, 9, 10, etc. Were the Jews alone, then, the spiritual heirs of Abraham, and to whom did God's covenant with him pertain? 11—17.

13. Why could there be no room for grace if men were to be saved by keeping the law? 4. How, then, are men saved? 5—8, 24, 25. Is this faith that saves, a belief in certain facts, or doctrines, or creeds, or even concerning the person and character of Christ? If it be a disposition of heart, what is the disposition and how is it related to the divine law?

14. What is the plan and method by which God rescues men from the condition in which the law leaves them? v. 6—11. What is the process? 1, 2. The effect? 3—5.

15. What contrast is drawn between Adam and Christ? 12—19. Does the redemption by Christ simply cancel sin, or does it avail something vastly more? 20, 21.

16. Does the fact that we have exercised faith and are under grace, render it of no consequence whether we sin or not? vi. 1—14. (See also topic 13 in this lesson, last question). Can one be under grace who does not purpose to renounce sin? If we are in the practice of any sin or desire to commit it, what is doubtless our condition?

17. What is the condition of him who yields to the service of sin? 16. The effect of faith and the character of Christ's service? 17, 18, 20, 21—23. What illustration is given of a converted man's relation to the law? vii. 1—6.

XVII.

Continuation of the Epistle to the Romans.

Chapters vii.; viii.; ix.; x.; xi.

1. What inference might possibly be drawn as to the character of *the law* from some of Paul's previous statements? vii. 7 How does Paul reply to such intimations? 7—13. Is the evil of a wrong course of conduct really any less because not known to be wrong? What is the office and effect of the moral law? 7, 11, 13. Is the law a creator or a revealer of sin? The character of the law and of the violator of the law? 12, 14.

2. What is the great conflict in the unsanctified soul in the presence of the divine law? 15—24. What is the only salutary outcome? 25. What are opposite effects of the carnal and spiritual victory? viii. 4, 6.

3. The first effect of the subordination of the carnal to the spiritual? 1. The second effect? 2. Can one be a Christian without the new spiritual life? 8, 9. What is the grand condition of those in whom the spiritual life has thoroughly subdued the carnal? 14—18. What is said concerning the sympathy even of the inanimate creation in the degradation and also in the redemption of man? 19—23.

4. What other and still richer advantages are implied in this life of the spirit? 26, 28, 31, 32. What is said of the predetermination of God concerning this salvation? 29—31. What exulting confidence does the apostle express? 35—39.

5. What intensity of desire does he exhibit in behalf of his own people? ix. 1—3. What exalted conditions were theirs? 4, 5. Were they all rejected?

6. Are the temporal conditions of men and nations altogether of their own appoinment, or of God's purpose? 7—24. Does God harden men's hearts that they may sin, or because they sin? Does he reject and elect men arbitrarily and capriciously, or does he elect those who believe and reject those who do not?

6. Why are the Gentiles accepted, while many of the Jews are rejected? Were the latter all rejected? 25—30. Why were any rejected? 31—33; x. 1—5.

7. What is the one condition of salvation, both for Jew and Gentile? 6—13. Is faith mere *belief?* What is necessary in order that men may believe? 14—21. How does this bear on missionary work?

8. What hopes does the writer cherish concerning the Jewish people? xi. 1, 2. What instance is cited of apparently universal apostasy, when there were still some faithful? 2—4. Were all the Jews shut out from the new covenant? 5. How were they saved, and why were the others lost? 6—10.

9. What does he predict concerning the future of the Jews, and their relation to the Church, and the Gentiles? 23—32. What exultation does the apostle utter concerning this? 33—36.

XVIII.

Conclusion of the Epistle to the Romans.

Chapters xii.; xiii.; xiv.; xv.; xvi.

1. Having completed his doctrinal statement, what is the character of the following chapter? What is the personal duty of each one? xii. 1, 2. In their relations as members of the spiritual body, what important fact is to be kept in mind? 3—8.

2. What dispositions are to be cherished? 9, 10. What particular virtues are enjoined? 11—16. Against what evil impulses are they advised? 17—21.

3. Relations of Christians to government? xiii. 1—7. Does this appear as though Christians in early times formed a community antagonistic to the civil power, as has sometimes been charged?

4. What is the teaching of the next passage? 8—10. Is it enough that we keep the bare letter of the commandments? What is the spirit and essence of them?

5. What exhortation concerning the redemption and economy of time; and what as to sobriety and virtue? 11—13. The grand summing up? 14. What is the full meaning of this?

6. What is the direction concerning persons possibly over-scrupulous concerning unessential observances? xiv. 1—6. What grand general principle is always to be remembered? 7, 8. On what ground is this brotherly consideration based? 9—13.

7. What good rule of charitable action is laid down? 14, 15. How is this further enforced? 16—23. What disposition founded on the example of Christ is enjoined? xv. 1—7. What is given as the doctrine of the Jewish scriptures concerning Christ as the Saviour of the Gentiles as well as the Jews? 8—13.

8. Under what especial title and office does he commend himself to them, and excuse the liberty of his exhortations? 14—16. What evidence is adduced of his apostleship? 17—21. What does he divulge concerning his future movements? 22—28.

9. What assurance is expressed? 29. What does he ask of them? 30—32. As matters eventuated, was there special occasion for this? Did Paul go to Rome in the manner here anticipated?

10. What is the first part of the last chapter taken up with? xvi. 1—16. What should you judge concerning Paul's acquaintance with the Roman Christians? Is not this singular, seeing that he had never been there? Are there any of these names with which you have previously met?

11. What caution is given, and what commendation? 17—19. What prediction is made? 20. Who join with the apostle in salutation? 21—23.

XIX.

The Apostle's Visit to Jerusalem, and the Persecution Stirred up against him by the Jews.

Very soon after writing the Epistle to the Romans, Paul took his departure from Corinth, and, accompanied by several brethren, journeyed through Macedonia, visiting the churches there, and spending some time at Thessalonica and Philippi. From the latter place, he embarked by ship and went to Troas, where, after some days, he re-embarked and began the voyage along the coast toward Cæsarea, stopping at various ports on the way. Of this journey and voyage as far as Mitylene, where he had the deeply interesting meeting with the representatives of the Ephesian Church, we have had a brief account in Number IX.

From Mitylene they pursued their course to Tyre on the Syrian coast, where they also found, as already in almost every considerable city, a company of disciples with whom they tarried a few days. From thence to Ptolemais, the modern Acre, it was a short voyage, and the remainder of the journey appears to have been by land. Paul himself had prophetic forebodings of serious experiences and sore trials awaiting him; and there were other inspired disciples, both men and women, who predicted much temporal evil as the result of his present journey. Yet he felt as though led by the Spirit to go on and meet whatever was ordained for him.

He had scarcely been at Jerusalem even a few days when the outcry against him began, and he was soon after arrested, and was doubtless only saved from violence by asserting to the Roman officer his rights as a Roman citizen. Foiled in their purposes to destroy him under color of law, his enemies laid a plot for his assassination. Fortunately this was discovered and brought to the ears of the military governor, who sent Paul away secretly with a guard to Cæsarea, the residence at that time of the governor of the province. Here he was detained for some time, and had a hearing before the magistrate, and should have been set at liberty; but, being detained on one pretext or another, and fearing that he might be again exposed to the machinations of the Jews, he appealed to the supreme authority at Rome, and thus precluded any further danger of a trial at Jerusalem. It was by this means, also, though in a way far different from what he had contemplated, that he was permitted to visit Rome.

Acts xxi.; xxii.; xxiii. Nero, Emperor, A. D. 54—68. Events of Lesson, April 16 to May 23, A. D. 58.

1. Voyage from Miletus to Tyre. Stopping-places on the way. Acts xxi. 1—3. Can you give any account of this latter city, either from sacred or secular history? What dissuasion was attempted by the brethren there? 4. Religious services at the departure. 5, 6.

2. Continued journey and arrival at Cæsarea. Family of a man of whom we have previously heard. Gift of the daughters. What were the predictions of the prophetic Agabus? 7—11.

3. What did Paul's friends endeavor to do, on this account? Journey to and reception at Jerusalem. 12—17.

4. Conference with James the apostle, and with the elders of the church, and report of the work among the Gentiles. 18—20. Advice of the elders. 21—25. What apprehensions had been created among the Christian Jews concerning Paul's teaching of the Gentiles? What did their rigid Judaism lead them to think concerning the Gentile converts? What had been previously determined by the elders on this subject? 21—25. (See, also, xv. 23—29.) Why, then, enjoin upon Paul that he should observe the ceremonies? 24.

5. What occurred while Paul was thus engaged? 27, 28. Who were the men crying out thus against Paul? What misapprehension was used? 29.

6. Excitement and riot. Attempt to kill Paul, and how prevented? 30—32. What did the officer do, and what followed? 33—36. Paul's request of the captain, and the latter's surprise when he found what kind of a man he was. Permission given him to speak. 37—40.

7. Paul's address. xxii. 1—21. What is the main topic? 5—16. In what language did he speak? How does the narrative of his conversion differ from that in Chap. ix.? What does he say took place when he returned to Jerusalem? What hearty and humble confession does he make? 17—20.

8. What remark greatly enraged the people? Why? What did they do? 21—23. Order of the officer? Why not carried out? The officer's apparent doubt. In what respect was Paul's citizenship superior to that of the Roman captain? 24—28. What was done the next day? 29, 30.

9. Paul's address before the Sanhedrim. Insolent violence toward him. Indignant rebuke. Remonstrance and apology. xxiii. 1—5.

10. Adroit announcement, which caused a division in the anti-Christian party, and the consequence. 6—9. Paul taken under the care of the Roman authority. 10.

11. Paul's vision and assurance. 11. Conspiracy and oath-bound plot of his enemies, and attempts to carry it out. How it was frustrated. 21, 22.

12. The Roman officer's plan for delivering Paul. Conveyance to Cæsarea and custody there. 23—35.

XX.

Paul's Continued Imprisonment at Cæsarea. His Appearance before the Procurators, Felix and Festus, and King Agrippa.

Felix, who was the Roman procurator or governor of the province of Judea at this time, was a freedman of the Emperor Claudius, and one of his favorites. He had been useful to his master in ways none too scrupulous, and had been rewarded by one place after another of emolument and power, till we find him the ruler of an important and extensive province, with almost the state of a king. The reports that we have of him indicate a profligate, unprincipled and thoroughly corrupt man. His government of the province for two years was distinguished for violence, disorder and discord. Though his treatment of Paul was personally courteous and humane, yet his management of his case was regardless of the rights of the prisoner, and with an eye to his own interest and emolument.

Of Festus, who came in the place of Felix after the removal of the latter, we have very little knowledge. He appears to have been an upright judge and an honorable man. His course with regard to Paul was straightforward and fair, though he evidently was desirous to ingratiate himself with the Jews at Paul's expense. Still it is not probable that he had any suspicions of the plots against the apostle's life, when he proposed his going to Jerusalem for trial before the Sanhedrim. It was this incident, however, that prevented Paul's being set at liberty, as he unquestionably would have been had Festus made an immediate decision of the case as he had a right to do. Paul's "appeal to Cæsar," while it prevented his transferrence to Jerusalem, also took him out of the jurisdiction of Festus, and determined his appearance at Rome.

The Agrippa who appears so conspicuously at this point of the history, was a son of the Herod who had persecuted and put to death some of the first disciples in Jerusalem and very soon after died a miserable death just as he had received the adulation of the citizens of Cæsarea. He was also the great-grandson of Herod the Great. He was governor and titular king of Chalcis, a region to the north-east of Jerusalem, and on the other side of the Jordan. He appears to have had some sort of authority in Judea, though no absolute jurisdiction. He was a descendant of the Asmonean princes, and, of course, had Jewish blood in his veins. He was also familiar with the Jewish polity and usages, and knew perfectly well how to appreciate Paul's relation to them.

The rancor and malignity with which the Jewish party pursued the apostle, is significant. It shows how important a factor he was in the establishment of Christianity in the place of Judaism, and how great was his influence in so establishing it that the Jews would have no pre-eminence over the Gentiles in admission to its privileges and advantages.

Acts xxiv.; xxv.; xxvi. Nero, Emperor, A. D. 54—68. Events of Lesson, May 25, A. D. 58, to July, A. D. 60.

1. Prosecution of Paul before Felix. Presentation of the Jewish side of the case by the advocate Tertullian. Outline of the speech. xxiv. 1—8. Was the compliment to the administration a just one? 2. Testimony submitted. 9.

2. Paul's defense. Give the substance of it. 10—21. Was there any effort to disprove this?

3. What was the action of the procurator, and on what pretext? 22. What reason is there to suppose he knew "of that way?" (See Chap. x.) Was Christianity at this time obnoxious to Roman law? Felix's leniency to the prisoner. 23.

4. Paul asked to set forth the system of Christianity before Felix and his Jewish wife. What seems to have been the character of the discourse? What was the character of the procurator? How did the discourse affect him? 24, 25.

5. What sordid hope animated Felix that he kept Paul in custody? Why did he not discharge him, on retiring from office? 26, 27.

6. Who was the new procurator, and what did he do? What petition did he receive, and the motive of it? What did he say to it? xxv. 1—5. What reason was there for this? 16.

7. The hearing before Festus. The accusers' failure to prove their charges. Proposal of the procurator, and the motive for it? Was it in his discretion to determine the case himself? What grand right did Paul exercise and how did he state it? Could any other apostle have done this? Could Festus exercise any further jurisdiction? 6—12.

8. King Agrippa's visit. Who was he? The case reported to him. 13—21. Festus' estimate of it as a whole? 19.

9. Agrippa's desire. 22. The appointment and preparation for the hearing. 23. Festus introduces Paul. What difficulty does he find in the case? Would it have been *more* or *less* difficult if Paul had been guilty, or even had any semblance of guilt? 24—27.

10. Paul's speech. Graceful compliment to the king. His account of himself? xxvi. 1—5. How does he represent his case as related to the Jewish nation? 6—8. His conduct before conversion? Account of the great change. 9—18. Does the narrative differ much from the previous recitals?

11. The apostle's life after conversion. Character of his teaching and doctrine. Appeal to the Old Testament prophets. 19—23.

12. What was the effect of his allusion to the *resurrection of the dead*, on Festus? How did Paul defend himself from the imputation of insanity? 24—26. Personal appeal to the king, and reply of the latter. Paul's rejoinder. 27—29. Retirement and consultation of the officials. Agrippa's conclusion. 30—32.

XXI.

Voyage and Journey to Rome. Residence and Experience there.

The voyage of Paul and his companions from Cæsarea to the coast of Italy, is given with the circumstantiality and minuteness of immediate personal observation. It is evident that the narrator was one of the company, and this accounts for the particularity of detail which characterizes the narrative. This, too, has enabled modern writers to trace with great exactness the actual course pursued, and to verify the places mentioned, even where the modern names differ from the ancient. It was a remarkable voyage, abounding in disagreeable conditions and perilous experiences. It was only a narrow escape from the destruction of the whole company of soldiers, sailors and prisoners; and but for the counsels of Paul, and the divine interference, most of them would no doubt have perished.

The journey from Puteoli, which was not far distant from where Naples now stands, to Rome was by land. It was about two hundred miles, and was over the famous Appian Road, over which the armies of the Republic and Empire, embassies, prætors and proconsuls, with vast throngs of merchants and citizens and travelers from foreign ports, had come and gone. The traces of this famous road still exist throughout most of its extent, and in the vicinity of Rome it is still traveled, and the entrance to the city is the same as of old. The voyage and journey occupied from the last of August till sometime in March.

Rome has been for ages one of the great centers of power and influence in the world. No city probably has drawn to it so much of the attention and interest of mankind, and none has been of so much importance even in the estimation of the Christian, save Jerusalem. Even now when its political power has been gone for ages, and its ancient grandeur lies in scattered ruins, it probably draws more travelers to it and is the object of more general desire than almost any other spot. For ages both before and after the beginning of the Christian era, its history was substantially the history of the world.

In the apostolic age, Rome was nearly at its greatest splendor. The city and its suburbs, within a radius of three or four miles, contained a population, as some of the best authorities estimate, of about two millions. There were many private residences of considerable costliness and elegance, and public buildings of much magnificence. There were temples, tombs, basilicas, aqueducts and fountains in abundance, while statues and monuments of many kinds were everywhere found. The ruins of many of these are seen at this very day.

At the time of our Saviour's advent, Augustus was Emperor, although the forms of the Republic were still maintained. He was a man of great force of character, as well as a broad, generous, and on the whole, a just man. Under him, literature flourished, and the arts were cultivated. His successors were of a different type. Tiberius, who reigned during the latter half of our Lord's earthly life and a few years later; Caligula, who followed during the next five years; and Claudius, the Emperor for the succeeding fourteen years, were, all of them, selfish, cruel, sensual and degraded specimens of humanity. Nero, who had been Emperor about eight years when Paul arrived in Rome, was doubtless a man of greater abilities than his immediate predecessors, but his moral character was of the vilest, and his conduct has seldom been excelled in infamy.

The population of Rome was made up of many different nationalities. There were many thousands of Jews. Some of these had been brought there as captives in war; others had come in the pursuit of business. As we have seen, Christianity had been for some time established there, and among its adherents were already some persons of reputation. There had as yet been no molestation sanctioned by the government, though two years later there began a cruel and savage persecution under the brutal Nero, which was to be followed at intervals by similar bitter hostilities for two hundred years.

Acts xxvii.; xxviii. Nero, Emperor, A. D. 54—68. Events of Lesson, August, A. D. 60, to March, A. D. 61.

1. Paul and other prisoners committed to an officer of the Prætorian Guard. What relation had this guard to the emperor? How was the con-

veyance made? The first stage? Treatment of Paul by the officer? xxvii. 1—3.

2. Second stage of the journey? Point out on the map. 4, 5. What change of conveyance, and with what intention? What hindered? Where did they find shelter? Where was this? 6—8.

3. What time in the year was this? 9, compared with Lev. xxiii. 27, 29. What advice did Paul give? 10 Why was it not taken? What was the design? 11—13. What occurred? The effect? What precautions were taken? 14—19.

4. Desperateness of the situation. 20. What does Paul now advise and what grounds had he for his encouraging prediction? 21—26.

5. After how long a time did they discover a change, and what did they discover? 27, 28. What precaution did they take? 29. What treacherous action did the seamen intend, and how frustrated? 30—32.

6. Paul's further advice and assurance. 33, 34. The effect? How many were there in all? What further did they do? 35—38.

7. What was discovered in the morning, and what was done? 39—41. Project of the soldiers, and how frustrated? The result? 42—44.

8. Name of the island? Where situated, and its present name? Character of the inhabitants, and their treatment of the strangers? What remarkable incident befell Paul, and how did it affect the people? xxviii. 1—6.

9. Hospitality of the governor. The miraculous healing of his father. Other miracles. What was the disposition of the people? 7—10.

10. How long stay was made here? Describe the voyage hence to the Italian coast. Where did they land? How far from Rome, and in the vicinity of what great modern city? 11—13.

11. Whom did they find here? Journey to Rome, and incidents on the way. 14, 15. Arrival at Rome. Delivery of the prisoners to the Prætorian Prefect. What special favor was shown to Paul? 16.

12. How did he use his privileges? Give the substance of his address. Reply of his countrymen. 17—22.

13. Paul explains to them the grounds on which the Messiahship of Jesus was based, and sets forth the Old Testament proofs of the Christian system. 23. How did they receive it? Does Paul find in their very disagreement and disbelief any confirmatory evidence? Why and how? What is his resort here, as usual? 24—29.

14. Paul's subsequent action at Rome? Was he still a prisoner, or discharged? How could he do this religious service? 30, 31.

XXII.

The Closing Years of Paul's Life, and his Last Letters.

During the two years that Paul waited as a prisoner for his trial, he appears, both from the closing remark of Luke and from sundry allusions in his letters, to have been actively engaged in advancing the cause of the Gospel in Rome. It is true that he was confined to his house, and always under the surveillance of a soldier to whom he was chained. But he had the privilege of receiving any who were disposed to wait on him, and his home evidently became the resort of great numbers, so that he had abundant opportunity to teach and preach. He dwelt doubtless within the limits of the Prætorium, or the quarters assigned in the city to the Prætorian guards, and his influence throughout these quarters appears to have been very great in behalf of the Gospel. To this he alludes, Phil. i. 13, where he says, "My bonds in Christ are manifest in all the palace" (or *prætorium*, as some translate it). In the same epistle, there is a clear intimation that he had some converts among the Emperor's own servants—slaves or freedmen. iv. 22.

The Scripture narrative breaks off abruptly with the statement of the apostle's two years of imprisonment in Rome, giving no details of the life except what has been already referred to. But we have some more or less trustworthy traditions, which, taken in connection with intimations in letters written subsequently to this time, give us a fair account of the remainder of his career. It appears from these sources that when his trial came on, probably in the year 63 A. D., he was readily acquitted and set at liberty. In his letter to Philemon, written not long before his discharge as well as in that to the Philippians, he had expressed the intention of traveling eastward and visiting the churches in Asia Minor. Philem. 22; Phil. ii. 24. This he undoubtedly did, lingering but a little among his friends at Philippi and the neighboring churches, and hastening on to Ephesus which he made the center of his operations among the churches in that vicinity. There is a tradition, which seems to be well-founded, that, having regulated matters in the churches in the province of Asia, he went to Spain and remained there about two years; but of the details of this journey, or his labors in connection with it, we have not the slightest account. In the year 66 A. D., he returned to Ephesus to find there grievous errors and disorders, such as were beginning to characterize many of the churches. Having spent some time in correcting these as far as possible, and leaving Timothy in charge of the work of further setting the church in order, he went to Macedonia. From thence he wrote his First Epistle to Timothy, giving him direction as to his course of conduct in the ecclesiastical administration, as well as much affectionate personal counsel. It is probable that he returned to Ephesus, but left after a brief visit, for a tour in Crete with Titus. Here there were also similar disorders to be rectified, and some time was given to the work, as we learn from the Epistle to Titus, written soon after his departure, and giving the latter instructions as to the administration of affairs among the Cretans.

In this letter, he speaks of a determination to spend the ensuing winter in Nicopolis, a city of Epirus on the eastern side of the Adriatic Sea, where also he wishes Titus to meet him. The probability is, however, that the apostle was not permitted to spend the whole winter as he had proposed. Some three years before this, a bitter, malignant and horrible persecution had been incited against the Christians in Rome, and the government had taken part in it. The infamous Nero, who, it was thought by many, had set Rome on fire and was the cause of the tremendous conflagration of that time, was willing to avert the rage of the populace from himself to the Christians. The sufferings of the latter were almost too horrible to contemplate. Paul had been set at liberty from his first imprisonment the year previous, so that he was far distant when the terrible outbreak came. But, though three or four years had elapsed, the hostility had not ceased, and it had spread, to some extent, to the provinces. It is probable that he was arrested at Nicopolis, in the winter of which he speaks, and taken to Rome. The charge was probably made by some one of his numerous enemies.

It is also likely that his imprisonment was short, and that the only account we have of him during this time is his Second Epistle to Timothy, written from his prison. He was probably tried at separate times, on two distinct charges; first, on being concerned in the burning of Rome. On this, he was acquitted. The circumstances and outcome of this trial we have in his own words. (See II. Tim. iv. 16—18). The second trial was doubtless on the charge of his being a Christian, which, as a *religio nova et illicita*, rendered him liable to prosecution, though the law in this respect had been a dead letter for a long time till revived by the bitter hostility against the Christians. On this charge, on which he evidently did not anticipate acquittal, he was convicted and suffered martyrdom early in the summer of 68, and not many months after his second letter to Timothy.

Besides the epistles to Timothy and Titus, of which mention has been made, he wrote during this period, and indeed during his first imprisonment at Rome, the epistles to the Ephesians, the Colossians and the Philippians. Of the first of these, there is much doubt concerning the church to which it was addressed, some contending that the address in the title is wrong, and that it is the epistle alluded to in the letter to the Colossians as having been sent to Laodicea. Col. iv. 16. The two epistles are very similar in their style and matter, and there are very few passages in either which have not something corresponding in the other. They are both, as well as the epistle to the Philippians, characterized by a glowing personal affection and sympathy, a hearty and sometimes intense enthusiasm for the cause of the Gospel and the experience of its power and influence. There are many passages of almost unequaled eloquence, in which he gives utterance to these feelings. They also abound in practical exhortations, in kindly rebukes and cautions. Of the occasions of the Pastoral Epistles, we have already spoken. The brief letter to Philemon was occasioned by the discovery in Rome of a slave of the latter, who, in absconding, had also stolen from his master. Philemon appears to have been one of Paul's converts to whom he was much attached. The slave, converted under Paul's teaching at Rome, is restored to his master with this remarkable letter, and in such a way as most likely to secure his practical freedom. Our limits will allow only a partial consideration of these epistles.

Philemon. Ephesians.

1. Where was Paul at the last previous account we have of him? How long did he remain there at that time? In what condition? How did he employ himself, and with what success?

2. What do we learn from apparently trustworthy traditions connected with intimations in his letters concerning his release and subsequent experience? What city appears to have been his headquarters for a time? Whither did he probably go afterwards, and what were some of the principal incidents of his life?

3. What intention does he express in a letter to Titus? iii. 12. About what time did the first persecution of the Christians at Rome begin? Under what emperor? His character, and the character of the persecution?

4. How long after this was Paul arrested? Where? What were the charges against him? Was he convicted on the former? How does he describe the outcome to Timothy? What was the second charge? Of what Roman law was it a violation? Had this law been practically operative?

5. What was the result? When and how was he put to death? What letters did he write during this period?

6. *The Epistle to Philemon.* Who was Philemon, and where did he live? Who was Onesimus? Where and when was the letter written, and what was the situation of the writer? Give some account of the contents.

7. *The Epistle to the Ephesians.* When and where was this written? What doubt is there concerning its destination? What are some of the grounds of this doubt? What other epistle contains almost the entire substance of this?

8. *Analysis of the Epistle. Part First.* i. 1—14. After the salutation, what are some of the several things in general for which the writer blesses God?

9. *Second Part.* i. 15—ii. 10. What does he thank God for, and for what does he pray concerning those to whom he writes? 15—19. What does he say of the exaltation of Christ? 20—23. What change had taken place in them? How had this been effected? ii. 1—10.

10. *Third Part.* ii. 11—iii. 21. What had been their former estate? 11, 12. Their present condition? 13. What had Christ done both for the Jews and the Gentiles, and in what relation did it place both? 14—18. What high privilege was thus theirs? 19. What figure is used? 20—22. What was the great new revelation concerning this, and to whom had it been specially committed? iii. 2—12. What grand spiritual gifts does he invoke for them? 13—21.

11. *Fourth Part.* iv. 1—16. What exhortation does he give? 1—3. How is the unity enjoined described? 4—6. What diversity consists with this unity? 7—15. What beautiful figure illustrates this? 16.

12. *Fifth Part.* iv. 17—v. 21. What was their former state? What radical change, and how figured? 17—24. What particular sins are they to put away? 25—31. What disposition is enjoined? 32—v. 2. What contrast between the light and darkness of the soul? 8, 11—14. What are some of the special exhortations? 15—21.

13. *Sixth Part.* v. 22—vi. 9. What kind of relations are here referred to? Mention some of the duties enjoined.

14. *Seventh Part.* vi. 10—24. What fine figure is here used to illustrate the Christian character and calling? What are the principal points?

XXIII.

The Last Letters—Concluded.

Philippians; I. Timothy; Titus; II. Timothy.
(The Epistle to the Colossians is omitted as being similar to that to the Ephesians.)

1. *The Epistle to the Philippians.* Where was Philippi? What have we in the history concerning the first preaching of the Gospel there? What disposition had the Philippians manifested towards Paul? iv. 14—16.

2. What disposition does he manifest towards them? i. 1—7. How does he describe his present condition? 12, 13. How had his persecution and imprisonment, on the whole, affected his usefulness? 14—20.

3. What opposite desires does he express? 21—24. To what does he exhort the brethren? 27, 28; also ii. 1—4. What beautiful presentation of the example of Christ is given? 5—8.

4. What was Paul's situation as regards companionship when he wrote? 19—22. What account does he give of his temporal advantages and former spiritual defects, and how does he regard them? iii. 4—10. What allusions are made to the kindness of the Philippians? iv. 10—16.

5. *The First Epistle to Timothy.* When and where written? (Introduction to XXII.) Where was Timothy and what was his office? For what purpose had he been appointed to this office? i. 3, 4. The condition of the Ephesian church at this time? 4, 6, 7, and Introduction. What instance of church discipline and excommunication? 19, 20.

6. Instructions concerning public assemblies of Christians? ii. What prayers are to be especially offered? Instructions concerning women in public? Why was this appropriate to that time and place?

7. What church officers are mentioned, and what character are they severally to have? iii. What remarkable statement of the character of the Gospel? 16.

8. What prophecy of evils in later times? iv. 1—3. How is Timothy to prove himself a good minister? 4—7. The advantage of genuine religion? 8. As a young man, what is Timothy advised to do? 12—16.

9. What wholesome directions to servants? vi. 1, 2. What is said of contentment? 6—8. Danger of avarice? 9, 10, 17 The better way. 18, 19. What grand ascription to Christ? 13—16.

10. *Epistle to Titus.* Where written? What happened to Paul soon after? (Introduction to XXII.) Where was Titus and holding what office? What evils were in the churches there? What vices does Paul attribute to the Cretans generally? i. 10—13.

11. What are some of the general directions to Titus concerning the management of affairs, and concerning what particular classes? 13, 14; ii. 1, 2, 3, 4, 5, 6—8, 9, 10, 15. For what reasons? 11—14.

12. What other practical injunctions are given? iii. 1, 2. What experience is cited? 3—7. What indication does the apostle give of his situation and intention? 12, 13.

13. *The Second Epistle to Timothy.* Where and when written? How long before the apostle's martyrdom? How does he address Timothy? i, 2. What is his feeling toward him? 3—7. What is the condition of Paul and his bearing in it? 11, 12. What is evident concerning some who should have stood by him? 15. Did this include all his friends? 16—18.

14. What are some of the special exhortations to Timothy? ii. 3, 14, 15, 22, 23. What errors of some teacher does he deprecate? 16—18. What future evils are predicted? iii. 1—5. Examples of perverted teachers? 6—9. How does he set forth his own example and the natural consequences? 10—12. Value of the Scriptures? 14—17.

15. The final charge? iv. 1—5. Paul's grand summing up and glorious expectation? 6—8. How do you think at this point Paul, a prisoner and soon to die as a criminal, would have answered the question, Is life worth living? What was evidently his condition in respect to many of his friends? 9—11. His confidence nevertheless? 17, 18.

XXIV.

The Epistle to the Hebrews.

There has been more controversy about some points in relation to this epistle than perhaps any other book in the New Testament. The discussion, however, has had to do mostly with its authorship, the language in which it was originally written and the parties to whom it was sent; for there is very little doubt about its canonicity and its inspiration. The notion has widely prevailed that it was intended as a kind of encyclical epistle for the Jewish converts generally, like the epistle of James which explicity states that to be its intention. The marked absence of any note of address at the beginning such as characterizes every other epistolary book in the New Testament, not only leaves this point, but also that of the author, in doubt; while it in some degree indicates a difference in the object of the writer. But as nearly as can be ascertained, the best authorities agree in this, that it was not addressed to the Jews, nor Jewish Christians generally, but either to a particular church composed principally of Jews, or to a particular circle or class of Jewish Christians, in Alexandria or Jerusalem. The best authorities also agree in the opinion that it was originally written in Greek, and therefore doubtless addressed to some body of Hellenistic Jewish Christians The last would seem to indicate Alexandria as the locality, while some other circumstances point to Jerusalem as the place, and a special class as the persons addressed.

As to the writer, the popular idea has been that it was written by Paul, although he is not alluded to in the book. Careful criticism, however, finds so much evidence against the validity of this opinion, as to, at least, make it doubtful. The thoughts themselves and the general course of the reasoning are sufficiently Pauline, but the language and style are dissimilar to Paul's. But whoever may have been the author, there is, as has been said, little room for doubt concerning the genuineness and inspiration of the book. There is another peculiarity about it; it is less like an epistle than any other book that bears that name. Though not destitute of epistolary characteristics, its style is somewhat that of a treatise having a particular subject to discuss. It is of the nature of a theological essay.

The object of the writing seems to have been to correct a tendency among those addressed, to slide into a formal Judaism and thus apostatize from spiritual Christianity; to rest in the ceremonies of the temple service, instead of entering into that higher experience of which these were only types and shadows. This gives the writer an opportunity to set forth in order the actual relation of the Mosaic system to Christ and Christianity. The book furnishes a masterly representation of the connection between the Mosaic and the Christian dispensations. The leading topic is *the grand preeminence of Christ, and his completeness for the deliverance of humanity from all its evils and the supply of all its spiritual wants;* as contrasted with the imperfectness, insufficiency and incompetency of the Mosaic system without him as its complement and the antitype of its principal ceremonies.

---

1. What difference of opinion has prevailed concerning this book? What has been a common opinion? Are there any reasons for a contrary opinion? How does the beginning differ from that of every other epistle?

2. What theory of some weight do we have concerning its character and the parties to whom it was written? What difference of opinion concerning the writer? What are some of the reasons for supposing it to be Paul's writing? What reasons against this supposition?

3. Do these diverse views affect the question of its authenticity or inspiration? What other peculiarity of the book? Its main object? What is set forth? The leading topic?

4. What two methods of revelation are spoken of? i. 1, 2. How is Christ compared with the angels? 3—14. What very forcible argument is drawn from this, respecting obedience to Christ? ii. 1—4.

5. What is man's rank as compared with angels? 6—8. Why was it necessary when as we have seen Jesus was infinitely superior to the angels, that he should be made inferior to them? What objects were to be achieved? What nature did he take on? 9—18.

6. In what respect is Christ greater than Moses? iii. 1—6. What is argued from this respecting the consequences of disbelief in Christ? 7—11, 12—19; iv. 1, 2. What remarkable description of the divine word? 12, 13.

7. How is Christ superior to the Aaronic high priests? 14, 15; v. 1—4, 5, 6, 7, 9; vii. 28. What is said concerning the superiority of Christ's priestly order to that of Aaron? v. 10; vii. 13, 14, 21, 22, 23—26. What is the argument to show the superiority of Melchizedec to Aaron? vii. 1, 2, 4—10.

8. How does the holy place or sanctuary of which the Jewish high priest was minister compare with that of Christ? viii. 2, 5. How do the two covenants compare? 6—9, 10—12.

9. Were the ordinances, and offices and appointments of the former dispensation effectual and satisfactory, or only typical? ix. 1—8, 9, 10, 12, 13;

x. 1—4. What does Christ do that the former can not do and which they only prefigure? ix. 11, 14, 23, 24—28. What is the inference, then, concerning the continuance or cessation of the Jewish ritual?

10. What is the real and effectual offering, the substance of which the Levitical sacrifices were the shadow—the antitype of which they were the type? x. 5, 7, 9, 10. Is there need for further sacrifice? 14, 18. The effect of this sacrifice upon those who in faith accept it? 16, 17.

11. What rebuke is administered to the heathen? v. 11—14. What is the process of the spiritual life when once begun? vi. 1—3. What peril is involved in remaining stationary or receding? 4—6. How does the great inheritance come to God's children? 11, 12. How does he represent the assurance of the inheritance and the value of the hope? 13—20.

12. (Having completed the doctrinal exposition, the writer now proceeds to apply the principles evolved.) How does he group the particulars in which Christ becomes the fulfillment of the types implied in the Jewish altar service, and what encouragement is held forth? x. 19—23. What is said concerning religious communion? 24, 25. What dangers are involved, and how do these compare with those under the old dispensation? 26—31.

13. What had these Christians already suffered; and to what does the writer exhort them? 32—39. What is the subject of chapter xi.? Mention some of the prominent examples of faith. 4—32. How does *faith* differ from *belief?* What power had faith imparted to many not named? 33—40.

14. What is the inference? xii. 1—3. What is said concerning the benefit of affliction? 4—11. What special exhortations follow? 12—17. What remarkable comparison is made, illustrative of the two dispensations? 18—29.

15. What particular virtues are commended? xiii. 1, 2, 3, 4, 5, 7, 16. Against what are they warned, and on what ground? 8—15.

XXV.

The General Epistles of James and Peter.

There have been some doubts concerning the epistle of James both as to its being a really canonical book and as to the writer. In modern times the chief objection to its canonicity has arisen from the supposed antagonism of a part of it to other writings of the New Testament. This objection, however, when critically examined is found to have little weight, and there is at present a nearly unanimous opinion among evangelical writers that it is a genuine part of the New Testament.

There appear to have been three or four prominent persons by the name of James among the early disciples. Two of these were apostles, viz., James the brother of John, and James the son of Alphæus. James "the Lord's brother" is also spoken of; and there is also a possible fourth James, Matt. xiii. 55; Mark vi. 3. The best authorities identify "the son of Alphæus" and "the Lord's brother" as the same. The only difficulty is in the family relationship, but the term "brother" is often used in the Bible to denote a near kinsman, and there are still other ways of accounting for the legitimate use of the term.

The epistle could hardly have been written by the brother of John the apostle, as he suffered martyrdom in the first persecution of Christians under Herod. There is not much doubt that it was written by James the son of Alphæus, who also appears, by the narrative of Luke and the letters of Paul, to have had a kind of primacy among the apostles at Jerusalem. It was probably written about A. D. 62.

As has been intimated, one great occasion of contention concerning this epistle is found in the author's comparison of Faith and Works, in which he has been by some supposed to be in flat contradiction to Paul. It is strange that such an impression could have so widely prevailed. Clearly enough to a careful and critical reader, while one writer makes *Faith* prominent and the other *Works*, there is no antagonism. The one is insisting on Faith as the vital and essential thing, as against those who teach a righteousness to be secured through observance of the ceremonial law. The other defends such Works as are implied in obedience to the divine commands against those who teach that moral conduct is of no consequence so long as the belief is correct, or so long as one trusts in Christ whose righteousness will then be substituted for one's own. Neither teaches that mere opinion or blind trust, or that legal obedience, will meet the want of the soul; both believe that such a trust in Christ is necessary as implies a purpose to do and be and bear what God requires.

The epistle is addressed to the converted Jews and Israelites who were scattered abroad among the nations, though some of the allusions point also to the Jews in their national capacity. It is evidently intended to convey to them positive instruction on the subject of *Christian morals*. It also guards them against the harmful notions which were beginning to be disseminated in certain quarters to the effect that a formal acceptance of Christ was all that was essential, and that the moral character availed nothing. It abounds in forcible appeals, bold rebukes, earnest exhortations and wholesome advice.

THE FIRST EPISTLE OF PETER was written, as the address indicates, to companies of Christians scattered throughout the world, though more particularly to those of Asia Minor. The phraseology might indicate that the classes addressed were the same as those to whom James wrote, viz., Christian Jews; but there are intimations in the text of the epistle which would not agree with this supposition. Such are those contained in ii. 10—iv. 3. The apostle appears to have been at Babylon when he wrote; and though there have been differences of opinion as to what particular place is meant, the majority of reputable authorities agree that it was the new Babylon built in the vicinity of the site of the famous imperial city. There were many Jewish residents there, and Peter had doubtless made that the center of one of his great missionary campaigns. The time of its writing was probably somewhere between A. D. 60 and 64.

The design of the epistle wherewith also the contents correspond, was: 1. To comfort and encourage the Christians, many of whom were passing through severe trials. 2. To enforce the practical duties involved in their religious profession. 3. To warn them against special temptations attached to their position. 4. To remove all doubt as to the completeness and soundness of the system which they had received. This last was the more needful as we have seen in Paul's epistles that there were parties opposed to the latter, and who endeavored to divert the churches founded by him, on the ground that Peter and the older apostles were of higher authority. The instructions and exhortations of this epistle were well calculated to set at rest any such agitations and dissensions.

It is also worthy of note that the churches to which the parties here addressed belonged, were founded chiefly by Paul, and this fact as well as the tone of the epistle wholly dissipates the ancient theory of any antagonism between the two apostles.

The style of the epistle is what we might expect in one written by Peter; earnest, fervid, impulsive and emotional; yet with all these qualities chastened and controlled. There are many passages of great power and glowing eloquence.

THE SECOND EPISTLE OF PETER, unlike the first, has been a subject of much controversy, both as to its authenticity and its canonicity. The chief ground of doubt concerning it is found in its supposed dissimilarity of style to the first epistle. It is true that there are some grounds for this supposition. The two epistles are in some respects unlike, yet this lack of similarity is not predicable of the whole of the two epistles. There are also some parts of this epistle which bear a striking resemblance of that of Jude, so that some have surmised that they had one author.

On the other hand there are internal evidences that the First and Second Epistles were both by the author whose name they bear. The opening passage of this epistle announces the writer to be "Simon Peter, a servant and an apostle of Jesus Christ." It is also said, (iii. 1,) "This second epistle, beloved, I now write unto you, in both which I stir up your pure mind by way of remembrance." He also alludes in a striking way to the Transfiguration, and the voice "from the most excellent glory;" and goes on to declare, "And this voice which came from Heaven we heard when we were with him in the holy mount." i. 17, 18. These passages would indicate the authorship clearly enough unless this was an intentional forgery, and we can hardly divine a motive for so audacious an act. Moreover a forgery would have been likely to have imitated the style of the assumed writer rather than to have differed so much from it.

This letter was evidently written to the same parties to whom the former was addressed. The time and place of its writing are unknown. If Peter ever came to Rome, it was probably written there. In any case, its date was probably not long before his death, or about the year 64 A. D. The design of the epistle was to remind those to whom it was written of the true principles of the Christian faith, and to warn them against the pernicious teachings of some whom the writer foresaw would undertake to lead them away from the simplicity of the truth. The characteristics of these teachers and their teaching are somewhat vividly set forth. There are some important doctrines which are brought out more fully here than elsewhere in the Bible. Among these are the statements concerning the final conflagration of the world, and the new heavens and the new earth.

James; I. Peter; II. Peter.

1. How many different persons bear the name of James among the disciples of Jesus? Which one is supposed to be the author of the epistle bearing this name? What was formerly the main ground of doubt concerning the authenticity of this epistle? To what other apostle was it supposed to be opposed and in what respect?

2. To whom is the epistle addressed? i. 1. What instruction does it convey? What cautions does it contain?

3. How may trials prove a benefit? i. 2—4. If we lack wisdom, what are we to do? 5—8. Will it do any good to ask for what we do not mean to use? What is implied in *faith* here?

4. What of the vanity of wealth? 10, 11. The cause of temptation? 12—15. Whence all gifts? 17. Difference between mere hearing and doing? 22—25. Genuine religion? 26, 27.

5. What is said of the greater probability that the poor will be acceptable to God than the rich? ii. 5—7. The royal law and its application? 8—13.

6. How does the writer represent the relation of *faith* and *works?* 14—26. How is this to be reconciled with the doctrine of faith as the condition of salvation? (Introduction.) There is a faith which is mere assent or belief, and another which implies the practice of the divine requirements; which does this writer mean?

7. What instruction is given concerning the liabilities of the tongue? iii. 1—12. What two kinds of wisdom and their difference? 13—18.

8. What do you find concerning selfishness in living and in religious effort? iv. 1—6. Rule for calculations of the future? 13—16.

9. What rebuke to mere worldly and selfish men? v. 1—6. Advice to the pious and persecuted. What great hope is expressed? 7. Examples of endurance. 10, 11.

10. Simplicity of speech? 12. Utility and power of prayer? 13—18. The good effected by converting a soul? 19, 20

11. To whom was the first epistle of Peter written? Where and when? What Babylon was this, and why was Peter there? What is there in the epistle and the circumstances calculated to dissipate the theory of any antagonism between Peter and Paul? (Introduction.)

12. What were some of the objects of the epistle? (Introduction.) Under the first design what encouragements are mentioned? i. 3, 4, 6, 7; iv. 12, 13.

13. What are some of the duties enjoined under the second head; as for instance, what duties of consecration? i. 13—16; iii. 15. Of society? ii. 13—17. Of domestic life? 18; iii. 1, 7. Of Christian brotherhood? i. 22; ii. 1—5; iii. 8, 9; iv. 8—11; v. 1—3, 5. Of watchfulness? v. 8.

14. What warnings against special temptations? Sensuality? ii. 11, 12; iv. 2, 3, 4. Vanity? iii. 3, 4. Vindictiveness? 9.

15. What confirmation does the writer give of the chief doctrines of redemption? i. 8—12, 18—21; ii. 21—25; iii. 18—22. Do you find any intimation in favor of those Jewish observances on which the enemies of Paul insisted?

16. What controversy has there been concerning the Second Epistle of Peter? The ground of the supposition that it is unauthentic? What internal evidence in favor of its genuineness? Introduction, and i. 1; iii. 1; i. 17, 18. What are the probabilities of a forgery?

17. To whom and when was it written? The design of the letter? What are some of the characteristics of the false teachers, against which warning is given? ii. 1—3, 10, 12—14. The style of their teaching? 17—19.

18. The results of such living and teaching, as illustrated by Old Testament examples? ii. 4—6, 15, 16, 21, 22. Against what does he particularly warn those to whom he writes? iii. 2—4. How does he illustrate this spirit? 5, 6.

19. What predictions, more explicit than we find elsewhere in the New Testament, are given concerning the termination of the present period? 7, 10, 12, 13. What exhortations are founded on this declaration? 11, 14, 17. What reference to Paul's writings? 15, 16.

20. Give the list of Christian virtues, in their logical order? i. 5—7. What is the character of the address and exhortation of the opening chapter?

XXVI.

The Epistles of John and Jude.

The Epistles of John do not bear his name, and there is nothing specific in them to indicate the writer, except the style. But this is so obvious that there can be scarcely any doubt as to the authenticity. They were probably written at or near Ephesus, and near the end of the First Century, or 91 or 92 A. D. The First Epistle was written primarily doubtless to churches in Asia Minor, over which John probably exercised a kind of supervision, and in which he was particularly interested. But it was also designed for Christians generally. It is supposed by many that one object of the epistle was to warn those to whom it was especially addressed against certain heretical teachings then being diffused among the churches. Gnosticism was the chief of these, and consisted in the doctrine of the inherent viciousness and corruption of matter, and hence as one of its tenets inferred that Christ did not come in the flesh, because this would be degrading to him. Out of this, there arose a variety of confusing and conflicting ideas which were full of mischief. There are several passages in which very likely this false doctrine is alluded to. The more prominent of these are i. 1, 2, and iv. 2, 3.

But probably this was only incidentally his object. The epistle is not controversial, but rather hortatory and instructive. It every-where inculcates and enforces that spirit of love of which this apostle was so eminent an example.

The Second Epistle is addressed to "an elect lady," probably some eminent Christian woman in the East. In it he gives similar warnings to those in the First Epistle. Indeed, it is said, that of the thirteen verses which compose this epistle, eight are the same in substance as an equal number contained in the first.

The Third Epistle was addressed to a prominent Christian by the name of Gaius. He is very likely the same person of whom Paul speaks, Rom. xvi. 23, as "mine host, and of the whole church." The same characteristics appear in John's commendation in this epistle. 5, 6. "Beloved, thou doest faithfully whatever thou doest to the brethren and to strangers; which have borne witness of thy charity before the church." He was probably a wealthy layman whose house was a home for the apostles and Christian evangelists. This epistle appears to be a personal letter of friendly and affectionate character, but written more especially to commend to the hospitality of the person to whom it is written some Christians who were traveling that way. It seems that he had before written to some of the elders of the church, but at the instigation of one Diotrephes, the brethren had not been received.

The *Epistle of Jude* has been the occasion of some doubt, both as to its authorship and its canonicity. The name given in the title is the same as that in the list of apostles given by Luke (vi. 16.) Some have thought, however, that this was not the apostle, but one of the same name, and a brother of another James. There is little doubt among evangelical writers of its right to be in the canon. It is not known at just what time it was written, but the prevailing opinion makes it about A. D. 66. It was addressed to Christians generally, but primarily probably to those churches in Asia Minor to which the Epistles of Peter and perhaps the First of John were sent. The contents of the epistle coincide, in a large measure, with a part of the Second Epistle of Peter.

The object of the epistle is expressed in the third verse, and the reason given in the fourth. The adversaries of pure doctrine and life, who at the same time professed to be Christian disciples, are portrayed, and the brethren are carefully warned against them.

First, Second, Third Epistles of John; Jude.

1. What is there in the three Epistles of John to show that they were written by the apostle of that name? Can you mention any phrases or expressions which are similar to some in the Fourth Gospel? About what time were they all probably written?

2. To whom was the First Epistle written? Its object and some of its contents? What was the heresy which John is thought to oppose? What are some of the expressions indicating this? i. 1; iv. 2, 3. By what term does he designate these errorists? ii. 18.

3. What is the great characteristic of this epistle? How does this comport with the character of the Apostle John?

4. Mention some of the passages in which this spirit of love predominates or is enjoined? What other important quality is largely referred to, and what is meant by it? i. 5, 7; ii. 9, 10.

5. What passages prove that faithful obedience is a means of light and truth? i. 6; ii. 3, 4, 5, 27, 29. What important office of Christ is declared? ii. 1. What reasons does he give for writing to the different classes mentioned? ii. 12—14.

6. What high privilege belongs to believers? iii. 1, 2. The distinction between those who are Christians and those who are not? 4—10. An essential mark of real believers? 14. How is hatred characterized? 15; iv. 20.

7. The mark of genuine faith? v. 1, 2. The power of such a faith? 4, 5. How do men know of their regeneration? 10—12. The prayer of faith and its effect? 14, 15.

8. To whom was the Second Epistle written? How does it compare with the First Epistle? What significant warning is given? 9, 10.

9. Who was the recipient of the Third Epistle? Do we probably meet this name elsewhere? What seems to have been the character of this man? The object of the epistle? 5—7. What rebuke to some of the officers of the church? What may we gather concerning the character of the family of Gaius? 4.

10. What difference of opinion has existed concerning the Epistle of Jude? To what other of the apostles was the first Jude or Judas mentioned by Luke related? Is it certain that this is that one?

11. To whom was it written? To what other epistle is it similar? Point out any similarities that you find.

12. The object of the epistle? 3. What reason was there for this? 4. What lessons are we taught concerning those who have once been subjects of saving grace, but have afterwards forsaken the faith? 5, 6.

13. What were some of the characteristics of the perverters concerning whom Jude writes? 8—10, 12, 13, 16, 19. What had some of the apostles foretold concerning such characters? 17—19.

XXVII.

The Revelation of John.

The Book of Revelation was written by "John, a brother and companion in tribulation, and in the kingdom and patience of Jesus Christ," to some of those to whom he wrote; who was also under banishment to the island of Patmos for his adherence to Christ. Certain German critics and some others have denied that this was the Apostle John. The chief ground of this denial is the difference of style. But this, in so far as it exists, is readily accounted for in the vastly and radically different character of the subjects. A simple narrative of events readily conceived by any one, or a letter to familiar friends on topics concerning which they were accustomed to converse, would not demand a style like the stupendous and astonishing visions and utterances which the writer of the Book of Revelation was called upon to record. Besides, a careful examination will reveal not a difference, but a striking similarity of style in the simple narrative parts of the book, as compared with the Fourth Gospel and the Epistles. This, taken with the almost unanimous traditions of the early Christian centuries, secures the majority of authoritative suffrages in favor of the Apostle John as the writer.

As to its date, the authorities are more nearly equally divided. Many names of great weight are found in favor of the opinion that it was written in the time of Nero, and not long after the death of Paul. The main reason for this early date, is the belief that much of the prophetical part of the book was fulfilled in the destruction of Jerusalem and the life and death of Nero; this belief being founded on the intimation that the things here revealed would "shortly come to pass." i. 1. (See also xxii. 6, 7, 10, 12, 20.) But a number of weighty facts and circumstances militate against this. In the first place, there is the nearly unanimous voice of the fathers and of those nearest John's time who assign a later date. Then there is the fact that the expression of "the Lord's day" for Sunday did not begin to be used till near the end of the first century. In the third place, the condition of some of the churches could not have been so early such as is represented. Finally, the fulfilled prophecies of the Bible, it would seem, should be more obvious in order for the edification of believers.

These and similar considerations furnish weighty reasons for believing that the book was written by John the apostle during the reign of the Emperor Domitian, under whom the second fierce persecution of Christians occurred, and in which John had been banished to the island of Patmos.

The contents of the book may be loosely grouped as follows:—1. After the title of the book (i. 1—3) and the salutation to the seven churches (4), the writer sets forth his fundamental idea, viz., *Jesus Christ as the central figure and power in the government of the world.* (5—8.) 2. There is the vision of the seven golden candlesticks with the Son of Man in the midst of them, whom he describes (9—20), and who dictates the messages which are to be sent to the seven churches in Asia, of which John seems to have had the general supervision. (ii. 1; iii. 22.) 3. Then comes the second vision—that of the throne of God,—the slain Lamb opening the otherwise insoluble seven seals of the book, which, as they are severally opened, furnish each its appropriate revelation. (iv. 1—viii. 1.) 4. Next is the vision of the seven angels with trumpets, the sounding of which in order is the signal of successive judgments. (viii. 2—xi. 19.) 5. A series of visions of varied character. (a.) The woman and the child, persecuted by the dragon, and protected by divine power. (xii.) (b.) The living creature with seven heads and ten horns, persecuting the people of God, and a two-horned beast of the same spirit and having a mystical number. (xiii.) (c.) The Lamb and the 144,000 who celebrate his praises; the angels proclaiming the fall of Babylon, blessing the faithful dead, and pronouncing the doom of the wicked; the harvest. (xvi.) (d.) The saints who had overcome the beast, sing the song of Moses and the Lamb. The seven angels pour out the seven vials of divine wrath upon the several objects of it. (xv., xvi.) (e.) The harlot sitting on the scarlet beast with the seven heads and ten horns—a great and wicked city on seven hills and controlling many kings. The destruction of this city and evil power. (xvii., xviii.) (f.) The triumph of the Lamb. Satan bound for a thousand years. His release at the termination of this period, and vain attempt to regain his power. His final destruction, the resurrection of the dead and general judgment, with the new heaven and the new earth. (xix., xxi. 1.) (g.) The description of the eternal city, and injunctions to the prophet.

The interpretations of this book have been almost as various as the commentators. It is more than probable that the time for its complete interpretation, or the interpretation of any considerable part of it, has not yet come. The Bible was written not only for *all men* in all nations and conditions, but also for all generations in *all time*. Much that would not be explicable or applicable to one class or in one age, may be clear and well suited to another. It is more than probable that, as in the past progress of the world new truth has been constantly appearing in the Bible which no preceding age had discovered, so it may be in the future, and that many passages which are now partially sealed to us will be clearly understood by those who come after us. But this does not necessarily imply that any part of the Divine Word is useless to any generation. Even some of its obscurest parts have some lessons of instruction to all who prayerfully study them. So this wonderful and mysterious book of the Revelation conveys every-where to the devout soul intimations of the power and wisdom and perpetual providence of God.

---

1. By whom was the book written? What are the reasons against and in favor of the opinion that this was John the apostle?

2. What difference of opinion as to its date? The grounds of each opinion? To whom was the book addressed or dedicated? i. 4.

3. What is the fundamental idea of the book? 5, 6, and Introduction. The location of the "seven churches?" What is meant by *Asia?*

4. Give the subjects of the first two divisions of the book? (Introduction.) Take up severally the messages to the seven churches, and give in order the following particulars concerning each:—(a.) What is commended? (b.) What is censured? (c.) What is enjoined? (d.) What is promised to the overcomers?

5. What is the subject of the third division? How is Christ represented in v. 5? How in 6? What is the subject of the song of praise? 9, 10. What followed the opening of the first five seals severally? vi. 1—11.

6. What extraordinary events consequent upon the opening of the sixth seal? 12—17. What other important transaction during this period? vii. 2, 3. How many of each tribe, and in the aggregate, of the old covenant people, were sealed? 4—8.

7. Did these comprise all the glorified? 9. What had been the pre-

vious experience of these? 13, 14. Their glorified experience? 15—17. What followed the breaking of the seventh seal? viii. 1.

8. What series of events comprise the fourth division? What events in order followed the sounding of the first four trumpets? viii. 2—13. What terrible commotions were consequent on the sounding of the fifth trumpet? ix. 1—12. What would be the condition of wicked men in this period? 5, 6.

9. The sequence of the sounding of the sixth trumpet? Its effect on men? 14—18. Did the survivors repent? 20, 21. The final grand and awful catastrophe declared? x. 1, 5—7. Was this to take place in this period, or in the next? 8. The sounding of the seventh trumpet? xi. 15—19.

10. Mention some of the more conspicuous of the visions comprising the fifth division. What moral characteristics are embodied throughout, in the dragon, the beasts with many heads and many horns, and in the notable woman arrayed in purple and scarlet? What is always in antagonism with them, and finally overcomes them? xii. 7—11; xiii. 7, 8; xiv. 9, 10, etc.

11. What was the character of ancient Babylon? (See Old Testament Prophets.) Could these predictions apply to it? What then must have been the character of the power or agency designated by this name here? What are some of the things said of it? What was to be its fate? xiv. 8; xvi. 19; xvii. 5, 18; xviii.

12. What is the subject of the song of the glorified, in view of the judgments before described? xix. 1—8. What judgment of Satan is spoken of? xx. 1—3. Was this to be final? 7. What is the final doom? 10.

13. How are the general resurrection and judgment described? 11—15. What are some of the characteristics of the heavenly Jerusalem? xxi., xxii.